# The Miracles *of* VAASTU SHASTRA

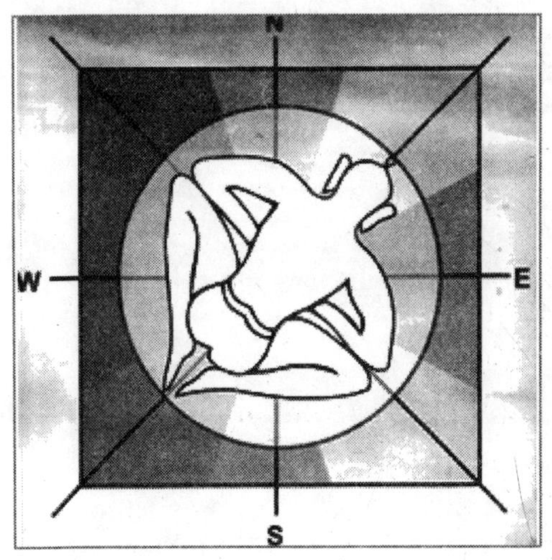

# The Miracles *of* VAASTU SHASTRA

Shanku Shiva Dass

PUSTAK MAHAL®

*Publishers*
**Pustak Mahal®**

***Administrative office and sale centre***

J-3/16 , Daryaganj, New Delhi-110002
☎ 011-23276539, 23272783, 23272784, 23260518
*E-mail:* info@pustakmahal.com • *Website:* www.pustakmahal.com

***Branches***
**Bengaluru:** ☎ 080-22234025, 40912845
*E-mail*: pustak@airtelmail.in • pustak@sancharnet.in
**Mumbai:** ☎ 022-22010941, 22053387
*E-mail*: rapidex@bom5.vsnl.net.in



ISBN 978-81-223-1465-6

**Edition 2022**



***Printed at :*** Glorious Printers, Delhi

# Foreword

India has been a land of great scholars. Ancient texts on Astrology, Art, Architecture and Ayurveda are a storehouse of knowledge. And, today with the advent of the 21st century when man in his unquenching thirst for knowledge has achieved hitherto unimaginable breakthroughs and opened up newer frontiers of research, these ancient texts are very much relevant.

Vaastu Shastra has been in practice increasingly in India today. Vaastu Shastra, the science of creating built environments incorporating the Pancha Bhootas (Earth, Water, Fire, Wind and Space) and Pancha Rasas (Jyotisha, Vedaanta, Yoga, Ayurveda and Vaastu Shastra) is an holistic approach towards creating homes and offices for people, enabling them to lead a happy and contented life.

Shanku Shiva Dass in his book has made an attempt to present the basic concepts to the uninitiated reader briefly and concisely. He also gives easy and quick guidelines for practising Vaastu Shastra in today's context for all types of buildings and plots.

I wish him all success in his endeavour "*The Miracles of Vaastu Shastra*" and hope readers will appreciate his maiden work and his earnest attempt.

10 February, 2008.

Sd/-

Sqdn.Ldr.(Rtd.) C.P. Soma Sundaram

CC.20/3110A, Perumpadapu,

Palluruthy, Cochin-682006

# Preface

*Aum Namah Shivaya!!*

In "Aarsha Bhaarat," innumerable text scripts explicitly preserved the ancient wisdom in palm leaves books "Thaliyola Granthams" written with the pen known as "narayam". That was the sole method of keeping the innate and inherent source of wisdom of the enlightened Rishis of yore. Such unique grassroots information of inheritance vanished with the passage of time before transferring it to the next generation through suitable disciples or followers.

Such precious and matchless ancient knowledge of the Thaliyola granthams should have been preserved and persisted with human beings

1) by Shrutis or Knowledge retained through the tradition of continuous recital and memory and
2) by Smritis or Knowledge preserved in recorded or written texts.

It was an excellent encouragement symptom and method of preservation in specific areas notably to Ayurveda, Astronomy, Philosophy, Veda, Vedaanta, Upanishads, Samhitas, Yaagams, Yogams, Mantras, Tantras, Vaastu Shastra and Architecture, etc. In Ayurveda, for instance, ottamooli (panacea) single doze medicine treatment and cure are unique in nature with its special formulations and diagnosis for several kinds of diseases like leukemia, jaundice, aids, hepatitis, leprosy or leucoderma. Such remarkable successes have remained a distant dream of accomplishment for modern medicine and scientists.

Vaastu Shastra is one among the many sciences propounded and propagated by the sages over hundred and thousand years ago like other arenas of Astronomy, Philosophy, Astrology, Mathematics, Sciences, Vedaanta, Yoga, Ayurveda, etc. The Vaastu science prescribes on the basis of the combination of the pancha bhoota elements of nature and the theme of land size, its selection, constitution and construction of a Vaastu. The canons of

Vaastu tentacles are spread over a number of factors that commence with levelling of the landscaping, rectification of the required size and selection of square/rectangular form of shape. The 'paada vinyaasam' has to be calculated for the main gate positioning, the front main door location paada proportion, and the selection of Deva or Manushya Khanda zone. The most important part of house construction should be a well-designed plan, drawn, rectified or corrected by Vaastu experts according to the available land area, the actual owner's requirement, location of the rooms as per paada Vaastu limbs, the best age and perimeter measurement.

The Yajamaana (the house owner) has to arrange to perform the Vaastu Bali pooja a day before the commencement of house warming ceremony to please the Vaastu Purusha. The Vaastu Bali Pooja has to be performed regularly in continuation once in every three years. The circumstances will bestow happiness and prosperity throughout on all, including the house owners, the inhabitants and others associated with. It also insists on keeping a gold icon of Pancha Mrugasira (five animal heads) underneath the Northeast house floor or wall base where any Marma Suthra Veda occurs or touches with the wall or pillar during construction or at a later stage for rectification or Vedha constraints.

This Book "The *Miracles of Vaastu Shastra*" focusses mainly on the house (Saala) Construction and owes a great deal to "*Manushyaalaya Chandrika*". The author, Thirumangalath Neelakantan Acharya deserves thanks and appreciation for the exalted degree of fact finding techniques that he had applied even during 1565 A.D. Of course, the Acharya possessed an excellent knowledge of Sanskrit, Tantra Samucchayam and temple architecture.

Credit and benevolence is offered and accredited to Kanippayur Krishnan Nambudirippad Thirumeni for his enduring encouragement, unstinted support, and his suggestion to write this book basing authentic Vaastu book *Manushyaalaya Chandrika* for apt evaluation on the subject in a simple format . The real base of Vaastu is "the actual practical experience" that conforms to one's learning and experiences. The most essential rectification is required to be carried out in accordance with the experts' advice to location, placement or other changes. In this modern era, certain ancient concepts have to be considered as the norms of Vaastu rules but irrevalent to be adopted in actual practice like that of making a house roof, utharams (wall plate) pothika (support bracket), aarudam (Pivotal point) reapers, old methods of soil examination, caste bifurcation, flowers, etc. These assume no value in the case of re-enforced cement concrete top roofing, or structural tiles by using ceramic, granite, marble, or mosaic floorings.

This book contains Nine Bhaagams (Chapters) and annexure of Five Tables which are detailed fully to the satisfaction of readers. Perimeter Table must be utilized in selecting the excellent position of prosperity before finalizing the drawings and taking approval from Governmental authorities.

Certain aspects have direct link with karma results which were performed in the past, and are being performed at present and will also be performed in the future. The end result should always match with the outcome of the Vaastu follower's accomplishment.

The readers are the best judge to suggest any improvements or corrections on the work that I present to them. I submit the book "*The Miracles of Vaastu Shastra*", with the grace of God and blessings of Gurus, to the public to ensure happiness, peace and prosperity to the followers.

Shanku Shiva Dass

# Contents

## Bhaagam 1



## Bhaagam 2

## Bhaagam 3



## Bhaagam 4



## Bhaagam 5



## Bhaagam 6

## Bhaagam 7



## Bhaagam 8



## Bhaagam 9

# Bhaagam 1

## prayer

*"Om Hari Shri Ganapataye Namah Avikghnamastu Shri Guruve Namah"*

*"Suryaya Sheeta Ruchaye, Dharani Sudhaya Saumyaya, Devaguruve, Bhrugunandanaya, Suryatmajaya, Bhujagaaya, Cha, Ketuve, Cha, Nityam Namo Guruve Varaya"*

*"Shri Shri Vaastu Purusha Raaja Vallabhaya Pranamam"*

This book "The Miracles of Vaastu Shastra" is submitted before the Holy Feet of Brahma, Vishnu, Mahadeva and Vaastu Purusha and its presiding deities of every part of the body, for its extraordinary perfection and boon.

## The Meaning of Vaastu Shastra

In Sanskrit dictionary, the word 'Vaastu' means "a house constructed on land". In Malayalam language, the word 'Vaastu' means "a landed property with or without house or buildings". The Tamil Vaastu shilpi Maayamayan in his book 'Maayamatam' mentions 'Vaastu' as "an ancient science of divine nature visible in the form of a dwelling, a site or a building for human living".

The word Vaastu is derived from the word 'vasu'. The Vasu is symbolically or utilitywise known as 'the earth'. The earth is the principal point of Vaastu; and all the buildings, altars and complexes constructed on the earth are also Vaastu.

Vaastu Shastra is a divine science linked to the nature comprising of sun rays, water, wind, earth, fire and the open space. Of course, Vaastu is a combination of art, science and architecture. It has the association of several factors contributed to the flourishment and favourable aspects which ultimately lead to a happy and prosperous life.

The word 'Vaastu' means 'a house contructed on land. The book 'Maayamatam', authentic on the subject, means Vaastu as a dwelling, site, building, or any other living place. As per the book 'Manushyaalaya Chandrika', the Vaastu Shastra has four classes: land (bhoomi), buildings (harmya), vehicles (yaana) and furniture (sayana) based on desirable biotic, terrain, and climatic conditions.

Vaastu is considered as Shastra, duly tested and proved by practical and natural phenomena. It is an art of construction and architecture of well designed houses, buildings, well planned sites and factories etc. which are created in accordance with the panch bhoota elements of nature i.e.: Earth, Water, Fire, Wind and the Space.

The theme of Vaastu as a combination of art, science and architecture has been prevalent in India from time immemorial and remains even today with its ancient glory in modern designing and carving. The name of Vaastu Vidya is known by various forms as Vaastu Shilpa, Gruha Nirmaana Sutram, and Thatchu Shastra etc. The Vaastu, hence, is associated with soil, trees, buildings, sculptures, elevation of places, temples, shops, hotels etc.

## The Principles of Vaastu Shastra

The principles of Vaastu Shastra apply in the selection of plots, construction of houses, flats, apartments, offices, shops, factories, industries, restaurants and temples. Basically, Vaastu Shastra deals with the exercise of architecture and building science, and, in fact it gives a fair touch in every aspect of life.

The principle of Vaastu Shastra is a combination bye-product of pancha bhootas of nature and Pancharatras of dormant norms or rules framed after the divine derivations of several eminent sages. This will cover the entire phase of human thought, spirituality or aspirations of vivid forms to make the life of every one happy, peaceful and contented. The Pancha Rasas – Jyothisha, Vedaanta, Yoga, Ayurveda and Vaastu Shastra plays an important role in Vaastu principles. The relationship of Vaastu Shastra is very simple and friendly as compared to Astrology. The relation between the Space Factor of Vaastu Shastra is very much correlated to the Time Factor of Astrology. Both Sciences will always move together, hand in hand, in determination of pertinent aspects of every individual's life and varied style of functioning.

The principle of Vaastu Shastra is illustrated by means of certain elements which are to be explained separately. The rules are very decisive and very difficult to follow in practical view point. Certain norms are given below to practise the following:

• **Selection of Land:** Land size, shape and form should be divided either in square or rectangle without cutting, deformation and depletion of any corner or sides. No diagonal land form is acceptable unless rectified for the purpose of construction. The land will be separated in rectification and may be used for gardening by making a wall or base boundary line within the premises.

• **Cardinal Direction:** Follow the Ashta Dik directions of planets. Their controlling deities area of operation should be analyzed before the commencement of the construction activities.

• **Land Cells Division or Marma Mandala:** The correct Marma sutra mandala and land cells divisions should be decided.

• **Placement of House Location:** The Location of house khanda is to be decided on Manushya or Deva Khanda and its marma settings with road directions.

• **Avoidance of Veethi Shoola etc.:** Care should be taken on all possible ways to avoid the Veethi Shoola, L bend or T-cut shape vedha troubles or Muttu vedha disturbance.

• **Placement of Rooms:** Placement of rooms should be given prime importance especially to bed rooms, kitchen room provision, pooja rooms, living place and reception hall or dining portions.

• **Water Sources Location:** Re-check the exact location of well, bore well, sump provision, septic tank arrangement, or overhead tank provision on the top of the roof of the buildings.

• **Perimeter or Basement Measurement:** Correct evaluation is to be made for the measurement of Uthama (Best) Perimeter, house foundation both padukam and basement.

• **Paada Principles of Measure:** Strictly follow the principles of Vaastu calculation measure applicable to main front door and to the gate paada.

• **Combination works of Pancha Bhootas:** By giving correct position of shape, dimension, cells division, khanda selection, placement of rooms, position of water sources, main door-perimeter or main gate measurement with the working lines of Pancha Bhootas will reflect and emit miracle of happiness and prosperity in a single or in joint nature action.

• **Provisions of Toilets and Bathrooms:** There is the need to analyse the location of toilets or bathrooms when they become part of the main house. Its position should be re-checked to avoid dangerous afflictions by accidents or marriage blockade and unbearable difficulties.

• **No Cuts on Southwest or Northeast:** It is strictly to be adhered that no cut on Southwest or Northeast corners is permitted in land plot size and shape.

The above principles are necessary for getting the desired results. Since the rules of Vaastu Shastra are very rigid and vivid its applicability should invariably be tested in a chemical laboratory as chemical compound or mixture. The results of Vaastu are amazing in practice leading to a progressive or a destructive reaction in combination function of all elements of nature. If it works well and progressively, every occupant will be happy and satisfied at home, and, if not, it will result in a complete devastation and dangerous outcome.

## Vaastu Shastra is a Gift of God

There are six points of reason to establish that the Vaastu Shastra is a "GIFT OF GOD"

• **Gift of Nature:** The Vaastopati is none other than the creator of the universe and humans "The LORD PARABRAHMA" who is also the originator of Astrology. So Vaastu Shastra is a gift of God through sages.

• **Power of Space and Time Magnitude:** It is simple to say that Vaastu Shastra is a magnitude of space with the influence of the five elements of nature called Panch bhootas of Fire, Wind, Earth, Water and Space, their mutual cooperation, coordination or combination will end in a mixed reaction as a miracle.

• **The Solar Rays:** Solar Rays of the Sun entering through North, Northeast, East or Southeast regions of the house will energize during morning hours. The entry of Sun rays conjoins to attain the material comforts of every human being and to live in an atmosphere of peace and harmony with the nature. Different forms of the Sun rays penetrating in morning hours by 'vibgyor', (Violet, Indigo, Blue, Green, Yellow, Orange and Red colours), ultraviolet or cosmic rays, definitely will influence the entire surface which is totally different from evening Sun light.

• **Water Sources:** Eshana corner is always good for placing water well, borewell, storage sump or pond except the corner joint Karna Sutram marma vedha point. Water bodies, situated in the Northeast corner region, increase the strength of financial stability, creditability and equilibrium to all inmates. Thereby, a self-balanced, good living is certain to all family members. The will and pleasure of the nature is allowed to act on a positive interaction between self and others.

• **Rishi or Sage Culture:** Maha Rishis' enlighted wisdom and its involvement in practice are considered the best for a progressive combination of living, ensuring a happy and peaceful life to all common masses. The divine power factor of sages is important aspect to recheck minutely in all texts of ancient Vaastu works. Enunciated Vaastu Principles are the best criteria to decide in the right direction. This Gift is offered to humanity in the form of Vaastu rules and principles to practice. They are the 'Divine Revelations' of Rishis pronouncements accepted whole heartedly. This treasure knowledge is hard to grasp and difficult to follow; however, it is welcome as it is of immense use in Vaastu Shatra. We are deeply in debt to our sages.

• **Directional Lordships:** The eight cardinal directions and their lordships are important to make the Vaastu Shastra as Gift of God.

| **Direction** | **Lordship** | **Domain region for** |
|---|---|---|
| East | Indra | King of Kings- Blessings |
| South | Yama Raja | God of Death/Dharma Raja help |
| West | Varuna | God of Rain/Water |
| North | Kubera | God of Wealth/Health |
| Northeast | Eshana | God of Supreme Energy/Power |
| Northwest | Vaayu | God of Wind Power/Strength |
| Southeast | Agni | God of Fire/Ignition- Saviour |
| Southwest | Demon | God of Sarpa/Nairuti -Spirit/Enthusiasm |
| Centre | Sun | God of Dharma/Truth/Boon Satisfaction |

## The Base of Vaastu Shastra

To bring extraordinary happiness and peace to humanity is the real aim or motive of Vaastu Shastra. The Maharishis enunciated a set of norms to observe the Vaastu culture as a way of life. Every Indian feels proud of the unique intellectual legacy and Vedic cultural heritage. The Vaastu wisdom is bequeathed from generation to generation as a hereditary tradition and culture, which is evident from the findings of research conducted at various levels in different countries. The Vaastu knowledge and its tentacles will continue to reach each one individually, nationally or universally.

The essence of Vaastu is visible by form of feelings in Wind or Space and by vision in Fire, Earth and Water elements of nature. The process of evaluating the normal functions of Vaastu is possible by judging with actual happenings and feelings to the inmates. The combination of five elements of nature and their way of functions are totally invisible but the resultant aspects of good or bad experiences will be possible to make a judgment about inmates' happiness, satisfaction and a sign of prosperity and also about a stage of melancholy, unhappiness in turn and total destruction. Water, Air, Fire, Earth and Space coordinate the mutual combinations, and connectivity to the actual propulsion of Divine Power is evident from results.

The Chinese Feng Shui is based on Indian System of Vaastu Shastra and the working lines on the positive and negative powers with the constant interaction of all five elements of nature. The elements are mentioned in Feng Shui. Earth element controls Southwest and Northeast. Metal element presides over West and Northwest, Water element controls only North region, Wood element presides over Southeast and East. Fire element is vest with the control of South. Each element has a function that moves productive or destructive based on the cycle of rotation.

The other factors are also decisive in matters of the Land surface, Atmosphere, Sun's temperature, Air, Fire and Water. The end result is certainly good and favourable if one follows the Vaastu Principles.

## The Concept of Vaastu Forewalls

The concept of Vaastu is very ancient and highly interconnected with the Hindu way of living. The wisdom of ancient Rishis is the real basis for the Vaastu norms formulations, and such knowledge is transferred to generations to live in peace and harmony.

The essential features of Vaastu Shastra have grown powerful through eminent people of several countries and series of experiments over the years. Vaastu Shastra has been proved as a science beyond doubt. It has established a peaceful, worthy practical life, varying from persons and mode of life, houses, places and circumstances.

One should possess first hand information on Indian tradition and culture, the wisdom of Vedas, the law of Karma and rebirth theories, which is necessary to grasp the in-depth knowledge on Vaastu parameters.

## Indian Tradition and Culture as Basic Concept

The Saints have maintained a unique and intellectual legacy and imparted a standard Vedic tradition to India. All Indians ought to be really proud of such cultural heritage, traditional thoughts and refinements innovations of the past. The characteristics of the ancient cultural heritage and tradition are considered unique throughout the world. The findings from excavations conducted in the selected sites bear testimony to India's cultural heritage as the greatest in the world.

The following are the intrinsic facets of Vaastu, immutably embedded in our culture and traditional values:

The Vedas and Upavedas
Astronomy, Mathematics and Astrology
Yugas, Vedaangas and Upanishads
Soorya Siddhaanta and
The Law of Karma and Rebirth Theory

These are the best parameters to evaluate the nature of inputs and outcome of one's own karma or deeds.

• **The Vedas:** The word "Veda" means 'vid' (to know) or the knowledge of gods, the universe, nature, birds, animals, oceans, land, dharma and of course "THE ABSOLUTE". The Vedas are considered to be the oldest embodiment of knowledge based on our ancient culture and civilization. It is an essential manifesto of purified human life activations enriched by Karma Kanda and Jnana Kanda. The Vedas are mainly classified into four: 'the Rig-Veda, the Yajurveda, the Samaveda and the Adharvaveda'. The Ancient Rishis have obtained the knowledge through a continuous tapasya and were granted divine revelations known as *Srutis*. Such knowledge is preserved and placed by oral traditions through Vaidika Brahmins known as *Smritis*.

The Lord Parabrahma has transferred the divine revelations to Sage Vyasa. The enlightened Vedas illustrate the universal pattern of human spirituality, and quest for reality, peace, fulfillment and salvations. Vedic hymns embody the highest and loftiest human aspirations.

In the Upaveda classifications, the Vaastu Shastra is linked with the Upavedas during the period of Rig, Yajur, Sama and Adharva Vedas respectively:

Sathya Veda Tradition – the knowledge of building science.
Ayurveda – the knowledge of life and medicine.

| | |
|---|---|
| Dhanurveda | – the knowledge of weapons and warfare. |
| Gandharva Veda | – the knowledge of fine arts and music. |

• **Astronomy, Mathematics and Astrology:** Jyotisha, Ganitha and Vaana Shastra are three sisters conjoined together very often, functioning in cooperation and coordination. The classical work "*Brihat Samhita*" clearly defines the acts together coming under one subject called "Jyotisha Ganitam".

***Astronomy (Vaana Shastra):*** All ancient works on astronomy are written in unambiguous terms. Aryabhatta (476 AD) pioneered the work of extracting the Tantra Shastra (Astronomy and Mathematics) from the Vedas in his book titled '*Aryabhatiya*'. Vaana Shastra plays an important role in the modern era for locating planets and stars with exact distance between the earth and the sun. Communication satellites and geostationary stations in the orbit are an outstanding testimony to the present day material advancement made in this field linking vast networks of all mobile, telephone and television channels.

***Mathematics (Ganitam):*** Ganitam is mathematics comprising of all branches of arithmetic, algebra, geometry, trigonometry and any other branch. '*Bhaskaracharya*' (1150 AD) wrote a comprehensive composition "*Siddhaanta Shiromani*" containing a number of theories and mathematical solutions. His famous work "*Leelavati*" is a very useful book on mathematics, algebra and geometry with theories and solutions for the teachers, students, researchers, scholars, historians and all individuals working for the cause of mathematics.

***Astrology (Jyotisham):*** Jyotisham means knowledge of light from logic or reasoning. It is clearly depicted by Sage Paraasara in *Naarada Samhita* (Part 1 in 4) that Jyotisham is an intellectual legacy. It is considered to be the eye of Vedas. The Jyotisha Ganita calculations spread over three dimensions by:

| | |
|---|---|
| 1. Horoscope | – Janam Kundali or Thalakuri. |
| 2. Jaataka Samhita | – Natal effects of natural phenomena. |
| 3. Prasna Horary | – Hora Shastra. |

These calculations are based on place, time and date of the individual (native) and nation (places affiliated as per countries codification).

• **Yugas, Vedaangas and Upanishads:** Yugas, Vedaangas and Upanishads influence everyone in daily life in some form or other.

***Yugas:*** The culmination of years in Yugas was already formulated even before thousands of years ago, and the sequence of the yugas was predominantly recorded by:

| | |
|---|---|
| Krita (Satya) Yuga | contains 17.28 lakh years, |
| Treta Yuga | contains 12.96 lakh years, |
| Dwaapara Yuga | contains 8.64 lakh years and |
| Kali Yuga | contains 4.32 lakh years. |

This means that the Kaliyuga has a total of 4,32,000 (Four lakhs thirty two thousand) years. The proportionate length of Dwaapara, Treta and Krita Yugas is respectively twice, thrice and four times more than that of Kaliyuga. Together it adds upto a total of 4.32 million years, which constitutes a major time cycle. The year 2013 AD equivalent to the Kaliyuga year is 5116.

The sloka says as below:-

"..........Shubhey Shobhaney Muhurta Adhya Brahmaney,
Dwitiya Praharaat Sweta Varaahkalpey,
Vaivasvat Manvantarey Ashtaavinshatitamey,
Kaliyugey Pradhamey Padhe, Jambu Dwipey,
Bharatha Varshey, Bharatha khandey,
Meroho, Dakshiney Bhage..............."

6 manvantaras (27 mahayugas) are over. Now we are in the first phase of 28th mahayuga. As per above sloka, fourteen manvantaras will constitute one Kalpa or Brahma Dina.

***Vedaangas:*** An anga or part of the Veda has different functions to perform and each one has its own importance in its functioning. They are classified as six limbs:-

| | |
|---|---|
| Jyothisha | – the eyes (the time of such Veda rituals) |
| Kalpa | – the hands (the procedure of sacrifices) |
| Nirukta | – the ears (the special meaning of words) |
| Shiksha | – the nose (the phonetics) |
| Vyakaran | – the face (the grammatical peculiarities) |
| Chhandas | – the feet (the treats of prosody and meters) |

These are considered to be the parts of personified Veda Purusha. The Vedaanga Jyothisha is considered to be the eyes of Veda Purusha, which are instrumental in finding out Thithis, Nakshatras and Luni-solar movements.

The Paaniniya's Shiksha contains a 60 sloka compilation and there are other Slokas available in Rigveda and Yajurveda.

The Nirukta of Yaaska is a commentary on an older theme called Nighantu. Without this science there cannot be any understanding of the Vedic mantra (1-15) Yaaska collections.

The Vedaanga Vyakaran deals with grammatical studies and it is associated with pioneer Paanini and other 64 predecessors.

Pingala's Chhandah Sootras deal with the Vedic meters in general. The Kalpa Sootras are connected with special manual for priests, which contains

- The Srauta Sootras dealing with sacrifices based on Shruti,
- The Smarta Sootras dealing with household ceremonies (Graha Sutras like Pancha Maha Yagna Samskaaras),
- The Dharma Sootras dealing with the duty or law of Dharma – moral or religious laws, and
- The Sulbha Sootras dealing with the rules of the construction of altars and other buildings etc. enabling to testify the knowledge of geometry. Gruha Sootras, Dharma Sootras and Sulbha Sootras are based on Smruti.

***Upanishads:*** Upanishads means "sitting at the feet of the guru and learning knowledge from him". Upanishad is the Jyaana Kanda portion of Vedaanta. It contains an elaborate description of the core essence of "TRUTH" which enables to eradicate ignorance. The Upanishads will give us the answers to the questions "Who are we? Why are we here? What is this work? Who is God? What is freedom? Misery? Bondage? Ignorance? "

*"Sarvam upanishadam aatmaa yathaathmya*
*Nirupane naiva upanishayaat"*

**By Aadi Shankaracharya**

This sloka means that all the Upanishads exemplify themselves in glorifying the aatman. The human being has a body and a mind, but the aatman is everlasting and that is the only truth. The Upanishads deal with the supreme source of everything (body and mind) including aatman.

*"... Universe is the evolution of Primal nature. According to some of the advaitists (followers of Guru Sankaraacharya) whole of the universe is evolved from God. The Upanishads are the mine of strength". (The complete works Vol-I pp 362 to 363)*

**By Swami Vivekananda**

Out of the total available 108 well known Upanishads, prominence is given to eleven Upanishads. The names of these eleven Upanishads are:

***Iswhavashyopanishad:*** It contains eighteen mantras from the shuklayajurveda base for all Vedaanta secrets.

***Kenopanishad:*** It consists of nine chapters of a Saamaveda Guru-shishya discussion on Brahma Jnaana (wisdom).

***Kathopanishad:*** It mentions the Krishnayajurveda in six chapters of performing vishwajit yaagams, cow daanam and brahma paadam attainment for reasonable solutions to all problems.

***Prashnopanishad:*** It mentions praana, energy and matter to the disciples Sukesan, Sathyakaman, Garyan, Kausalyan, Bhargvan and Kabhandi from Guru Rishi Pippalatha.

***Mundakopanishad:*** It contains the ideals of Gnaana and Brahma descriptions from the Guru Angiras.

***Mandukyopanishad:*** It contains Moksha and Mukhti in twelve mantras with "Om" Mahathyuva and Brahma Chaitanyam. It comes under the Atharvaveda branch.

***Aitareyaopanishad:*** It has three khandams (chapters) in Rigvedha division.

***Taittireyopanishad:*** It spreads over three Vallies (chapters) of Shiksha, Brahma and Bhrugu Vallies in Krishna Yajurveda branch.

***Chandogyopanishad:*** A Saamaveda branch Upanishad of eight chapters which contain Sooryopaasana, Praana, Veda, Puraana subjects.

***Shvetashvataropanishad:*** Krishnayajurveda branch Upanishad margas has six chapters including Jnaana, Bhakti and Karma.

***Brihadaranyaka:*** A Shuklayajurveda branch Upanishad consists of six Brahmanas with vivid Bhagam Brahmanas.

The Brihadaranyaka Upanishad is the longest of all; followed by the second Upanishad, which is the Chandogyopanishad. These Upanishads contain the eternal truth of nature and each sloka or mantra is a medicine. In the words of Swami Vivekananda, in his book *"The Complete Works" Vol I, pp 452),*

*"The Upanishads point out that the goal of a man is neither misery nor happiness....*

*We must be masters of the situation and at its very roots.........*

*To show us how to be the masters is the end aim of the Upanishads.........."*

• **Soorya Siddhanth (The Principle of the Sun)**: The basis of the Soorya Siddhanth is the movements of the sun. Due to the sun's motion combined with the earth's rotation there are variations in time from one place to another. The placement of several planets in the orbits, i.e., Mercury, Venus, Jupiter, Mars, Saturn, Neptune etc., has incurred changes in latitudes and longitudes. Sunrise, Sunset, temperature and Greenwich Mean Time (latitudes and longitudes) are subjected to the principles of movement of the sun. It is necessary for calculating the Thithis, Nakshatras, and Vedic rituals and even all Panchanga calculations.

• **The Law of Karma and Theory of Rebirth:** The law of Karma and theory of rebirth of the soul are an intrinsic part of Sanaatan Dharma, and completely subjected to the laws of nature and one's actions over innumerable cycles of birth. This part is an important and inseparable section of the Vedic thought and wisdom. The advice of Lord Krishna to Arjun during the Mahabharat War is produced as a message in the book 'the Bhagavad Gita', the embodiment of the Soul and rebirth incarnation. These messages have become the theory of birth, rebirth and the law of karma.

***Karma:*** Karma is the law of cause and effect. Each effect produces further effects.

*"One indeed becomes good through good work and evil through evil work. Karma connects the past, present and future. Sattva Guna, Rajo Guna, Tamo Gunas will make the difference of the individu personality. Good deeds and benevolent work predominate in Sattva Guna. Extreme passion or desire to grab or appropriate the others wealth will dominate in Rajo Guna. And reckless behaviour provokes talks, acts without thinking promote in Tamo Guna"*

**From the Brihadaranyaka Upanishad (III 2-13)**

The classification of Karma is spread into four categories which are as follows:-

| | | |
|---|---|---|
| Sanchita | – | Compilation of all Karmas. |
| Praraabdha | – | Karmas of one's previous life carried over to the present life. |
| Kriyaman | – | Current Karmas that are to be performed. |
| Aagami | – | The future and forthcoming Karmas. |

The present, past, future and codified Karmas will make a difference in individual identity from one to another.

*"The Karmas are to be performed at free will."*

**From the Bhagavad-Gita**

If it is performed, that Karma will become fate for tomorrow. The first two above Karmas 'Sanchitha and Praraabdha' are fated Karmas which are already done. Any remedial measures to combat the evil effects of such Karmas by ritual or pooja or wearing precious stones or Yanthras are prevalent and useful.

Katopanishad (Ref 5-7.9) reveals the great hidden truth regarding birth and death. The entire edifice of the Astrology is built on the basis of the theory of re-birth and law of Karma. Karma is explained in the Bhagavad-Gita

*"As a man discarding worn-out clothes, takes other new ones, likewise the embodied soul, casting off worn-out bodies, enters into others which are new."*

**From the Bhagavad-Gita (II-22)**

The nature of Karma is explained in the Bhagavad-Gita

*"He who has fallen from yoga, having obtained the higher worlds (heaven etc...) to which men of meritorious deeds alone are entitled, and having resided there for countless years, takes birth in the house of pious and wealthy men."*

**From the Bhagavad-Gita (VI-41)**

Such a lesson is important to reveal that the mighty rishis have reincarnated like celestials in human form for specific propagation of values and departed after the mission. The first Bhaagam is depicted in brief to reiterate the effectiveness of the Karma during one's lifetime and its Vaastu application of the native or nation, whosoever concerned.

## Necessity to Observe Vaastu Shastra

The observance of Vaastu leads to a happy and prosperous life. The need for acceptance of the shastra of Vaastu is to lead a pleasant, prospective and a comfortable life without any kind of problems. The benefits of Vaastu Science are noteworthy:

- Vaastu Shastra leads to sound health and sleep.
- It facilitates excellent job, services or profession.
- It regulates the inflow of finance.
- It creates a congenial and peaceful atmosphere.
- It encourages good education for one's progeny.

- It ensures prompt and timely decisions.
- It enables to acquisition of landed properties and knowledge.
- It helps to upkeep better relations and understanding with all.
- It promotes good behaviour and action.

Above all, Vaastu helps to achieve more prosperity, peace and happiness. The real effect of Vaastu Science is invisible directly to human eyes. The hidden prosperity in Vaastu observance can sustain when living in a house. The inmates experience happy feelings with the food they eat, the shelter they live, the profession they practice and the relations they maintain with relatives or friends. The native will gain special inborn strength and stability of mind and body, and takes accurate and timely decisions or actions whenever necessary.

The inmates of a Vaastu house will be generous and always sympathetic to the poor and needy. And, that in turn will bestow on them peace and prosperity.

The following aspects are necessary to be considered in Vaastu rules:

1. The point of entry of the Sun's rays into the house.
2. The Northeast sunlight entry is important.
3. A Northeastern well point, pooja room, and more open space are to be provided.
4. The sides of West, Southwest or Southeast parts are not auspicious for certain types of work and are to be avoided for free spaces, openings, projections or cuttings. These areas are utilized for the use of staircase.
5. Temples can be constructed in thick forests or top of hills and mountain regions in order to achieve fame, prosperity and popularity.
6. The flow of water is steady in eastern and northeastern areas, and there will be a tremendous influence or good symptoms of prosperity and happiness to the inmates and neigbhours.
7. The potency of Vaastu results is to be felt by the house inmates, but prediction is only possible while in stay within the area, zone or side of the land or house. Paada (Cell) Vaastu details are provided with the nature defects and the parts to be affected thereafter.

## Sages' Views on Vaastu

The divine vision of ancient Sages was far more deeply based on the realities and values of life. These are the prominent sources of Vaastu wisdom. The rishis were aware of the different types of energies radiating from the Sun and planets or field forces. The first field force has the relation of Time and Space connecting an important role of Astrology with Vaastu. The Pancha Bhoota elements, i.e., Earth, Water, Fire, Wind and Sky along with the eight cardinal orientations, directions, sides or corners greatly affect the owner of the house. The various sources of energies radiating from each element will affect or influence the inmates of the house progressively or reversely.

The ancients devised simple and inexpensive methods for examining a site, its measurement and orientation. According to sages, the Vaastu application includes the soil, the land size, the shape, levels, angles, water points, growing trees, mounts, projections, extensions, cuts, veedhi-shoolas etc. which are subjected to microscopic scrutiny and examination.

Ancient rishis classified the architects into four types of craftsmen, entrusting various levels of work with:

1. Sthapati for layout and designing,
2. Sootragraahi for supervising the functions,
3. Takshaka for refining and shaping material for construction, and
4. Vardhaki for wood and material work.

The Sthapati is responsible for all master planning and construction and usually takes advice from acharya and the Yajamaana of the family. Some of the devoted craftsmen maintain a high degree of precision in making idols or structures. Among the architects, specialists are assigned for carving stones, designing, wood, etc.

The perimeter of the building is specifically calculated to derive the Ayadivarga. The Ayas are obtained by number calculations to find out the fitness of the structure. The terms like Dwajaya, Simhaya, Vrushaya and Gajaya are auspicious for entrance. According to Deva Shilpi Vishwakarma, sixteen types of bad effects are possible to doors, windows or pillars during the construction of a house like andhaka, rudhira, kubja, kaanam, bhadheerika, digvakra, chipitakam, vijangajam, maranam, kudilam, kubjakam, suptam etc. Another ten types of bad effects like frequent illness karmic diseases of leprosy, kanavedha or blindness will obstruct the good fortune.

The patterns and size of the village, towns or cities are devised with divisions convenient to the ancient rulers. The Vishwakarma Vaastu explains the towns near the seashore suffixed with 'pattanam' at the end name, i.e., Vishaka, Chennai, Bhimuni, Machili, Naaga, Mumbai.

## Sources of Vaastu Shastra

The main sources of Vaastu Shastra have come through ancient sages from Lord Brahma.

There are many more sources which are scattered in different regions of India, to supplement with. Most of the works are ancient and written on palm leaves in Sanskrit. The varied forms and works drawn from different environmental zones are venerable and outstanding. They facilitate exposure to the beneficial aspects of Vaastu to millions of its followers. Some of these sources are given below:

- **Brihat Samhita by Sage Varaahamira:** The book elaborates the structure of the buildings, their composition and strength. The *Brihat Samhita* enunciates the strength and thickness of pillars and beams with partial division of designs. Some structural buildings are curved in various designs, especially bottom base, in gold. The Utpala complementary on the *Brihat Samhita* refers to Vaastu Vidya as an anga or limb of Jyothisha and that "Vaastu falls in the category of samhita teachings".

- **Maayamatam by Mamuni Maayamayan:** *Maayamatam* is a general treatise on architecture in puraana and aagama references. Manasaara represents the University of dwelling. This book on Vaastu Shastra was in Sanskrit and authored by Asura Shilpi Maayamayan during the Chola period. This coherent work defines Vaastu as "anywhere where immortals or mortals live". *Maayamayan* was an expert both in Vaastu and astrology. Hence, he was recognized as a 'Divine architect' like Vishwakarma. His famous astrological work "*Soorya Siddhanta*" is famous even today for daily reference as a source book and for all panchanga calculations.

- **Manasaara by Manasa Muni:** Like the "*Brihat Samhita*" and "*Maayamatam*", the book "*Manasaara*" is also considered to be the source of all presentations of the Vaastu Tradition and it also contains the iconography of Jain and Buddhist images. However, this is universally accepted for consultation. In fact, this treatise "Manasaara" is identified as the first Vaastu script available on earth.

• **Samaraangana Sootradhaara by Bhoja Deva:** The book *Samaraangana Soothradhaara* has 230 stanzas. The principle of constructing vimaanas (aeroplanes) and their use have been well explained during war and peace time. The definition of Vaastu taken from this book says that earth is the principal of Vaastu and all buildings situated on the earth and whatever is created from Vaastu or objects of the earth are also called Vaastu. Bhoja Deva explained clearly the calculation of Ayas, Vyayas, Thithi, Nakshatra, Vaara and Dina etc., in the book to select the best to avoid 'doshas' (disadvantages or perils) and to ensure happiness to the owner. Dr. Robert Pinotti II, an Italian scientist is of the opinion that it will be better to examine Hindu texts in detail than dismiss the traditional scripts as myths. Bhoja Deva has also given a clear picture of town planning, construction of forts, palaces, underground war passage dungeons and several attractive crafts through his works *Samaraangana Soothradhaara.*

• **Vishwakarma Vaastu by Divine Deva Shilpi:** The divine Viswa Shilpi Vishwakarma's capability of constructing marvellous and magnificient altars, and palaces by using ultra modern designs with diamonds, pearls, emeralds, white or yellow saffire stones was remarkable and renowned.

Deva Shilpi Vishwakarma and Asura Shilpi Mayan have the same view that the basis of 32768 units of paramaanu was on the central point of the globe with a slight deviation of the pole region. The essential food requirement of a human being is clearly mentioned in the Charaka Siddhaantam Paramaanu-wise. Such minute calculations, weights and measures were used by the ancients, which assumed high value in Vaastu Shastra. Vishwakarma is believed to be the self-born supernatural architect of the Devas.

The *Vishwakarma Vaastu Shastra* has explained in detail the mode of construction of houses. The area has different divisions of twelve kinds of villages and twenty seven types of towns. Seven towns are taken as fit and proper models for the rulers, while the other 20 types of the towns are allocated for other groups. There are a number of cities constructed for the people as per the specifications of Vishwakarma Vaastu near the potable water sources or near the seashore.

• **Matsya Puraana:** The *Matsya puraana* contains an elaborate picture on architecture and sculpture. It specifically mentions eighteen enlightened rishis who enriched Vaastu Shastra. These eighteen rishis and their contributions to the material knowledge of directions, architecture and cosmology are engraved in letters of gold in the history of Vaastu Shastra.

- Bhrugu
- Vasishta
- Maayamayan
- Nagnajit
- Indra
- Kaartikeya
- Eshaka
- Krishna
- Shukra
- Atri
- Vishwakarma
- Naarada
- Vishalaaksha
- Brahma
- Nadiswara
- Garga
- Anuradha
- Brihaspati

The names of these rishis have been provided for the first-hand information of the subject of Vaastu. Their admirable vision and knowledge have contributed greatly to the enrichment of the divine science: Vaastu Shastra. Vaastu methods and applications were passed on to the common masses by several rishis and their disciples through a number of generations.

- **Tantra Samucchayam (Shilpa Bhaagam):** Chennas Narayana Nambudiripad wrote this book *Tantra Samucchayam* by codifying the available Idol worship practice of Saivism (Aagamas) and Vaishnavism (Samhitaas). Such agamas and samhitas of ritualistic compilation are known as Tantras or Shakti worship, and they are mainly centralizing the temple architecture and Vaastu designs in its shilpa bhaagam section.

- **Manushyaalaya Chandrika by Srimangalath Nilakantan Acharya:** The book Manushyaalaya Chandrika has created a building structure as per Vaastu shilpa principles with a valid foundation and construction parameters.

The book '*Manushyaalaya Chandrika*' is a unified version of the principle and practice of Gruha Vaastu wisdom prevalent in different regions/states of the country. The scripts of this book were written in palm leaves with description of technique of residential construction and temple architecture during 1565 AD.

• **Naatya Shastra by Bharat Muni:** The *Naatya Shastra* of Bharat Muni gives details of construction of open theatres, marriage halls, conference halls, community cafes with the facilities for dance and music. Cinema theatres, open public theatres for meals, prayers and for cinema or drama troupe's gathering halls are available in Naatya Shastra with diagrams and specific construction details.

• **Gruha Sootram by Rishi Vyaasa:** The *Gruha Sootram* gives details of marma sootram, Brahma naabhi and other sootrams and the ways to rectify if so occurred. Vyaasa Mahamuni's book on shilpa samgraham and buildings is renowned for temple measurement and construction.

The book elaborates the mandala of sootrams and rajjus in detail along with brahma naabhi touch during the construction time. Such touch will end in dangerous consequences. The main Paada Mandala classification of 64 cells (8x8), 81 cells (9x9) and 100 cells (10x10) respectively for Manduka, Paramsayika or Aasana Paada Vinyaasam is clearly mentioned in the book.

• **Artha Shastra:** This book on Arthashaastra provides a full view of measurement of yoni, ayam, vyayam, age, perimeter calculations and formulae. The book provides the entire measurement functions of one hasta or kolu which is equivalent to 72 centimeters. Nowadays, measurement of land is done in square meters and rooms size also measured in terms of meters. A bhaagam is fully devoted for Arthashastra prescription and perimeter formula details.

• **Padma Samhita:** This book mentions the different ways and methods of constructing houses and their architectural designs. The text also describes the ancient Vaastu Samgraham and landscaping methods. A special emphasis is accorded to the types of houses and their beautification through structural designs for stability and attraction. Some houses have accepted such designs and most of the temples have adopted natural architectural designs and sculptures which were very prominent in ancient period.

• **Ishta Shiva Guru Deva Paddhathi:** This book elaborates the idol-making for gods and goddesses and installation of Shri Ganapati, Shri Ayyappan and other deities for their krupa or boon as per Vaastu vidya.

The details of various types of metals and stones used for making 'Vigrahas' (idols) from brass, gold, panch loha metal, black stone, black saffire stone, black diamond stone of several modes and kinds are given in this book. Expert craftsmen are authorised to make such gods/goddesses shapes, image of idols for home usage, public places, and temples. Temple idol making, by carving stone and metal compound mixture for embossing is the most tedious work. Such Idol making requires specified number of days of penance to the craftsmen and the observance till the completion with the purity, piety and devotion.

• **Sooryan:** The Soorya provides sun rays fall, its brightness reflections and vibrations, rainbow and the ultra violet rays of vivid colours. In Vaastu Shastra, the Soorya as a source provides protection from impurities, darkness and laziness. The Soorya with brigh light is symbolized for super power of humanity, charity and help.

• **Pithaamaha Bhishma:** The Pithaamaha's advice is condensed in the Vaastu wisdom giving optimum elaborate information on the subject. This advice is given to humanity to follow as a guideline of house building culture to achieve progress and prosperity to all believers who practice it. Such formal advice is stricrly followed even today in the observance and practice of Vaastu principles.

• **Shilpa Ratna:** A Vaastu Vidhaana granth by Kumara describes the entire facets of the Vaastu science. In this book, the basic construction parameters of houses or buildings and various types of complexes, multiplexes or flats are given in detail. The size of the house varies from a small family, to a big joint family and is shown in the book with the implication of its use. Mr.Kumara warns all house builders or inmates that no toilets should be constructed inside the chatusaalas.

• **Naveena Shilpa Concept:** The *Naveena Shilpa* Concept outlines the details of modern housing styles and gardening methods. The latest form of modern architectural pattern, akin to designs which are of a costly nature, is mentioned in the book. The expenditure incurred on a particular design and its approximated measurement and value are also provided in detail.

• **Madhana Suthradhaara by Bhoja Deva:** Bhoja Deva's book on Vaastu Vidya methods mentioning the village, individual, house, numbers and luck of each is a worthy work in the science of Vaastu. The calculation of a house, gramam, village, taluka, district and the state in the order of (1) execellent progression, (2) ordinary life, (3) difficult living, (4) occupation or (5) the land of dead is exactly shown in the book. In a village, if a house is constructed on the dead or barren land, life in that habitation resembles a dead world. Luck and progresses are calculated with numerological methods and the concepts are sometimes difficult to grasp, since the language used for writing the palm book is colloquial Telugu.

• **Raaja Simha Vaastu:** This book contains full information on kingdoms, capitals and the details of modern designing fashions of construction manuals. The *Raaja Simha Vaastu* book is famous among contractors, builders and those who are interested in Vaastu. The Sultans of Hyderabad, Mughal architects and local kingdoms collected the first book to be published. The Forts, underground passages for movements of soldiers and Darwaja of Rajadhani (Entrance Doors), beautiful gardens, parks and public places are reconstructed with the help of the guidelines given in this book.

• **Vaastu Raaja Vallabham:** This book explains principles and norms of Vaastu with the constraints of making royal capitals, residences, palaces, altars, and temples etc. The book is considered a handbook for ready reference. Synopses of each point on Vaastu rules are available regarding land, trees, marma, paada vinsyaasam, number of doors in a room, total windows, ventilators or doors for calculations as a ready recknoner.

• **Aparaajita Pratcha:** This is a model of Vaastu shilpa kala manuscript Manual which is meant for designing, planning, and the modern building concept. The book is also written in Telugu and is used by the common folks who are conscious about improvement. The popularity is enshrined in the Deccan, Vidharbha, Bhopal and Jaipur areas in construction on the lines of Aparaajit pritcha designs and planning.

• **Dipaarpana Shilpa Ratna:** This is a condensed book on Vaastu vidya as a mirror for Vaastu designs on sculpture, sopaanams, pillars, etc. A number of varieties of sopaanam (staircases), pillars, wooden or metal craftsmanship work, structural designs, architectural attractions and use of mirrors are all mentioned for Vaastu Shastra guidelines. The nature of modern construction techniques or various modifications is vividly accommodated in abundance.

• **Gruha Chitraavali:** A detailed description of measurement, yoni gruhas and various kinds of saalas is given in this book. Usually Simha yoni, Dhwaja yoni, Gaja yoni and Vrushabha yoni are used for South, West, North and East facing houses. The book gives a complete description and calculation of Ayam, Vyayam, Constellations (Stars), Tithi, Karanams, Yogams, Dhruvathis, etc.

• **Shilpa Vidya Saaravali:** This Vaastu Vidya book is containing land size, sand test methods, house making, gate, door, paadams calculation etc. Several land test modes are given as examples to select the best land. Colour community selection of best land is also provided in this book as a caste-wise land division.

• **Vaastu Vidya by Sunaka Mahamuni:** The *Vaastu Vidya* book by Sunaka Mahamuni is very specific with regard to the availability of good land, curse land or prishta land including explicating land afflicted with several problems and troubles.

Vaastu source materials are scattered. However, efforts are being made to compile the available palm leaves or books of Gruha Sootram or Arthashaastra. Traditionally, several sages like Bhrigu, Atri Vasishta, Vishwakarma, Maayamayan, Varaahamihira, Soorya, Shaunaka, Pitaamaha Bhishma and Naarada have developed the science of Vaastu. Much information on Vaastu roots is available mostly in Sanskrit in varied forms drawn from the different environmental zones of India. The approach of the ancient rishis is comprehensive, integral and holistic. This source is a very solid foundation for the basis of Vaastu Shastra. According to Vyaasa Muni, "time does not exist independently, it moves with the space but it has a relative material existence". The concept of existence of matter has been corroborated by Einstein.

The law of Earth's gravitational forces discovered by Sir Issac Newton, and scientifically proved, will be useful for the study of Vaastu.

# Bhaagam 2

## Cardinal Directions (Orientation)

Cardinal Direction or Orientation means the numbers of sides and corners that exist in a land plot. One will accept only the best plot of land among the many chosen for the house construction. Vaastu Shastra is very particular about the orientation, shape and road location to ascertain whether the symptom of the selected land is good, self-projecting or in progression. Generally, methods of Orientation selection of land are simple by determination or understanding of definite direction in response to eastern stimulus.

Usually a square or rectangular shape having four sides or four corners is selected.

• **Ashta Diks (Eight Directions):** The Land is a significant factor, either purchased or chosen for proposed construction. The Ashta Diks have to be understood clearly as they are needed to locate the land in terms of direction or dik determination. In Vaastu science, the direction, or location of dik is very important to determine its presiding deities and controlling planet in each direction.

***Sides (Diks):*** In each side or corner, there will be one deity or planet to control and bless the environment. There are four sides in a land area, known by the name Diks. The Sides are NEWS, i.e., North, East, West and South with the presiding deities of Kubera, Indra, Varuna and Pitrupati respectively.

***Corners (Vidiks):*** Likewise, there are four corners in a land plot known by Vidiks, Moola or Kone. They are Northeast, Southeast, Northwest and Southwest controlled by their owners Eshana, Agni, Vaayu and Nairuti respectively.

The particulars of eight sides, corners with one middle joint section and their controlling deities are given below:-

| | | |
|---|---|---|
| 1. Northeast | NE | Eshana Corner |
| 2. Southeast | SE | Agni Corner |
| 3. Northwest | NW | Vaayu Corner |
| 4. Southwest | SW | Nairuti Corner |
| 5. North | N | Kubera side |

| | | |
|---|---|---|
| 6. East | E | Indra side |
| 7. West | W | Varuna side |
| 8. South | S | Pitrupati side |
| 9. Centre | M | Brahma sthan |

At the centre of the land one owner or controller permanently occupies the space with his dignity and power. The owner of the middle portion of the Land is the Brahma. The location is called Brahmasthan.

• **The Planets and Corners:** The sides (diks) and corners (vidiks) controlled by each planet in direction, will have pertinent significance in Panch Bhoota reflective actions.

For example: the sun rays enter at the eastern sector especially in Northeast, East and Southeast during morning hours. And the rays touch Western sector at Southwest, West and Northwest during evening hours. The angle and brightness of the sun rays falling on each sides or corners will have different modes and ways which are given below:

| | | | | |
|---|---|---|---|---|
| East | : | Shukra | (Venus) | Indrasthan |
| Southeast | : | Chandra | (Moon) | Agni Devan |
| South | : | Mangal | (Mars) | Pitrupati |
| Southwest | : | Sarpa | (Raahu) | Nairuti (Kanni Moola) |
| West | : | Shani | (Saturn) | Varunasthan |
| Northwest | : | Shiki | (Ketu) | Maruti (Vaayu) |
| North | : | Guru | (Jupiter) | Kuberasthan |
| Northeast | : | Budha | (Mercury) | Eshana |
| Centre | : | Soorya | (Sun) | Brahmasthan |

The Vaastu experts generally use the mariners' compass (the North showing needle machine) to recognize the exact location or direction for enabling them to analyse before pronouncing the alteration or rectification steps.

The details of sides and corners are given:-

| | | |
|---|---|---|
| Southwest (corner) | : | planet-Raahu, Nairuti corner, Sarpa Naathan, Kanni moola. |
| West (side) | : | planet-Saturn, Paschim side, Shani Naathan, Varunasthan. |
| Northwest (vidhik) | : | planet-Sikhi, Vaayu corner (Maruti), Ketu (Sikhi) Naathan. |
| North dik | : | planet-Jupiter (Guru), Kuberashtan, Jupiter Naathan. |

| | | |
|---|---|---|
| Northeast corner | : | planet-Mercury (Budha), Eshana Moola, Budha Naathan. |
| East side | : | planet-Venus (shukra), Devendra shtaan, Shukra Naathan. |
| Southeast corner | : | planet-Moon (Chandra), Agni moola, Moon Naathan. |
| South dik | : | planet-Mars (Mangal) Pithrushtan, Chouwa Naathan |
| Centre (middle) | : | planet-Sun (soorya), Brahmasthan, Ravi Naathan. |

- **Cardinal Orientation Chart**:

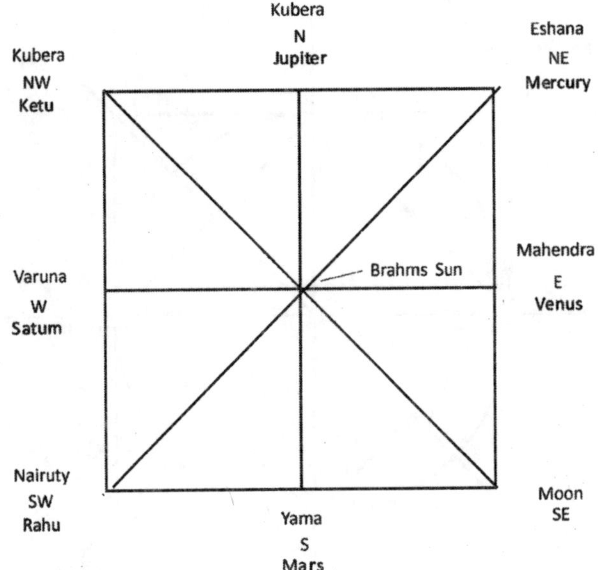


- **Sensitivity of Ashta Diks**

Why are the cardinal directions significant to sensitivity?

There are total nine sides, corners or brahma naabhi in every land plot as drawn in the above orientation chart. One must possess an idea of the direction of the diks, vidiks and centre position.

The four corners (vidiks), four sides (Diks) should be measured to locate the house point without any deviation of diks angles and diagonal dimension. Diagonal variations are not good for obeying the cardinal directions rules. To avoid all complications, it is desirable to follow the dik rules strictly during the layout time of colonies or plotting the land area.

In Vaastu Shastra, the rules are similar for both small and large area plots. The applicability of rules will not differ with land plots irrespective of land size or shape. The Vaastu Shastra norms once applied will tend to change its position and marma position with every further subsequent change, alteration or modification.

According to the marma Vaastu parameters, at first, outside house premise will be scrutinized fully to ensure arrangement, and then only the inside of house for rectification. Other wise, corrections are incomplete as per norms of Vaastu. Information received from consultation, the personal experience and the feedback reports of the actual users play an important role in the Vaastu Shastra.

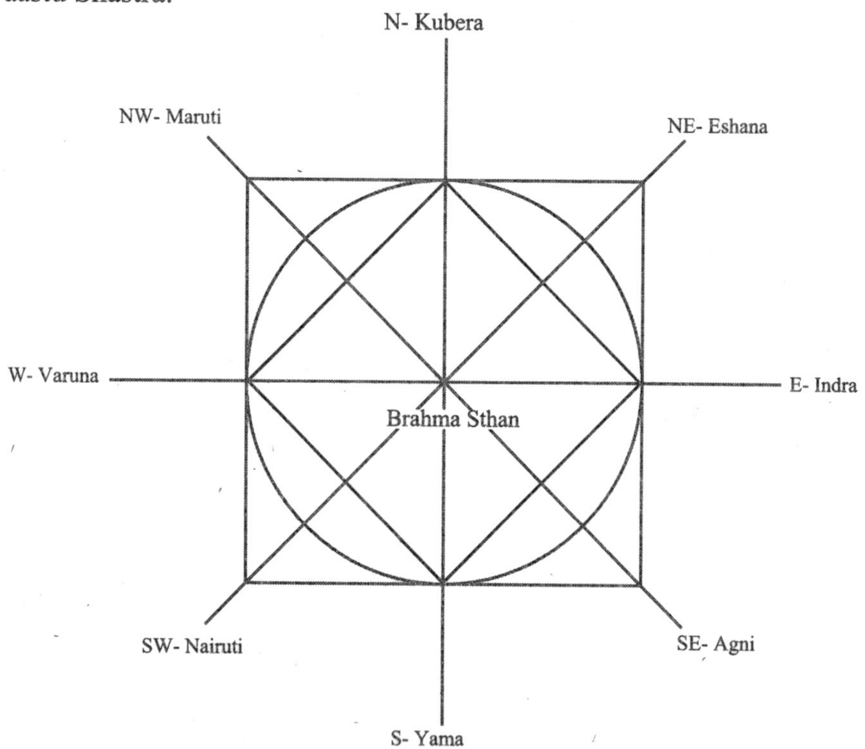


**Diagram of Orientation showing all Eight Directions and Centre**

## Primary Elements of Nature (Pancha Bhootas)

The Almighty has made everything including living or non-living things. Like human beings, Pancha Inthriangal (five sense organs) have vivid functions to perform i.e. Eyes to see, Ear to hear, Nose to breath, Skin to feel or Head to think. Similarly, Vaastu Shastra also has five primary elements of nature, i.e. Agni (Fire), Bhoomi (Earth), Jhalam (Water), Vaayu (Wind) and Aakash (Sky). These five elements of nature are considered to be the essential limbs of Vaastu. The participation of the Sun and other elements in the sky will automatically rejuvenate the functions of these elements. Each dik will be explained below one by one. All presiding deities and diks ensure a happy, sound sleep and all things at ease and peace to all inmates if the land and the house are in order as per Vaastu.

• **Agni (Fire):** Southeast Agneya Corner is allocated to Agni Deva in Roopa shape. Temperamental disorders and disintegration are bound to occur when the SE corner in the plot or house has any excessive projection or cut. The word 'agni' itself means the angry temperament of burning nature and human hot temptations. A natural healing touch will be provided by the control and manifestation of Vaastu parameters. The family members, especially women, will be able to sustain a very congenial and good relationship by keeping kitchen at the Southeast with East side platform. Scientist have recognized the Southeast corner as an ignition point when the Sun rays fall on SE region as red rays. However, in the view of ancient Sages, Agni ray is the promoter of efficiency and it bestows capability to the house owner.

The controller of the area is the Lord of Fire or Ignition. This area is an instrumental zone for getting help in all kinds of eventualities of Nature or fire and accidents. The Moon is the control deity of Southeast corner area. Moon will represent as Mother having purity of mind, great affection and strong will-power. The periodical fifteen days wax and fifteen days wane of the Moon will always carry with upward or downward travel either to pournami or amavasi.

• **Bhoomi (Earth):** The Earth is created by the Almighty, billions of years ago, with the ratio of three-fourth water and one-fourth land. The Earth is spread over 200 countries in seven continents. The Earth possesses Guna (Quality) when the owner constructs the house in square or rectangular size plot which bestows prosperity and betterment. The centre of the site is known as the Brahmasthaan which should be free from pits, boulders, pillars, walls or heavy loading areas. Then only the owner of the house will have a free life, fulfilment of the aspirations of job, service or profession with excellent finance, men and material. Controller of this area is the 'SUN' deity, the giver of ever shining light to all.

• **Jhalam (Water):** Water is considered as the most important portfolio of human financial aspirations. Money power is the best for confidence, health and social standing and good reputation. Vaastu, the real science, is a gift of nature which offered blessings to all in the form of water sources. The Water element stimulates the inflow of money. Since water has taste-qualities, pure or clear water-flow into a house symbolizes the inflow of honest money from NE, N and E sides. However, the West dik varuna is considered as a last resort for water sources, if there is no source of water at Northeast, North and East.

The Eshana (NE) zone is meant for water position. Meena Raasi, Kumba Raasi, Vrushava Raasis are good and progressive. However Soma, Indra, Varuna, Apa, Apatvatsa, Indrajit, Andariksha cells are also considered as auspicious for water sources. The Northeast Eshana corner is controlled by Budha (Mercury) the Karaka for wisdom, intelligence and educational success.

• **Vaayu (Air):** The Northwest Vaayu Corner is controlled by Sikhi also known as Maruti Corner. The Vaayu corner is very powerful felt only by touch and sound. Such invisible element has firm grip, extra-power and supreme energy. Such contributions are beyond the judgment of human beings. The inmates will be blessed with the positive prosperity and strength if one sticks to the norms of Vaastu. The control planet in the NW Vaayu corner is Ketu (Dragon tail). The Lord of Wind and his sons Veer Hanuman and Bheem Sen have shown their strength and vitality during their life as envisaged in the Epics- the Ramayana and the Mahabharata. Wind is normally very calm and peaceful but not welcome when it becomes extremely violent, dangerous and destructive.

• **Aakash (Space):** The universal concept of sky is beyond one's imagination and thinking. The space manifests God's creativity and it is comprised of many layers in the forms of atmosphere, troposphere, stratosphere, mesosphere, and thermosphere. High density, clouds formation, chemical composition of oxygen, nitrogen, hydrogen, oxides, etc., are compressed in the sky. Such comprehensive and multifarious activities were foresighted by the ancients and confirmed by scientists by giving more information on the sun, planets or stars in the orbit. The sky is the medium of effective passage of light, heat, waves, magnetic reactions, communications including gravitational forces of pull and push of earth and equilibrium.

The *Miracles of Vaastu Shastra* elaborates activation of environmental climate with the primal element of nature's combination, friction, multiplication and interaction of forthcoming the end output. In the combination of five elements of nature, if combined doubly or jointly, the output fraction will arrive in vivid formations. The ultimate end result will be awesome, amazing and it becomes just a miracle to the humanity. Given below are formative formulae:-

W= water, A=air, F=fire, E=earth, S=space or sky. In combination mixed up 'Plus + and Minus -':

- W+A+F+E+S = +5
- -W-A-F-E+S = -4, or +1
- -W-A-F+E+S = -3, or +2
- -W-A+F+E+S = -2, or +3
- -W+A+F+E+S = -1, or +4
- -W-A-F-E-S = -5 or 0.

The formative outcome formula will affect every house inmate or member by giving full satisfaction in practical life. The ultimate result whether good or bad will penetrate heavily to the life of each and every one either by inflicting its heavy burden or its positive miracle functions for high profile experiences or atmosphere. The final experience will be unbelievable; in normalcy, such combination has to be considered as wonder or miracle of Vaastu Shastra.

• **Earth and Water:** The Earth–Water combination has the real basis of gene for every life. The water content is the saviour of human beings, animals or plants or any microsomes. Nobody can survive without water. This combination has been emphatically mentioned with their inner connections. Water source has importance from the place where it is coming into the compound, storing, using and water distribution line connected to inside the house. All water source or distribution points will require minute observation. The money flow sources are reckoned carefully into the house and it has similarity with the water systems circulation.

The source of water in the vicinity has a direct link with the money power of the house occupiers and owners. The sources will influence irrespective of the nearness and nature or water is drawn from any of the available lake, river, tributary, canal, sea or a pond etc. Such availability of water sources in the nearby areas will enable all inhabitants to make use of water for irrigation, farming, agriculture or domestic requirements and other activities. The water-earth combination will always create an excellent social or professional status, elevation of present service with hefty salary package, and further more gain of contacts and co-operation from various angles. Over and above, this combination will encourage association with top personalities, feeling of brotherlihood, helping attitude, humanitarian or charitable tendency towards fellow-being and co-operation to all. And a special congenial atmosphere will prevail with wife, children and parents.

The location of water gives rise to several implications; the future developments will be affected adversely. Water is used for drinking, washing, cleaning or bathing. The health of the inmates or associates will be affected if the water in channels or pipeline is clogged. Dirty water stagnation or mixing with muddy water or other wastes will emit smell and suffocation. Health safeguards are provided with periodical regular cleaning and maintenance. The symptoms will reveal whether the water earth combination will do harm or good either due to lack of agriculture or loss of house edifice. Certain calamities will occur in the form of breakage of bunds, falling river rock, damages due to dam, rain havoc, sea-erosion, tsunami, floods, etc, causing devastation of the entire area.

• **Earth and Fire:** The Earth-Fire combination involves a hot atmosphere from the beginning to the end. Each and every object on earth is changeable to the vagaries of nature, atmospheric dilutions or global climatic alterations. The elements of earth differ from place to place and are available in the form of sand, rock, loose land, clay land, mud mixed soil, red soil or black soil. The mountain rocks can produce fire or desert sand can fully ignite with high heat and temperature. Nobody can easily walk over the hot black loose sand near the seashore during bright sunny hours. Barren or loose desert sand heat will hamper the human inhabitation and plant growth. In the case of forest fire, the devastation becomes wide spread. A large part of forest area will be destroyed causing heavy loss of life to humans, animals, forest wood or state income. The fire and earth combination will reveal the nature of the land, proximity to vegetation, mountains, rocks or valley, trees or plants, human occupation and agriculture. Such experience of the symptoms will be decisive to the earth-fire combination in considering whether good or bad to the inmates.

The Earth and Fire relation is dignified in making vivid varieties of clay utensils, earthen pots, bricks, and tiles, fashionable or decorative items of attractive proportions. Some of these materials are very useful for constructing houses and buildings. Possibilities of fire, rain, fire wind, and thick forest fire and volcano erruption are not ruled out under this Earth and Fire combination.

• **Earth and Wind:** The Combination of Earth and Wind elements relation is significant as it provides an explanation of various kinds of miseries in an alarming proportion to the house inmates. The nature of the wind blow as soft or hard will definitely influence the combination of Wind and Earth. And, presumably such combine will not be conducive to promote a good atmosphere of happiness or enjoyment. The powerful wind like storm will uproot even good old trees of forest area. The soft air will make more comfortable and fresh feelings to all; strong wind will become disastrous for the occupants' life, property or belongings.

The destructive power of wind can be understood only when the heavy loss of life of man, money and the assets are reckoned. Some of the important factors are considered in this combination of Earth and Wind for the nature of barren sand, desert storm, thick dense forest, dangerous occupational hazards, snake bite venom, etc. The wind power is very useful for generating electricity like other sources of solar energy from the Sun, thermal power from charcoal, hydro electric energy from water.

• **Earth and Aakash:** This Earth and Space combination is presumably excellent for several reasons. The light rays and sound waves travel faster in the space than in any other medium. Earth's gravitational pull or push attributes at a higher level of frequency in space medium. The relationship of Earth and Space is self-explanatory by recognition of the Laws of Motion and the Laws of Gravitational force. The physics students attach great importance to the nature of space–earth elements studies because of multiple composition and combination of layers or gases.

It is essential for all human beings to inhale fresh air in such free breathing space medium; the composition is provided with all types of gases including oxygen. Carbon dioxide, required for plants and trees, will be supplied by exhale of human beings; it shows their reciprocity. The most remarkable combination of Earth and Aakash factor is well connected to Vaastu Shastra with sun's sparkling rays. The Sun beams entering the house will radiate warmth and brightness eliminating the gloominess around and making the life of inmates cheerful. The Sun rays bright reflection plays a great role in space medium together with the timely occurances of vivid colours of vibgyor, cosmic, ultraviolet rays in Earth and Aakash combination.

• **Fire and Wind:** An open Fire and Wind combination will not be conducive to produce good result or progressive outcome. The Fire and wind blow will cause heavy destruction to the entire area. This Atmosphere of wind and Fire combination seems to be very dangerous and frightening. The occurrence of fire in uncontrollable circumstances will create extraordinary damage or loss to the life and property of many people. In such a condition, the gust of wind will be more aggressive. The fire extinguisher facilities are to be fully equipped for saving the life of millions.

The operation to control the crisis will become more severe and tiresome and may go beyond the control of humans despite the best efforts. The return of life into normalcy will become very tough and extreme attention is required for saving the victims from their state of devastation. This Fire and Wind Combination will do more harm than good. Hence, it is advisable to arrange and equip the house in order as per norms of Vaastu parameters. The rearrangement of the house in accordance with Vaastu should be done within the specified period span i.e. either in six months or in certain cases in a year to make the life in normalcy.

Southeast side kitchen with East platform will always have an impressive and promising combination of Agni and Vaayu. This will give a permanent and comfortable life for the ladies of the house.

• **Water and Aakash:** Rain water is closely associated with water-sky combination. Clouds accumulation and continuous raining are good symptoms. The role of the Sun and Sun rays, sky and stars, climate and atmosphere, oxygen and nitrogen, planets and shooting stars, satellites and solar-lunar energies, rain water and sea erosion, overflowing of rivers and lakes, cyclonic vibrations and negative pressure at the sea or tsunami, etc. will come under this water and sky co-operation umbrella.

This combination will protect a good friendship and living together for a long time. And at the same time, it will prompt to alter inmate's decision or attitude. Sudden change will cause angry temperament leading to abnormal tension or mental strain. The Vaastu Shastra helps to escape from such a difficult situation by self control and inspiration energies from within. The gain of self-confidence and inspiration will automatically solve all problems in a Vaastu principled roof, ensuring love, affection, relationship, finance, contact and status.

• **Fire and Water:** The Fire and Water combination will result in a normal cool but smouldering temperament with hostile or fear aspects which are tantamount to good or bad results beyond one's control. Fire is always self-purifier at the finish. Water element possesses the capability to normalize any kind of difficult situations by a process of slow and steady methods. The combination of fire with water brings an abnormal stagnation stage and often a feeling of insecurity to the inmates.

• **Water and Wind:** The Water and Wind, being the most favoured elements combine, have a far-reaching effect in Vaastu Shastra. This combination will be stimulating, inspiring and providing ingenuity and good friendship to all. The Chinese Feng Shui is based on the combination of Water and Wind. The Feng Shui represents the best combination with the elements of Water and Wind. The words Feng stands for Wind and Shui means Water. The Feng Shui is mentioning the functions of Water positions and Wind assistance to cater to the betterment of the follower. In Vaastu Science, money resembles Water, and Wind will assist to increase it.

The water and wind combine refers to word 'Chi' (energy) like the Indian form of 'praana' to every life.

• **Fire and Space:** The Fire and Space combination is mainly noted for the extreme heat of Sun, its sparkling rays, atmospheric alterations, stars movements, planets revolving changes, rain clouds formations, the existence of oxygen, hydrogen, nitrogen, etc. All are considered as God's manifestations. The example of such operations presently is available in the form of rain harvesting, drawing salt or sulphur from sky, separation of nitrogen and use of helium filled balloons. These are new inventions of some special nature. This combination has received global recognition.

• **Wind and Space:** The travel of Wind and Space combination is considered special for the close relationship and cooperation by keeping their functions in tact. The gentle or gusty blows over the space area will have repercussions on its touches and attachments. The relationship of the Sun, clouds, temperature, gases, and the orientation sides are significant as per Vaastu. The Northwest part is always controlled by Sikhi (ketu) where wind (maruti) occupies its supremacy.

A Special mention of all these factors is very important to the working of miracle functions in Vaastu norms. If one strictly follows Vaastu Shastra, definitely positive and progressive results will help to lead the entire life of the inmates happily.

## Vaastu Norms for Land (Site) Selection

The land (site) examination is an essential step as per Vaastu norms to ensure permanent peace and happiness to the owners/occupants. The scientific Vaastu concept is well applicable to the site (earth) as it has been classified by its nature and elevation.

The need of a well-selected site and positioning of the house plan is clearly envisaged by the ancients in vivid terms. The term land has been classified into four kinds on the basis of the factors of soil, water and flora. The land is called:-

1. Bhadra when it is near to water either sea or river etc.
2. Punna when near to hills and mountains .
3. Supadma when located in the plains .
4. Dhooma when having extreme climate with poisonous plants and rocks.

• **The Need for Classification of Earth:** The basic need and acceptance of earth selection should reveal positive symptoms by:

1. Maintaining the balanced winter and summer climate.

2. Availability of water even during summer time.
3. Over flow of the returned earth back to the same pit.
4. Sudden sprout of seeds if sown in the site within three days. If the seeds sprout in five days it is mediocre. The seeds may be of paddy, wheat mustard, sesame or barley.
5. Flow of water inside the site will be clockwise and finally towards East.
6. The earth should be glazy and soft.
7. The earth should have uniformity on all cardinal zones.
8. The presence of useful fruit bearing trees, good inmates, cow milk, fruits & flowers is added to the aspects favourable for good earth.

- **Size of the Land (Site) to be selected:** For the size or shape of the land bought or earmarked for the purpose of building construction, certain preliminary selection is a must. The shape of the land should be rearranged or rectified with the road in direction-wise. The maximum utilization of the entire land area without Vaastu principles observation or calculation will end in trouble.

In India, the division of land is guided by any rule. It is done consequent to quarrels between brothers, sisters or parents. Such fragmentation and partitions will pave way for a lot of difficulties and hardships even to the local planners and government agencies.

Size of the site should be ideal for the occupants, which derives positive symptoms.

The shape of the land (site) available should be as follows:-

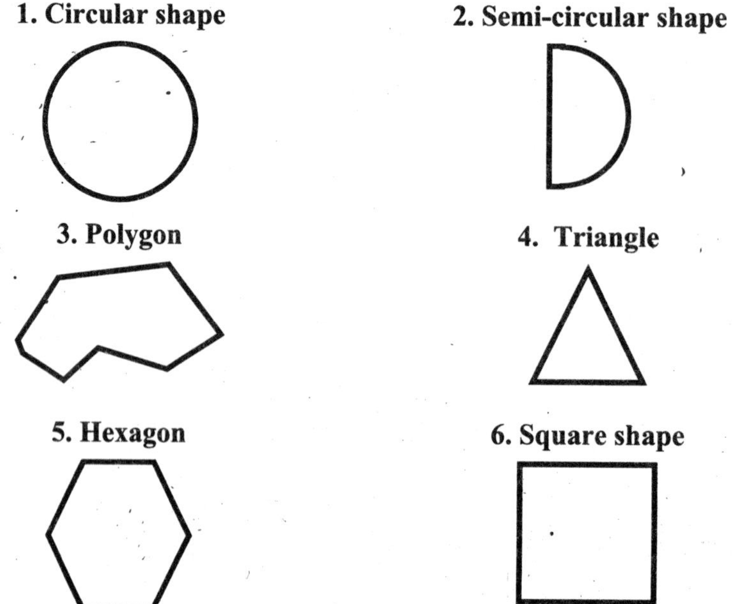

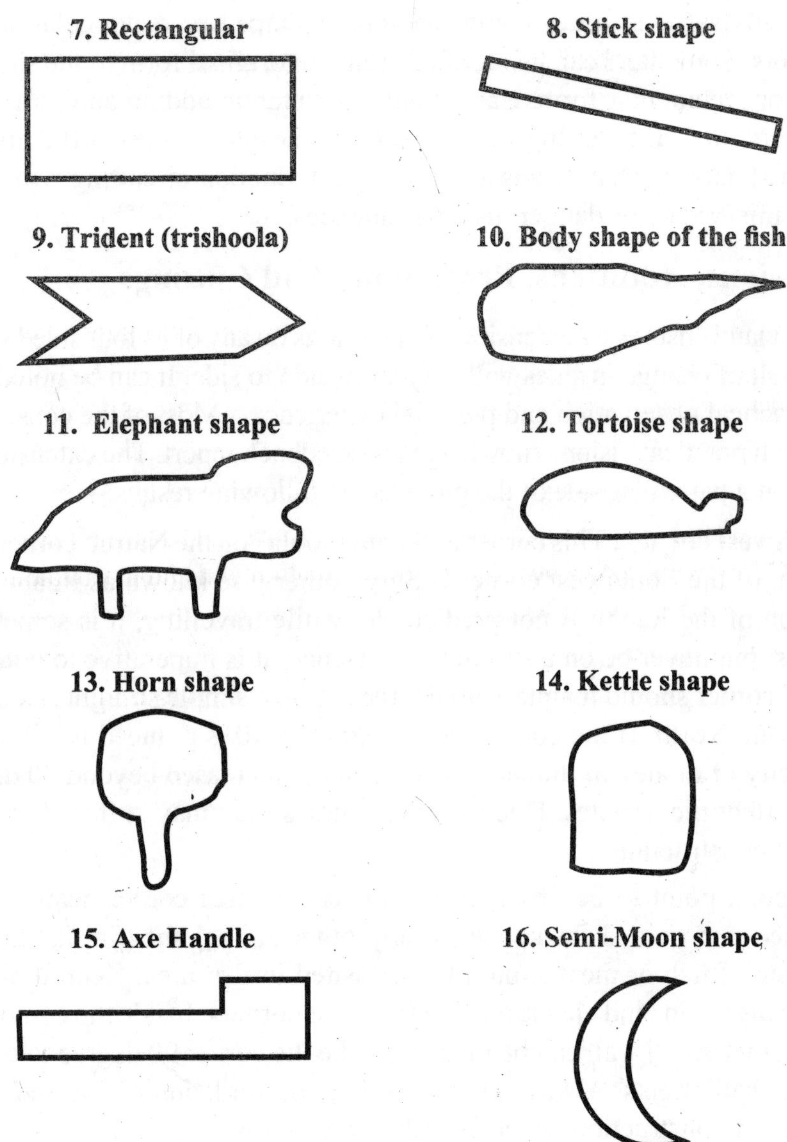


The best shape of land for the construction should be either square or rectangular shape. The land site having above specification other than square or rectangular shape will be prone to various illness and dangerous effects. The misery and agony will multiply when one occupies such site for living.

Likewise, there are several shapes of land: pot, cow, spoon, tiger tail, wood top, tube light, lamp, and many more. The personal luck of the individual depends largely on the best shape of the land one acquires or inherits. It is always advisable to accept only the square shaped or rectangular shaped land plots. Some land can be rectified from the original form to the shape of square or rectangular form. Care should be taken in adding and portioning for others, and any cutting on any side of the plot entails difficulties of combined nature. That means any addition; reduction or cutting will invite agony, misfortune or dangerous consequences.

## Extensions, Additions, Projections And Cuttings

The best land ensures no extension of or cuttings on any of its four sided shape. The result of change in sides will vary from side to side. It can be noted only with practical observation and personal experience. Most of the consultants have such practical vision, knowledge and feedback report. The extensions or cutting of a particular side of the plot has the following results:-

• **Southwest corner:** This corner is "kanni moola" on the Nairuti corner. The Naathan of the Southwest corner is Sarpa otherwise known as Raahu. The direction of the Raahu is not predictable; while travelling, it is sometimes very fast but never be on a straight line. Hence, it is imperative to note that the SW corner should maintain 90 degree angle, a simple straight line to the East or the North. If the corner angle degree of 90 is reduced it will result in scarcity of money or things. If SW corner is increased beyond 90 degree it will affect the inmates. Due to corner angles they may suffer after three years of construction.

The second point to be observed is to keep the area corner neatly clean. No space is provided for kennel or any other animal shed in that corner. No waste of fish or meat should be deposited in that area. Keep it always slightly higher in land elevation than the other corners. Inside the compound area another small wall can be made to make the corner 90 degree to escape from the bad effects. Always give consideration for kanni moola and avoid any type of construction attached with corner walls.

• **Northwest corner:** Northwest is Vaayu corner or Maruti moola. Sikhi or ketu is the Naathan of the NW region. Most of the time, Ketu will become the cause for bad remarks, pain, sufferings from the house, office or friends without any reason. The direction or power of wind is really not predictable to anyone. Such experience was recognized by all Indians in the Epics; Sri Hanuman and Bhimsen made wonders beyond one's imagination revealing their power. The Northwest region is submerged with the power of maruti. Any cut in the area invites the incapability or inefficiency of the owner and the members of the house. Such ineffectiveness of the members with lesser enthusiasm to initiate or commence certain new undertaking will be disastrous. An inefficient group will stay inside the house. This will affect not only the owner but also the tenant, only after six months of the occupation.

The Northwest area is generally used for wood storage, car parking, kennel, toilet, bath rooms, waiting shed, gardening etc. There should not be any permanent construction touching its corner walls. Temporary construction with air passage however is permitted.

• **Northeast side:** The extended Northeast corner known by Eshana Moola is considered to be the best corner favourable to the owner. The controlling deity is Budha (Mercury) who is the God of wisdom and knowledge. The Mercury is the Naathan of every discovery or invention or creation of new ideas. This corner projection provides help and happiness. It will always be good for peace and harmony. The Eshana moola will be very encouraging and it will raise extra intuition and progress in every step of life.

In the Northeast corner area, there should not be any 'cut' or lesser length in the eastern sector. The length in the eastern sector should be in no way shorter than that of western sector length. The troublesome bad effects will follow with the existence of cut in the Northeast corner. This will affect the gruha naathan (head of the family) or any other male of the house by way of accident on road or fall from a tree, quarrel or even blood shed and death. This will happen soon after three months of house occupation. The seriousness of the accident and nature will differ with the Northeast cut gravity. Cut in Northeast means sure danger. There should not be any construction on the extreme corner of NE permanently; it will hamper income sources of the owner. In case a construction is unavoidable, at least 2/9 portion of the total length on both side North or East side should be left free. Any projection of the land at the Northeast region will be the best progressive symptoms of progeny and prosperity.

It is always good to have an addition of land or extension on this Northeast Corner as projection. Such a projected Northeast corner, will call on the occupant in time an additional promotion or an excess amount of money by way of goodwill or bonus. This will bring an abnormal income sources to the occupants through other means. The inflow revenue is clean without any impurity attached to it. A happy mood and atmosphere will prevail at home, office or other walks of life.

• **Southeast corner:** The Southeast corner is the Agni corner moola, a fomenter of fire; the region is ruled by Moon or Chandra. The area is considered to be the region playing with fire. Usually Agni corner zone is earmarked for kitchen with eastern side platform. The Moon will wane in fifteen days till black or new moon or amavasi and wax in another fifteen days till full moon or vennala or pournami. When the Sun rays fall, the SE region is supposed to produce blue flames and ultra violet rays. Most of the ancient Vaastu books recommended the Agni corner area to be utilized for kitchen. The ladies very often work in the kitchen and their health is protected in Southeast area, more than in any other zone.

At the extension of the South zone, there will be a feeling to the owner or inmates that they are always standing over the fire, and will talk to others with fear. The SE cut always produces fear of fire in inner mind and in the entire body. In short, SE cut or extension or both will cause fear and freight of fire in the entire family members and all associated with.

• **East side:** East is the best among the sides for the main house to face. The East side facing house always has the morning Sun rays which bestows happiness and peace. That may be the reason why most of the Indians prefer East facing houses. If the house faces a different direction, the main door will be arranged in the eastward direction.

The friends and foes around will behave to the inmates decently. Co-operation and peace will prevail throughout. The controller of the East side is Shukra or Venus. Cordiality among the ladies will become a common phenomenon and their affection and love will lead to astounding heights. The Deity Indra's goodness or behavioural bad effects will be evident throughout.

• **North side:** If no East side entrance is possible, priority should be then for North facing. The controller of this area is vyazham (Jupiter). Jupiter, the guru of all gods, has trust, belief, spirituality, piety, cleanliness, brotherhood, sympathetic views and charitable nature or mind.

The North side facing house owners cannot refuse a request for charity. In certain particular circumstances, rejecting the people approaching for charity will result in 'curse'. The drawback of this area is that it will attract curse.

• **West side:** Lord Saturn is the owner of the West side. Saturn (shani) is the son of Lord Sun and father of Gulikan (Mandi). Saturn never forgets to give the bad conditions of each individual during the course of 'shani dasa', seven and half and kandaka shani periods. The hardships given to the people will vary from the shani in particular raasi placement. The Raahu placed at Southwest, Ketu positioned at Northwest and shani placed at western side cause sufferings more than happiness.

Lord Saturn will not disturb anyone without any reason. If the individual's bad times occur, difficulties can easily be reduced with prayer. The, offerings of mustard seeds, black cloth, mustard oil, etc. to Lord Shani is good, especially on thriodasi thithi and conjoining together with second Saturday pooja. Such days appear yearly twice or thrice in a year.

If the western side of the land is low or slopped down, it will result in less help from own children at times of real need. Hence, slight elevation in the western side is preferable.

• **South side:** The individual personality, courage, determination, industry, brotherhood and good decision in difficult time are assigned to this South zone. The side is controlled by Mars. The other names are Chouwa, Mangal, and Pitrupati etc. The Mangal planet is the most cruel and reddish. It will directly interfere in others problems and cause unnecessary troubles devoid of any reason. Pooja and prayers to Lord Mars will be helpful and beneficial. Usually, there will not involve any extensions or cut in normal circumstances. It will be better to keep the shape or size of land plot without any disfigure or deformity in all four sides.

• **Centre (middle part):** The middle portion is the Brahmasthan of the land where the sun is the presiding deity. In a house construction point, any wall or pillar, or staircase at brahmasthaan should be avoided. The Marma vedha section will apply to this centre part and bad effects will follow. Most of the architects are not acquainted with correct norms of marma Vaastu parameters and no co-ordination is available in their predictive conclusion. The masons, civil construction engineers and workers have to follow strictly the top-boss' or experts' orders. No responsibility is assigned to anyone who is making it. The owner alone faces its effects, good or bad.

## Goodness and Worthiness of Land

At the spot examination of the site, any normal person can notice the size, shape, slope, earth colours and overhead electric heavy line. Paddy field, canal side, kandal kaadu (thick forest or foliage), muddy land, graveyard, snake holed hips, barren land and ghostly area can certainly be avoided in selection. The site selection is an essential step as per parameters of Vaastu science, explained in vivid terms by the ancients in almost all texts.

The authoritative information is needed to categorize the matters pertaining to soil, water and flora availability. Five simple test parameters are prescribed by Vaastu Shastra for the symptoms of good soil examination. The symptoms are:

• **Ancient Method**

***The Colour:*** The soil is considered good if the colour of the soil is white or brick red. The soil should have the fragrance of flower or honey.

***The Smell:*** The soil should not have bad odors of meat or liquor.

***The Taste:*** If the soil tastes sweet then the plot is good. If its taste is bitter or salty, it is bad.

***The Touch:*** If the ground of plot is too rough for one to stand or if the clay is too hot or too cold, the plot should be rejected.

***The Sound:*** The plot should be rejected if one hears any fierce sound from the ground like those of fox, dog, ass, water fall. The plot is good if one hears melodious sounds like those of horse, elephant, bamboo, ocean, kettle drum or flute.

And the worthiness of land will be known by:

| | | |
|---|---|---|
| Bhadra | : | When it is near water (sea or rivers). |
| Punna | : | When adjacent to hills and mountains. |
| Supadma | : | When located in plains and vicinities of residences. |
| Dhooma | : | When having an extreme climate with poisonous plants or rocks. |

• **Desirable Method**

Plough the soil and notice the presence of charcoal, black stone, paddy, shell, human hair, bad smell, 'Asthy' (ash powder bones), hollow soil and ant hill (valmikam). Such lands are to be rejected. The soil elevations at West and South are considered good. The important factor is to note the Sun rise, arrivals of Arundhati Utharadhruvan, Saptairushikal and the moon sight from the inside house. These are primarily reckoned while selecting the soil and house building plan. Keeping in view of the above aspects, the ancients have recommended the method of keeping the North and East Zones at a lower height and avoiding any tall trees or obstructions.

If burned wood, coal, bones, husk, ash, leather or raw pieces or other such extraneous evil portent objects are obtained in the site, that plot should be rejected. However, if such ominous materials 'salyas' (remnants) are found beneath 12 feet or more in the ground, they will bear no evil effect.

## Classification of the Land (Soil)

The ancient works are very specific in Earth Classification according to the nature, elevation and slope. The Rishi Varaahamira had excellent information on twenty six types of land. The Vaastu Books have recorded the Varna groups allocating the slope of the land towards East to Brahmins,

South to Kshetriyas, and West to Vaishyas and North to Shudras. The land is classified by Veethi models as follows:-

- **Veethi Types of Land Classification**

According to the elevation and slope, the Earth has been classified into:-

*Goveethi:* Goveethi land is demarcated with West zone elevation and eastward slope. The high mount at the West sector and sloping down towards eastern part are very good symptoms of prosperity. The site having slope from the West (high) to the East (low) is considered good and prosperous and the occupants in the land will have long happiness over 500 years.

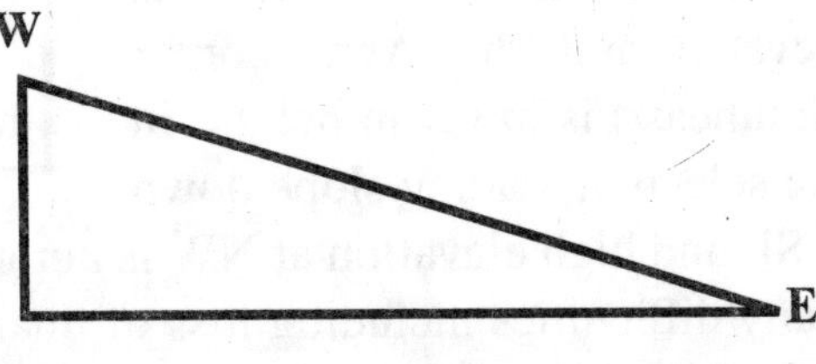


*Naagaveethi:* The Naagaveethi land is elevated at the Southeast (Agni Corner) corner and slope down towards the Northwest (Vaayu corner). The site having slope from the Southeast (High Level) towards the Northwest (low level) is not good. A stay in Naagaveethi land involves a total degradation of status or job.

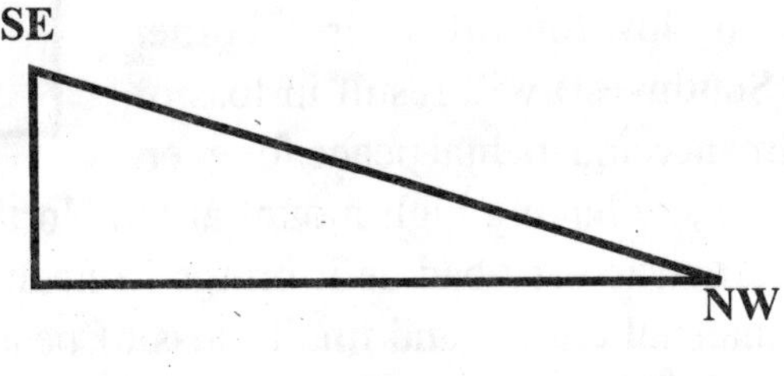


*Gajaveethi:* Gajaveethi land has high mount in the South and slope down in the North. The elevation of land at South is higher and at North lower. This symptom is very auspicious and it leads to more financial flexibility. Gajaveethi land is always good for fame and wealth and one who stays there will have long happy life.

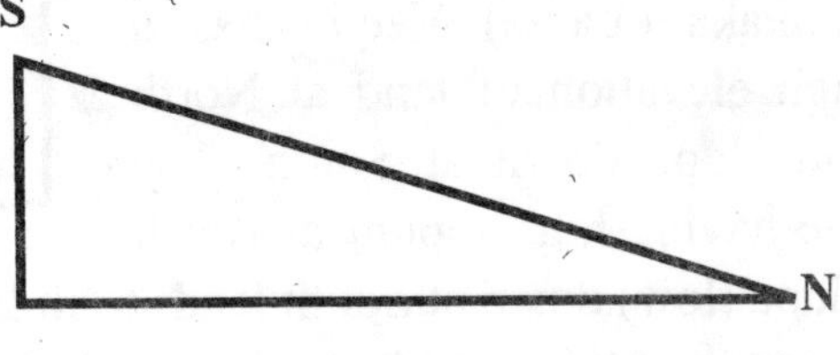


*Dhanyaveethi:*

This Dhanyaveethi land is the most prominent among the site location elevated at Nairuti (Southwest) corner and slopes down towards the Eshana (Northeast) corner. The site having sloped from Northeast to Southwest, is very auspicious and the inmates accrue beneficial symptoms

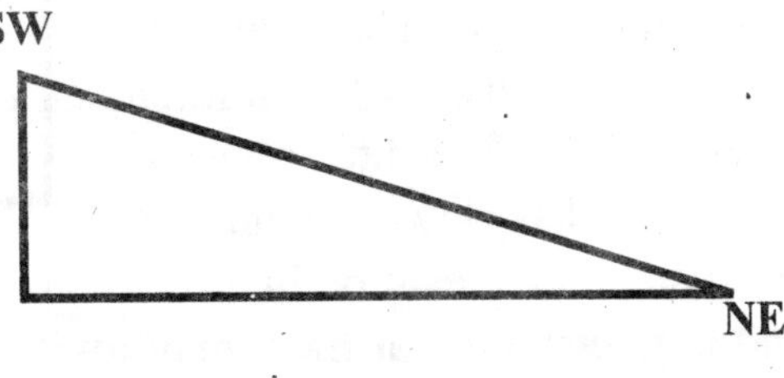

and plus points in natural way. All round prosperity will be bestowed on the occupants through good health, wealth, education, happiness over 1000 years.

***Vagni (Agni) veethi:*** The Vaayu corner (Northwest) is elevated and the Agni corner (Southeast) is lower in height. In site selection, having slope down at SE and high elevation at NW is not good for progress. This will result in many difficulties including loss of finance or accidents due to fear or fire. If the two corners of the site are identical in height, it will provide progress for the occupants.

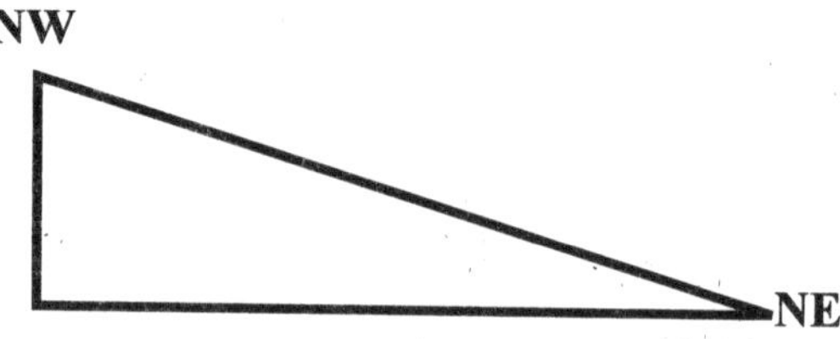


***Bhootaveethi:*** A highly elevated Eshāna corner (Northeast) and lying low towards Nairuti corner (Southwest) will result in loss of finance and mental peace for ever. The site having high mount at the Northeast and slope towards Southwest corner, is very bad as it brings ill health, by incurring heavy expenditure, financial crunch and finally loss of peace. The bad effects will commence after 6th year of occupancy.

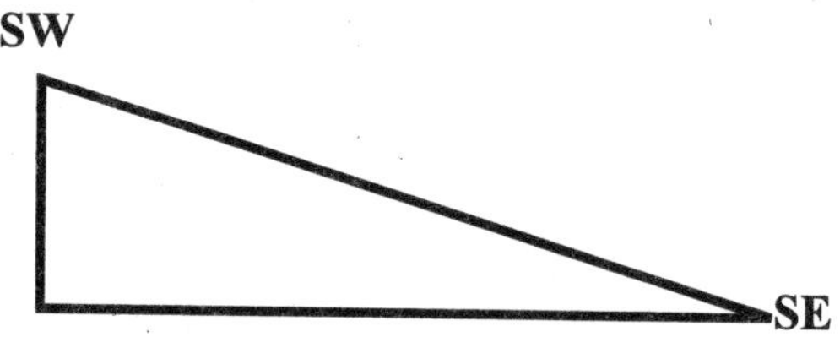


***Anthaka (Yama) Veethi:*** The Anthaka (Yama) Veethi has a high elevation of land at North and slope down at South. The site having high mount at North Slope (low) down at South leads to ill health and financial problems. It also causes bad things to the owner including death (Calling back to the world of YAMA)

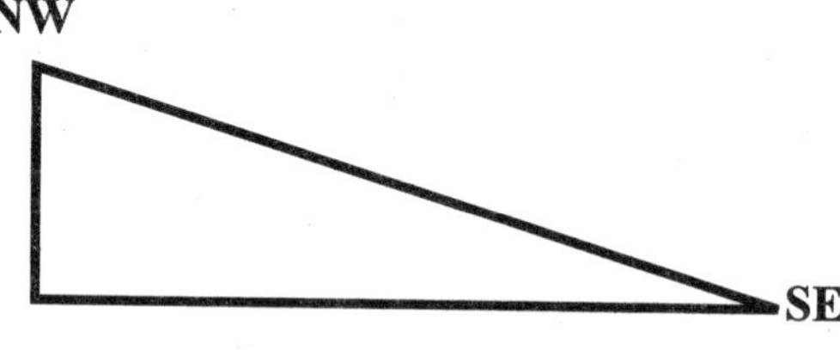


***Jalaveethi:*** The Jalaveethi stands for poverty. The occupants will have loss of children combined with acute poverty. The land has lower height in West and high elevation in the East zone. The site having low level at West and high elevation at East, may invite difficulties of progeny and internal troubles.

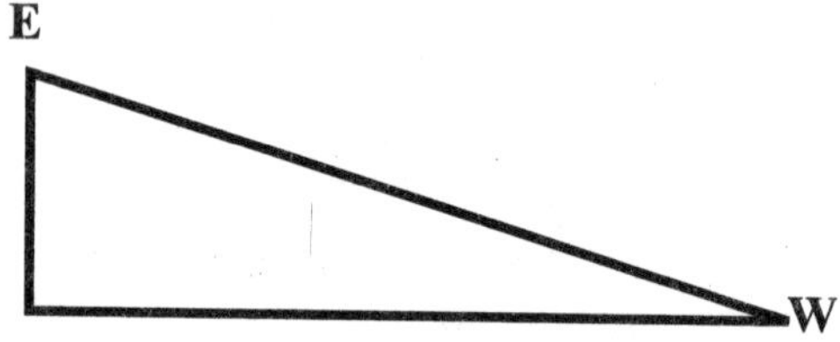

• **Elevation types of land classification:** In the Manushyaalaya Chandrika and other Vaastu works, several combinations of land elevation and slopes are mentioned. In brief they are given below:

| Nos. | Name of Vaastu land | Elevated At | Slope down at | After effects |
|---|---|---|---|---|
| 1. | Swamukhi Land | NE/SE/N Up | SW Down | The land owner becomes pauper and seeks others help or begs. |
| 2. | Brhmagnam Land | SW/SE/ NE Up | NW Down | This land is of no material benefit to the owner. It will lead to hardship and pain. |
| 3. | Sthavara Land | SE Up | SW/ NE/ NW Down | The Sthavara land is good for human occupation. |
| 4. | Shyaneka Land | SW/NE/ NW Up | SE Down | The Shyaneka land causes destruction and death of the owner . |
| 5. | Shamshan Land | NE/E Middle Up | W/SW Middle Down | This land will destroy lineage (vamsa) of the owner. |
| 6. | Rogakruth Land | NW/N Middle Up | SE/S Middle Down | The inhabitants take to unhealthy habits causing diseases of serious nature. |
| 7. | Apathi Land | NW/W Up | SE/E Middle Down | Diseases, quarrel, enmity among inmates and with others will be quite usual and troublesome. |
| 8. | Punyaka Land | SW/W Middle Up | NE/E Middle Down | This Punyaka land is useful for prosperous life to Brahmins, Kshetriyas & Vaishyas. Not good for Shutras. |
| 9. | Dheerghaisu Land | SW/S Middle Up | N/NE Middle Down | This land is good for progeny and vamsa parampara (good lineage) and for happiness and prosperity. |
| 10. | Pithaamaha Land | E/SE Middle Up | W/ NWM/ middle Down | This Pithaamaha land is good promoter of happiness and prosperity to all inmates, associates, relatives, etc. |
| 11. | Supatha Land | SE/S Middle Up | NW/N Middle Down | The Supatha land is best suited to all types of human beings and their activities for prosperity and happiness. |

| | | | | |
|---|---|---|---|---|
| 12. | Arugula Land | NE/N Middle Up | SW/S Middle Down | The land owner will undertake most heinous crimes, sins (even killing) that will lead to a total mental frustration or guilty feeling. |
| 13. | Shandula land | NE Up | SE/SW/ NW Down | This Shandula land of unhappiness will create problems one after another. |
| 14. | Sthandila Land | SW UP | SE/ NW/ NE Down | The Sthandila land is good and auspicious for every human being. |

• **Varnam Type of Classification of Land:** The Manushyaalaya Chandrika classifies the land according to Varna into four types:-

***For Brahmins:*** Brahmin community will concentrate to stay at gajaveethi and susthan land where athi trees (Indian Fig) and dhruva grass. Grass used for pooja functions grow in abundance. The land may be of square type with white colour, ghee smell, sweet taste and melodious sound. Favourable land to Brahmin group should have elevation of southern side and slope over northern parts.

Susthan Land: If the land has SW/NE elevations with (NW) lesser in height it is also favourable for Brahmins.

***For kshetriyas :*** The Kshetriyas should choose the goveethi and sutal lands areas where there are plenty of arayal trees (Aswattha) and turtle collections. The goveethi or sutal land suited to this community should have red colour sand, blood smell, sweet taste (kshetriya rasam). The length should be eight times greater than the width of the site with mount on West or South or Southwest slope leaning towards East or North.

*Sutal Land:* The land with SW/NW corners and West side elevated and slope down at Eastern side is suitable to kshetriyas.

***For Vaishayas:*** The Vaishyas are business community and they prefer centralized living near jalaveethi region. Mount from East and slope towards West, feeding grass, yellow colour sand and charaland (dry land) are suitable to Vaishya business community. Arayal trees (Aswattha) are considered good for the Vaishyas. Specialities of food (rice) smell and tastes of bitter are favourable to Vaishayas. The plot should be one-sixth extra length from width of the site leaning from East (lower) to West (mount).

*Charaland:* It has elevation at N/NE/NW and slope down at South. It is also acceptable land for Vaishya business community.

***For Shudras:*** The Sudras collectively settle in areas of jala veethi and sumukha lands, where dharpa grass is abundantly grown. Ethi Tree (Plaska) is a good symbol of this community. The special features of this community group are having black colour sand, presence of river, dharpa grass, liquor smell, chilli taste and one fourth extra length from width of the site leaning towards East (high mount) from West (low mount).

Swamukha- This land elevated at NE/E/SE and sloping down towards West, is also favourable to them.

If the land does not satisfy the requirements on the basis of colour, taste, sound, smell or touch to a particular Varna group, it is better to reject the land and undertake experimental tests methods which are detailed in the next bhaagam (chapter).

- **Surface Classification of Earth (Land):** The word Prishta refers to the difficulties arising due to different land surface level. The site (earth) is irregular with middle portion. There will be no coordination of all sides in surface level. The position of Prishta leads to either prosperity in good surface according to its nature, position or situation. Certain levels such land will cause more severe difficulties or sufferings. Given below is a description of difficulties or prosperities, classified into 4 known by the name 'prishta'.

***Gaja Prishta:*** If there is a mount on surface in S/SW/W/NW area without any slope, then the land is said to be Gaja Prishta. The speciality of the land is to have only elevation. It has no slope. The owners of this land have the advantage of living longer and can acquire enough property.

***Kurma Prishta:*** The middle of the site looks like round ball leaving all the eight directions at lower level. This land is suitable for residence. It brings peace and happiness to the owner.

***Daitya Prishta:*** The land with depression at West zone and elevation at NE/E/SE sides and corners is called Daitya Prishta. This Daitya Prishta causes always sufferings. The owners are inclined to lose wealth and have more problems of progeny.

***Naaga Prishta:*** The Naaga Prishta land is specifically noted for extreme bad effects that may afflict the owners. Naaga prishta land is lengthy from West to East, lesser with North to South. The land is having more length towards East from West direction. Naaga Prishta land is characterized with lesser width from North to South and elevated at Southeast portion. To rectify naaga prishta land as trouble free, it is required to divide it into two by making the length portion towards South from North, and width from East to West. This Naga Prishta land tends to increase:-

(1) Enmity,

(2) Loss of wife and children,

(3) Death of inmates.

By rectification of the prishta land, no bad effects will crop up to any of the inmates or owner of the land, instead happiness and prosperity will come up.

• **Land Selection Rules in General:** There are certain land selection rules to be followed:

1. Land with depression at the centre is not good. The owner will have to leave the place soon.
2. If the NE Eshana is depressed, it will beget wealth and prosperity.
3. North and East slopes will result in wealth and progress simultaneously.
4. South slope will invite sorrow and death.
5. Southwest slope (Nairuti) will result in destruction of the family.
6. Down of West side will reduce wealth, potency or social status.
7. Naga Pristha land is lengthy from West to East with lesser width from North to South. This will cause bad effect to wife, children, death or increase in number of enemies.
8. Lengthy land from North to South is good for prosperity.
9. Lengthy land where one end is less and the other end is more will destroy cattle.
10. 'Murram' (hard and dry) land with three roads will encourage Epilepsy and Tuberculosis
11. The tortoise shape land symbolizes Jail life for a short period.
12. Bow shaped land will cause fear in inmates.
13. Pot shaped land symbolizes TB disease.
14. Round or circle type land will pave the way for poverty and sorrow.
15. Triangle shaped land will always cause the fear of rulers.
16. Bent land always stands for loss of wealth.

• **Bad Omen in Houses after Occupancy:** The omen is invisible at first sight. These are visible during excavation of land. However, the bad effects will be applicable only if the 'salyas' (remnants) or bad omen as troubles still exist in the ground at the time when the house is fully occupied. The direction-wise, bad omen will show its ugly head after house warming and occupancy in new house.

Sided or corner-wise brief details are given below:

***East:*** Human bones in the East cause death in the family once in every three years.

***Southeast:*** If the 'salyas' of donkey is found in the Southeast, it indicates frequent troubles from the government like suspensions, dismissal from service.

***South:*** Any human body particles traced from the South may cause sufferings or diseases to the head of the family.

***Southwest:*** The canine bones lying in the Southwest will cause frequent infant mortality.

***West:*** If infant child's bones are found buried in the West side of the land, members of the family may get lunacy.

***Northwest:*** Any husk of animals or pieces of coal found in the Northwest region, the head of the family is in trouble with enemies or litigation, etc. for more than twelve years.

***North:*** Human bones buried in North side will invite heavy losses to the head of the family even though the owner possesses abundant money, valuables, landed properties, royal wealth. High professional status will diminish gradually in twelve years period.

***Northeast:*** The bad Omen will cause loss of cattle if there is presence of human bones in the Northeast.

***Centre:*** Any human bone, ash or coal in the middle of the land will result in the extinction of the entire family or they will be compelled to move out of the site.

A site mostly cracked or a site with 'salyas' or with termite hills or hillocks thrown up by white ants, moles etc. should be rejected for house construction. At the time of the plugging, digging or leveling of the land for cleaning the site, the sight of stones, or a gold brick etc. augurs happiness and prosperity for the owners.

The sight of the pieces of fuel wood presages fire accidents. Such omen or ominous substance should be removed from the site and possibly the site should be covered with fresh red brick or white sand. If any deep trench or pit is found near the house, it causes thrift and diseases. Good omen is predicted for progress if gems, stones, gold, copper, cow horn, 'shank' (conch shell), oyster, shell of tortoise are found at the site while digging. The construction of residence near oceans, mountains, paddy-fields, temple, hermitage, cattle shed is unsafe and dangerous in many ways.

• **Residences Near Temple Premises:** Residences adjacent to the temple premises and vicinities are considered important for the ancient belief and tradition as per Vaastu Shastra. The temple means the abode of God or Goddess. They have their own way of daily routine work for which no human beings are supposed to disturb by staying in nearby vicinities. The spiritual purity is maintained in an atmosphere of their activities within the premises built for. Therefore, Vaastu Shastra is firm on the family staying near or around holy temple premises to observe certain conditions strictly.

There are two types Murthy's (Deities):-

***Angry and Hot tempered:*** There are very aggressive natured gods/goddesses like Maha Deva, Maha Vishnu's incarnation Narasimha Swami, Goddess Bhadra Kaaliyamma, etc. Temples with deities having angry and hot tempered expression on their faces like lord Shiva are not ideal locations at the right side as well as in front sides for the purpose of human stay. Family stay is fully restricted on right side or in front of the temple premises. However, left and back are allowed for residence stay or some other construction and the inmates can live there happily with some observance.

***Peace Loving Natured Idols Temple:*** There are pleasant and peace-loving natured gods or goddesses like Maha Vishnu, Maha Lakhsmi, and Devi Saraswathy, etc. Residence at left and backside of these temples is fully restricted. Human habitation is strictly prohibited on left side or back of adjacent of Temples of such gods and goddesses. No house is to be constructed on left or back of the temple with the idols of Maha vishnu, Maha lakshmi, Lord Murugan and Durga Devi with peaceful and pleasant face. A family occupation is permitted to the right or in front of the 'shanti and soumya' natured god/goddesses especially at outer temple premises away from the complex.

A good stay is promised on the right or in the front of such holy temple of shanti loving idols outside away from the complex of shanti loving idols. Such residences are permitted in backside or left sides of the temples of Hot tempered idols. If any one ventures to occupy the restricted side premises, the stay will be fraught with dangerous consequences.

• **Effects On Stay Near The Temple Premises:** The residence for human beings is against the temple side rules, the violation will have the following effects:-

1. An unnatural fear among all family members.
2. All inmates of the house will become weak in concentration of mind. They will get little help and fellowship from beloved people if the house is constructed almost par or beyond flaghoisting mast height.
3. Such stay is bound to face frequent accidents, death and quarrel, litigation among family members, relatives, friends or neighbours.

Inhabitance near the temples is forbidden even if one has no faith in the temple. All hurdles can be easily overcome if all the house members are highly devoted to God and doing frequent visits to the temple for prayers or performing poojas at home as per stipulations.

# Bhaagam 3

## Location of Trees

In Vaastu Science, a specific location for trees in residential premises has been given. The availability of land is the criteria for planting trees in the residential premises. A diagramatic description is given below:

The location of trees is marked direction-wise as follows:

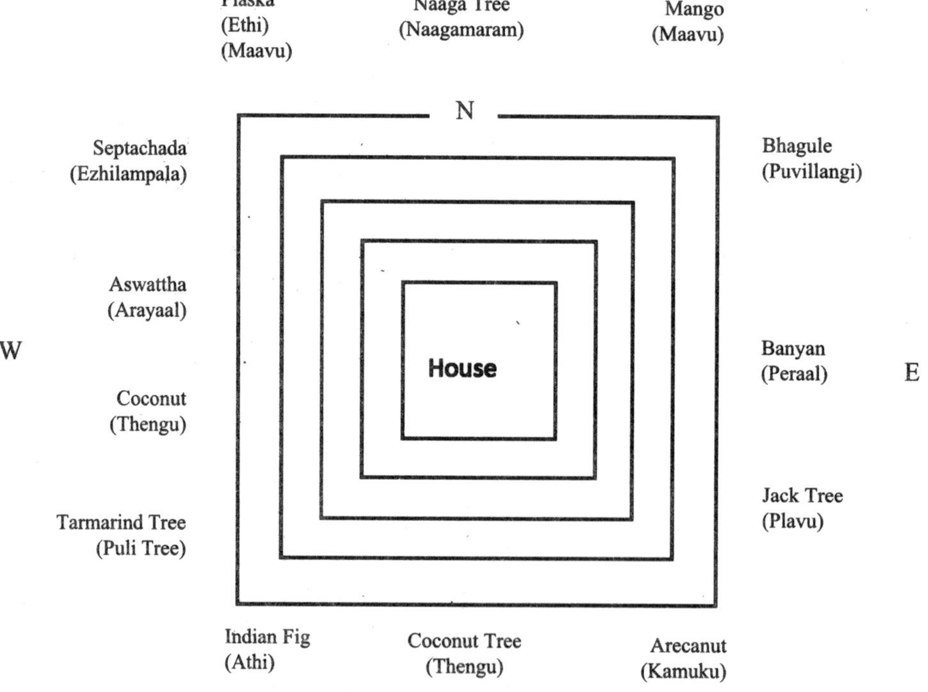


The above diagram shows a larger area, having four layer segments in all sides of the house. Trees and plants are permitted in all three sectors except the nearest to the house. Certain types of trees are not allowed in and around the house. The Vaastu Shastra insists on the direction-wise planting of trees as shown above.

All types of trees are not welcome in a residential compound. The following trees and plants are acceptable in the four sides of the house.

• **Trees Permitted To Plant Around Houses:** The type of trees allowed to plant around in residential premises is given below:-

a) North: Plaska (Ethi), Ficus Microcarpa, Mango (Maavu), Mangifera Indica, Naaga tree or Mesua Nagassarium and Punnaka (Punna) Calophyllum Innophullum.

b) East: Bhagula (Puvilangi) Mimusopas, Banyan tree (Peraal), Ficus Bengalensis and Jack tree (Plavu) Panasa, Artocarpus heterophyllus.

c) West: Saptachada (Ezhilampala), Alstonia Scolaris, Aswattha tree (Arayaal), Peepal-Ficus Religiosa, Tamarind (Puli) Tamarindus Indica and Coconut tree (Thengu) Naarial tree, Cocos nucifera.

d) South : Indian Fig (Athi) Udumbara, Ficus Racemosa, Coconut Trees (Thengu) Naarial tree Cocos nucifera and Arecacut tree (kamuku) Puga, Areca catechu.

The ancients have clearly stated the names of trees in each side of house. Wrong placement of trees will result in some kind of fear, fire, or danger to the inmates of the house. Aswattha trees planted in the West are always good. Trees with thick foliage are to be planted in the North to resist the cold wind from the North. Trees without foliage are to be planted in the South to allow sunlight.

Aswattha tree will cause fire, Plaska insanity, banyan tree cut or blow from enemies, and Tamarind tree stomatch trouble due to change of its location or direction.

The peepal tree, if placed at South instead of its position in the West, will generate mental disorder. The banyan tree placed in the West, will invite enmity. And if Indian fig tree is placed in the North it will attract stomach disorders. These are applicable only when the trees are situated around and inside the compound. Such trees are to be cut and removed within the distance equal to its height.

• **Restricted Trees Around Premises**: The following trees and plants may be avoided around house premises:

Kanjiram (karaskaram)
Cheru (Arushkara)
Naruvari (Slesmataka)
Thanni (Vibhitki)
Kappi (Coffee)
Aari Veppu (Neem tree)

Erumakkalli (Cactus)
Murinjaka (Drum stick)

• **Plants and Trees Allowed Around Compound:** All types of bananas, (Plantain), Malli (Jasmin), Pichakam (Moogra), Jyathi (Jathika), Betel leaves (Piper Betel) etc. are propitious and good anywhere in the premises.

The following trees are propitious and good on all four sides of the house.

Kumizhu (Sri Vruksha)
Koovalam (Bhilwa)
Kaduka maram (Abaya tree)
Nelli (Indian Goosebery)
Devadharam (Deodar)
Plavu (Panasa)
Ashokam (Ashoka)
Chandanam (Sandal wood)
Venga (Asana)
Punna (Brinjassal)
Chempakam (Chempak)
Karinjali (Kathira tree)

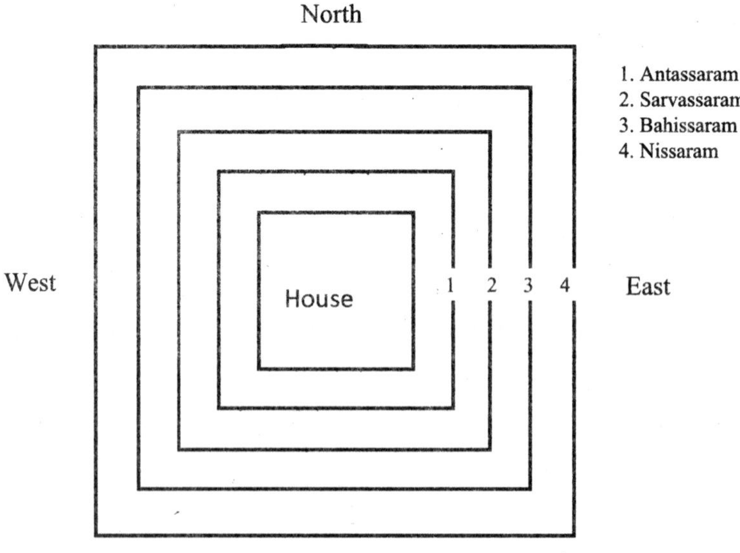


A diagram of the four zones of the House premises and the location of Trees and Plants:

The layer segments of land are marked as 1, 2, 3 and 4 starting from the house. The trees and plants of different structure and strength have specific location in Vaastu Shastra. The distance from the residence is not specific especially in small size of the land. The nature of the trees and plants are very particular as per stipulation, structure and strength. These are classified into four main divisions.

The layer sector bifurcation is provided according to the distance from the house position towards :

(1) The house compound premises,
(2) The house compound outer layer,
(3) The space outside of first outer layer and
(4) The extreme outer space layer.

***Antassaram Trees (Internal Strength):*** The hard wood trees having strength and firmness in the interior part of the wood like jack fruit tree (plavu or panasa), Aanjali (ayani) etc. are planted at distance twice the length of the tree away from the middle of the plot.

***Bahissaram Trees (Outer Strength):*** The bahissaram are trees with strong outer and weak inner like coconut tree, karimpana tree, arecanut tree, etc. The outer portion is used for construction of houses, sheds or fencing. Such trees are planted at the outer space of the antassaram trees and sarvassarams.

***Sarvassaram Trees (Internal & External Strength):*** These types of trees are strong to the core, having full wood strength both internal and external without any blank. The examples are teak wood, irumullu (double hook) and other trees. These trees are usually located in the outer space of antassarams.

***Nissaram Trees (Breakable & Perishable):*** Nissaram trees are fragile and easily breakable. This soft wood widely used for making match-box sticks. Trees like drum stick tree, ezhilampala (saptachada), mango tree, etc come under this catagory. Such kinds of trees are to be planted at the extreme outer portion of the house, away from all other types of trees.

## Land (Site) Testing

In olden days, people adopted numerous land-testing methods for human occupation. The Manusyaalaya Chandrika text also prescribes various ways to conduct the same. Most of the tests are conducted on the basis of colour-caste combination which assumes no significance in this flat and multiple complexes era. However, the knowledge of soil testing methods will prove to be very useful and worthy of public interest.

• **Desirable Methods of Land Testing**

***Method 1:*** On a chosen auspicious day, dig a pit of one kolu square pit. Take a raw mud pot, fill paddy in it fully and keep it in the pit. On the top of the pot keep four lamps marked with coloured cotton cloth of white, red, yellow and black facing East, South, West and North directions respectively. Carefully close pot for one hour. Check the lamps kept inside the pot by opening the closed pit.

If the white lamp is burning, the land is best suited for Brahmins. Likewise, red colour lamps for kshetriyas, yellow for vaishyas and black for shutras. If all lamps are burning, it refers to the suitability of the land to all Varna groups and vice versa, if none of the lamps is burning, the plot has to be rejected.

***Method 2:*** Soil testing is also done by filling up the pit as in method 1, with full water and keeping four flowers on it. Its colour distinction of the flower is to be followed by Varna group's specification. The point where the flower stops, is desirable factor for that community and the land is best suited to them.

***Method 3:*** Dig a pit of a cubic meter and fill it again with dug out clay. If the clay falls short on filling, the plot is not good for house construction. If the clay exactly suffices to fill the pit, it is mediocre, if excess clay remains after filling the pit, the plot is good.

***Method 4:*** Fill the pit with water, if water remains for a day the plot augurs prosperity, if the mud remains without water it forebodes poverty. If the water is completely dried and shows no indication of water in the pit, it portends death.

***Method 5:*** Fill the pit with water for the time a person takes to walk of a hundred feet and return. The plot is good if water remains half the pit. It is mediocre, if the water level is more than the quarter pit and the plot is very bad if water level is less than quarter.

***Method 6:*** Plough the land in morning hours, the excavation reveals the contents inside the land and one will get a clear picture of bad omen as per Vaastu norms.The rejection or acceptance can be easily decided.

Prof. L. Ranganti Rangacharya, Director of Telugu University, Hyderabad, has revealed his wisdom of testing the land. The site belongs to the living or dead as per calculations from varga numbers. Such varga numbers are available with each person, village and direction. The calculated total divided by three, is if equal to one it means alive, two means dead and three means neither alive nor dead. The entire varga number formulae are given as soil testing methods.

• **Shanku Sthapana (Gnomon Fixation):** In olden days, there was no method to find out the cardinal directions. Hence Gnomon method is used very often to find out the sides, corners, timings and other changes. The Shanku sthapana recommends the method of tool used in olden days to ascertain the location and direction known as Gnomon (Shanku). The Shanku is made in the shape of lotus, its stick forms out of honge, mud and neem wood. The top segment is of round shape, the middle segment is square, and the bottom is of octagonal shape. Though, several kinds of shanku shapes are available in various parts of India, the common ancient types used are shown below:-

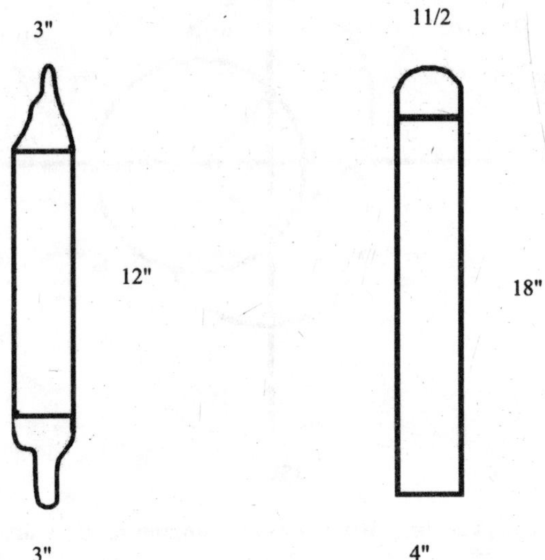


**Ancient model shanku sticks**

• **Use of Gnomon:** The use of Gnomon is simple to keep in an open place like a cricket stump stick.

Draw a circle with two angulam and fix the shanku stick firmly at the centre of the circle. When shanku shadow's top touches at any point, draw a circle in the western sector, mark that point during morning hours. Likewise mark gnomon shadow of the top in another circle in the evening hours in the eastern sector. Follow the same procedure next day morning to differentiate the changes in the sun's motion.

Draw circles on all points joint and connect West circle with East circle of the second day. This will be a vertical straight line. The variation in the circle will show the movements of the sun on a day. Changes will occur approximately1/3 of the circle of its size. Likewise a horizontal line from the South to North and vertical line from West to East can be drawn. The difference between 1st day and the next day would occur due to variation time of Utharayana and Dekshinayana of movements of the sun.

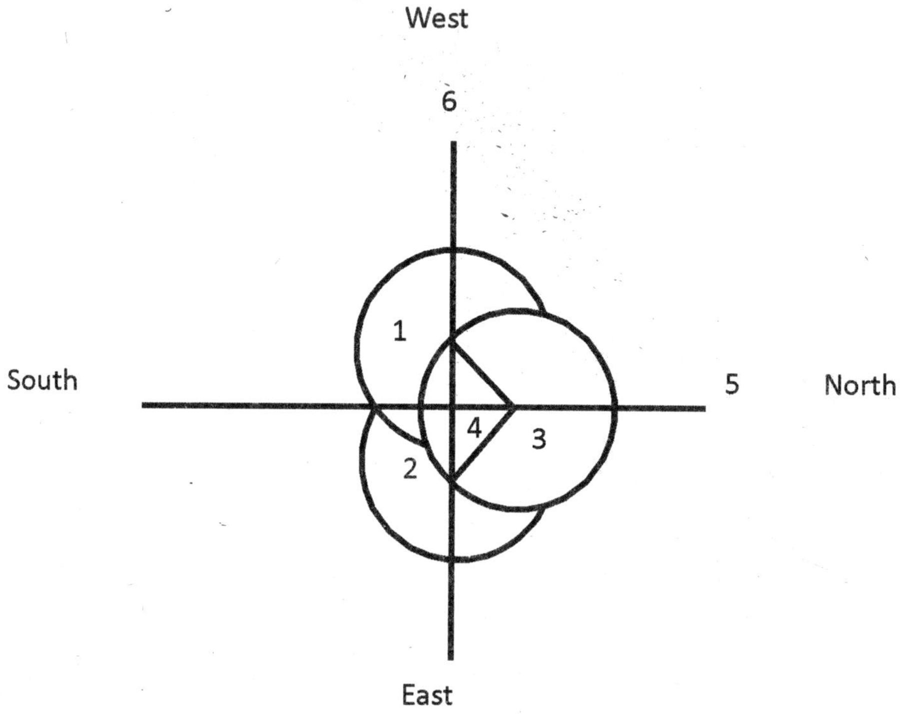


**Fixing Cardinal Directions by Gnomon in sun's shadow**

**Morning shadow circle 1st day.**
**Evening shadow circle 1st day.**
**Next day morning circle.**
**Variation of the shadow.**
**South-North horizontal line and West to East horizontal line.**

This method is adopted to find out East-West or North-South directions. Nowadays degree of the angle will determine the side and direction of land plot.

• **Levelling the Ground:** The Manusyaalaya Chandrika has mentioned the customary practice to offer pooja to deity, i.e. Swati and Jaya. Such pooja has to be performed for commencing the work of levelling the site.

An instrument known by Avanta is used to mark the direction and levelling. It has a calibrated frame with water level and plumb bob. It is almost similar to simple thread bob like the instrument nowadays using. Nowadays, water filled with thin pipes are used to find and fix the height level of area during construction.

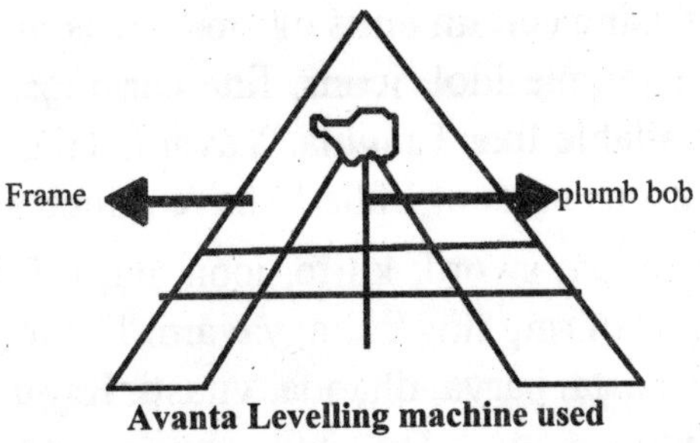

**Avanta Levelling machine used**

In the present day, Earth pooja is conducted before starting the earth excavation or measurement process. The owner will arrange pooja on that day. For mud or sand removing, JPC machine services are available. JPC services are time saving and cheap compared to the present physical labour.

## Measurement Methods

The ancients used the land measurement by Hasta or Kolu. However, different ways and names prevailed in India according to the local conditions. The names Kista, Hasta, Kolu, Kisku is prevalent in India. But as a standard measure a Kolu has 72 centimeters measurement or 24 matrangulam. The names given below are to be noted for different matra angulam:-

| | | | |
|---|---|---|---|
| 1. | 24 angulam | Kisku | 72 cms |
| 2. | 25 angulam | Prajadhipatyam | 75 cms |
| 3. | 26 angulam | Dhamur Musthi | 78 cms |
| 4. | 27 angulam | Dhamurgraha | 81 cms |
| 5. | 28 angulam | Prachayam | 84 cms |
| 6. | 29 angulam | Vaideham | 87 cms. |
| 7. | 30 angulam | Vaipulyam | 90 cms. |
| 8. | 31 angulam | Prakirna | 93 cms |

That means one kolu has 72 to 93 cms. One hasta is the basic measure used distinctively by Varna groups and its variations range from 72 cms to 93 cms to maintain the gap of 24 into 31 angulam. Such measurement stands to reveal the effectiveness of unit Vaastu perfection.

A Hasta means a measurement of a man's both hand' full stretch length. Equivalent to a fully developed body hands' stretch is considered to the complete length of Kaaya Vyama (hand swings). An angulam measure is equal to one section of forefinger length i.e.30 mm or 3 cms. The practice of using certain units of measure is prevalent for making specific cases only for temple idol, icons, fine carvings, vehicles or jewels. More names are available like Tangula, Yavam, Tila, or Talam etc. which are practiced in various parts of India to have minutest test measure.

Weapon, sword, knife, icon and pithal (brass) are made by measurement units of ring finger dia, yavam. The measurement of land buildings are done by hasta, parva, dhanda, vitasti, Rajju danda etc.

Clothes, silk and blankets are measured by vitasti (muzham). Yaagadhivan's, vessels, and utensils have the unit measurement of Yaagadhivan's hand. Such microscopic unit of measurement, devised by ancients was depicted clearly in Vaastu tests.

**Measurement Tables**

| | | |
|---|---|---|
| 1 | Angulam | 3 centimeter |
| 1 | Hasta/Kolu | 24 angulam |
| 1 | Hasta/Ko lu | 72 cms. Or 2.36 ft |
| 1 | Yavam | 3.75 mm |
| 1 | Perimeter | 1 Yochana |
| 8 | Paramaanu | 1 Tresa Renu. |
| 8 | Tresa Renu | 1 Romaagram/Lisa |
| 8 | Yugam | 1 Thila |
| 8 | Yavam | 1 angulam |
| 8 | Angulam | 1 paadam |
| 8 | Parva | 1 Hasta |
| 8 | Paadam | 1 Vyama |
| 3 | Paadam | 1 Hasta/Kolu |
| 12 | Angulam | 1 Vitastiti |
| 4 | Hasta/Kolu | 1 Dhandam |
| 8000 | Dhandam | 1 Yochana, 23040sq.mts. |
| 1000 | Dhandam | 1 Nagaram |
| 2000 | Dhandam | 1 Pattanam |
| 8 | Dhandam | 1 Rajju |
| 1 | Yochana | 1 Gramam/Village, 5750 sq.mts. |

## Land Divisions

• **Khanda (Quarter) Divisions:** A land, proposed to construct a building, may be square or rectangular in form. The earmarked land should be divided into four segments equally on all sides. If the square or rectangular plot bifurcation is not available with the present form, the shape should be rectified as shown below: Khanda means division. Here the division is in four segments or quarter in each portion

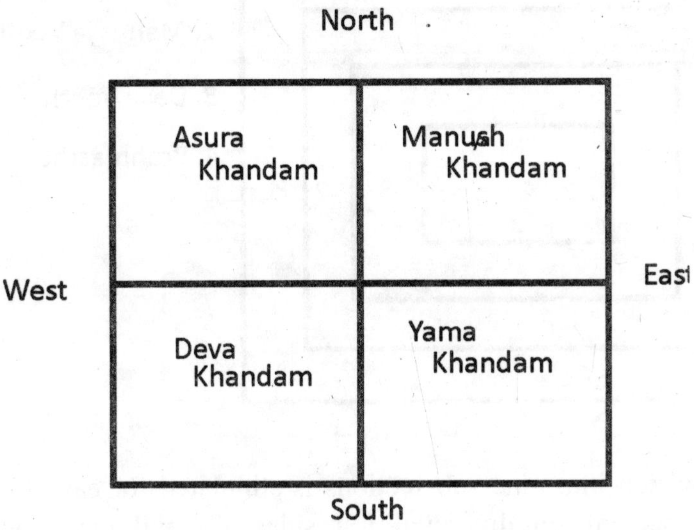

North

| | |
|---|---|
| Asura Khandam | Manush Khandam |
| Deva Khandam | Yama Khandam |

West

East

South

**Total land area is divided into four quarters**

| | | |
|---|---|---|
| SE | Agni | Yama Khanda |
| SW | Nairuti | Deva Khanda |
| NW | Vaayu | Asura Khanda |
| NE | Eshana | Manushya Khanda |

Both Asura Khanda and Yama Khanda are not good for locating a house in which khanda is proposed to construct. However, Manushya or Deva Khanda is the ideal location for the new proposed construction work. During construction process a little encroachment to other khandas is permitted.

The reason is that the entire construction area will not contain in the decided or selected quarter. It becomes imperative to extend the projection by observing certain factors of Brahma sthan, Brahma, Karna, Mruthyu and

Yama sutrams. Most of the sutrams, rajjus and sandhis are easily avoided in construction without walls, pillar or beams or staircase.

• **Land Plotting Divisions (Veethi Vinyaasam):** One should have the knowledge of the inner segments of the land. It has eighteen sections ranging from all four directions. The four fold divisions are Paishacha veethi, Manushya veethi, Deva veethi and Brahmasthan

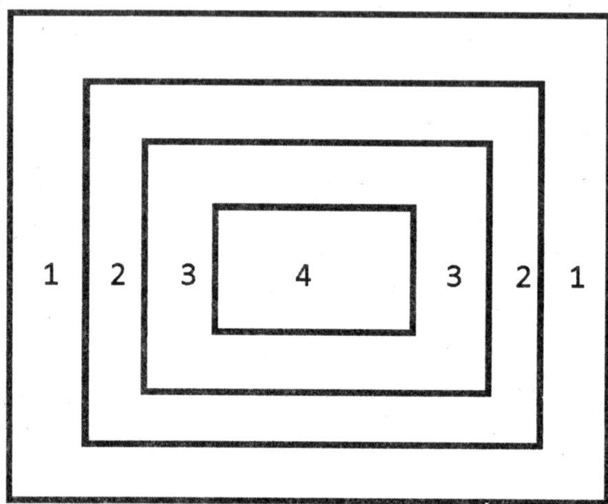


1. Paisacha Veethi
2. Manusya Veethi
3. Deva Veethi
4. Brahmasthan

The land division into nine sub-sections is stipulated for easy method of distiquishing the vulnarability on all four sides. This will make the total of eighteen sectional lines representing land area. The eighteen inner columns will provide a perfect square combination. These squares are represented to the total land plot area to decide on sections before planning for construction. The house location plan is drawn on the basis of the required buildable area and favouring good cells nature.

At the center 9th column is Brahma sthan.

| | |
|---|---|
| 8th cell | Ganesha |
| 7th cell | Agni |
| 6th cell | Jhalam |
| 5th cell | Naaga |
| 4th cell | Yama |
| 3rd cell | Kubera |
| 2nd cell | Deva |
| 1st cell | Paishacha |

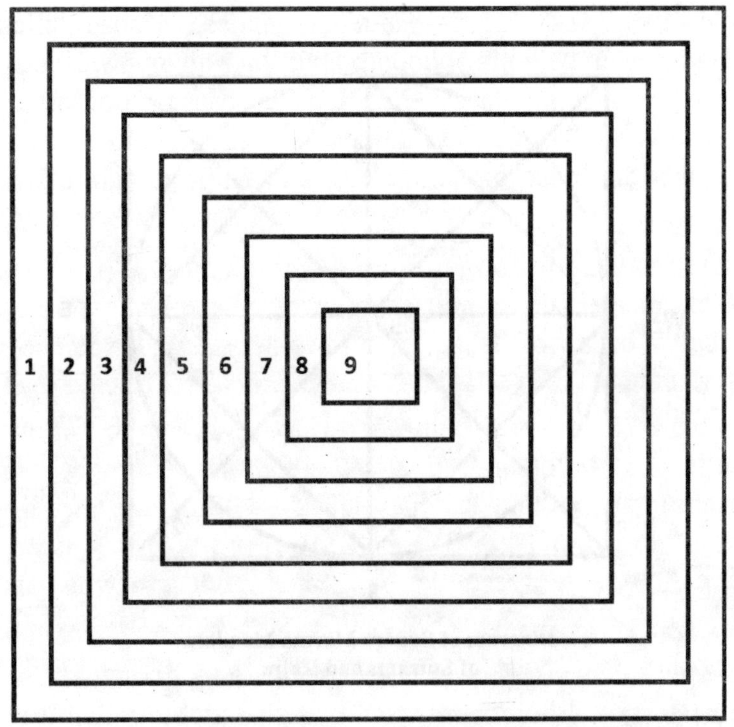


The eighteen inter cells columns will make 9 squares of 9 paadas making 81 square grid. It is the Paramsayika veethi vidhana mandala (81 cells profile classification). Further grid details will follow in the subsequent bhaagams (chapter).

## Mandala of Sutrams and Rajjus (Marma Mandala)

Mandala of sutrams and Rajjus are very significant to land plot like the nerves and veins of the human body. What will happen to human beings when veins or nerves are cut or touched? So also, the land plot has marma veins and nerves in certain junctions. That has to be avoided at the time of construction.

The entire land area is covered by Marma Mandala. Care should be taken in carrying out the construction work in all sensitive portions. Given below is a diagram of sensitive mandala of Sutrams, Rajjus or Brahma Naabhi. Each Sutrams or Rajjus is numbered from 1 to 8:-

Numbers given in the below diagram are:-

1 Karna sutram

2 Mruthyu sutram

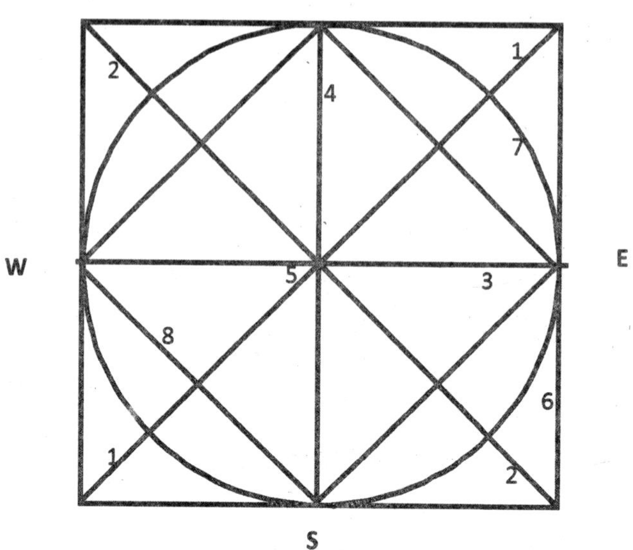


**Diagram of Square Marma Mandala of Sutrams and Rajju**

3 Brahma sutram
4 Yama sutram
5 Brahma naabhi
6 Paryanta sutram
7 Naaga sutram
8 Shoola Sutram.

**Karna Sutram:** A straight line from Southwest (SW) nairuti corner to Northeast (NE) Eshana corner is known as Karna Sutram.

**Mruthyu Sutram:** A straight line starting from SE Agni corner to the NW Vaayu corner is called Mruthyu Sutram.

**Brahma Sutram:** A straight line commencing from East-Indrasthan to West Varunasthan is known by the name Brahma Sutram.

**Yama Sutram:** A straight line from South Pithrupatisthan to North Kuberasthan is called Yama Sutram.

**Brahma Naabhi:** The exact centre of the square plot that touches Karna, Mruthyu, Brahma, and Yama Sutrams is called Brahma naabhi.

**Paryanta Sutram:** The outer boarder of all four sides of the plot is known by Paryanta Sutram.

**Naaga Sutram:** A circle line drawn touching all the four points of Brahma, Yama Sutram is called Naaga Sutram. This circle also touches the four sides of shoola sutrams.

**Shoola Sutram:** The four sides of square inscribed in the circle are called Shoola Sutram. Diagonal square four sides touch with Naaga (7), Yama (4) and Brahma (5) sutrams links or point adjoins with the same in all side Sutrams including square sides touching Karna (1), Mruthyu (2) Sutram lines are also known by shoola sutram.

The circle of Naaga sutram and diagonal square Shoola sutram are mutually linked at certain points. Rajjus means rope and the sutram means cord. The major diagonals are called karnas. The lines inclined at 45 degree to Brahma Sutram and Yama Sutram is called Rajjus. The main lines of Vaastu mandala are demarked in a square site and each is assigned to a specific regent (lokpala) in Vaastu science.

The boundary lines of the square are paryanta sutram and all the rounds of the circle are naaga sutrams, the square four sides inside the circle are called Shoola sutrams. Any touch or defection is occurred during the construction to Sutrams, Rajjus, Sandhis or naabhi is considered as marma vedha (obstruction) and the paada (Cell) rules of 16, 24, 32 square deities of Limb chart (given in end of this bhaagam) will be applied. An available remedy or rectification will be done immediately by correct prediction of limbs.

## House-Khanda and Placement

Location of the house is very important like the selection of khanda from Manushya, Deva, Asura and Yama khandas. If the house plot is bigger and each quadrant is bigger, its width 64 hasta each khanda is again subdivided into four upa (small) khandas. In Alpa kshetra (smaller plots) the entire area has to be considered as a gruha mandala.

**Small Mandala**
Manushya Khanda
Deva Khanda
Yama Khanda
Asura Khanda

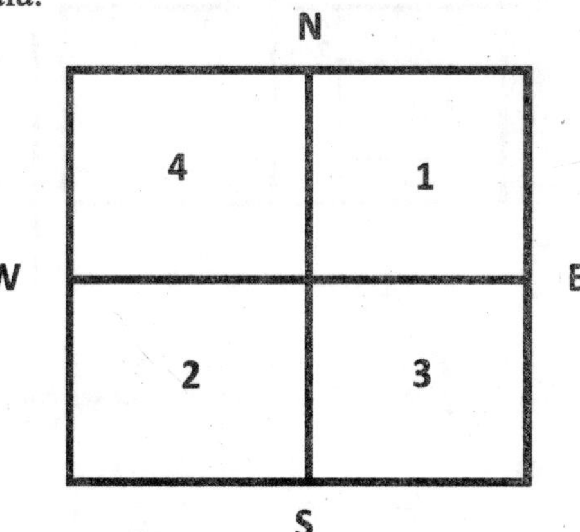

**Bigger Mandala**

1(a) Manushya Upakhanda
1(b) Deva Upakhanda
1(c) Asura Upakhanda
1(d) Yama Upakhanda

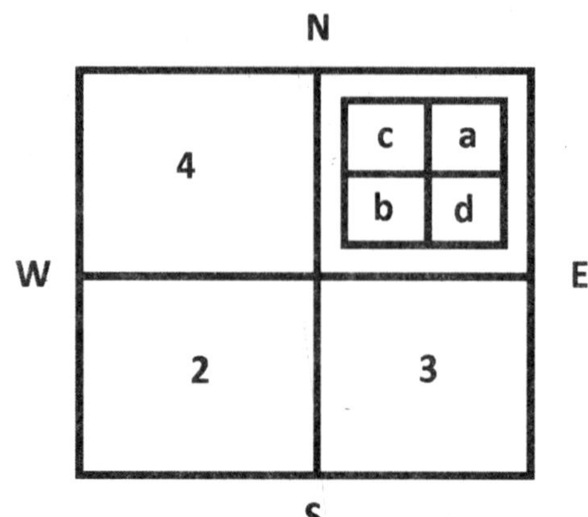


**Location of residence to decide on manushya khanda (small)**
**And manushya upa khanda (bigger)**

• **House - Location Point:** Placement of house location depends largely on the basis of the road available to the plot direction. Based on whether the road is situated on North-South or East-West, the suitable placement has to be selected. In a South road situation, the quadrant has to be selected as per details below:-

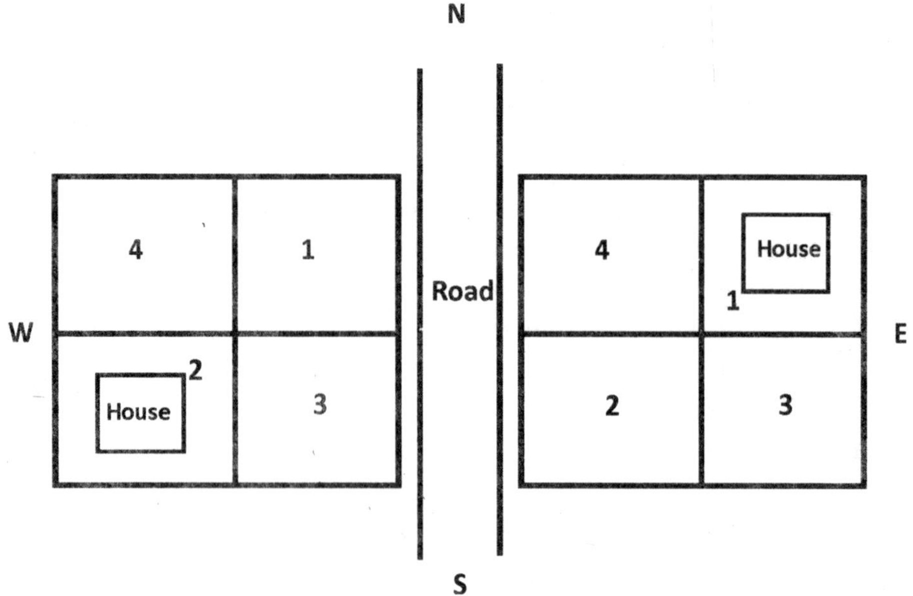


**Road point selection of Gruha mandala**

In East side house plot should be placed in the Manushya khanda and in the West side house plots should be placed only at Deva khanda. In East-West road, the house should be placed in North house plot in Manushya khanda and the South house plot in Deva khanda.

• **Small Plot Khanda Selection:** In every small plot, it is desirable to select the Manushya khanda zone for the gruha mandala. However the position of the road access to the plot, will be a deciding factor for its location in Deva Khanda which is also good.

In Vaastu Shastra, the place of the house has great important.

A small diagram is given below:

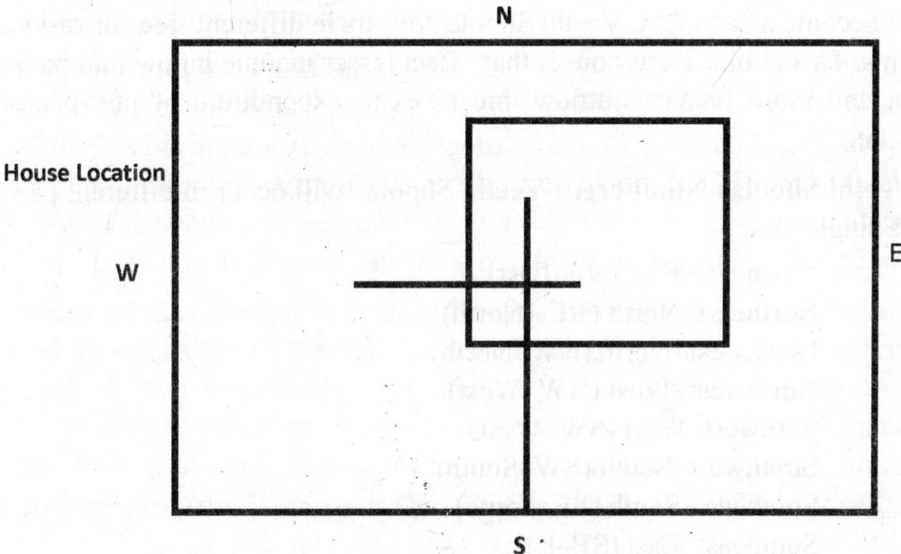


In certain cases, the construction area will be projected beyond selected quarter Deva or manushya khandas.

In this plot, the gruha mandala extended beyond Manushya khanda including Brahma Naabhi (even in Deva khanda) is considered for house location placement. To avoid all sutrams, Sandhis or Naadis it is quite essential.

• **Cremation - location and birth placenta placement:** In olden times, a portion of the land is kept vacant for cremation of dead bodies in Yama zone Southeast agni region especially for family members. And North-side is kept for disposing placenta after child birth in Soma cell zone. The rear or front portion of the Vaastu mandala, the sutras or rajjus involving vedha (hindrance) in diks and vidiks houses has to be avoided while designing and drawing the house plan. It will become difficult to conjoin the side houses and corner houses without a corridor.

## Veethi – Shoola (Road Obstruction)

The Veethi (Road) Shoola (Trident) (Road Obstruction) refers to a road that thrusts into a site as a sphere. They are the roads that jet into the plot straight to that particular side or corner. The result of Veethi Shoola may bring good or bad effect to the house occupants depending on the area side it jets into.

The disadvantage of Veethi Shoola is that it will block the inmate's peace and prosperity. It is also known by Marma Vedha where the plot or house will become as a trident. Veethi Shoola appears in different sides in various forms. This is like T-cut houses that effect lesser income inflow into house plot and more finance outflow due to extra expenditure of unexpected nature.

• **Veethi Shoolas Numbered:** Veethi Shoolas will occur in different parts of a single plot.

Northeast–East (NE–East)
Northeast–North (NE –North)
Northwest–North (NW–North)
Northwest–West (NW–West)
Sothwest–West (SW–West)
Southwest–South (SW–South)
Southeast–South (SE–South)
Southeast–East (SE–East)
East–East (E–East)
North–North (N–North)
West–West (W–West)
South–South (S–South)

• **Types of Veethi Shoolas:** Veethi Shoolas are of twelve types. This can be in a side or in a corner. The corners or sides shoola will appear in the following ways:-

| | | |
|---|---|---|
| NE–North | Northeast –North | Veethi shoola is good |
| NE–East | Northeast –East | Veethi shoola is good |
| NW–North | Northwest –North. | Veethi shoola is bad |
| NW–West | Northwest– West. | Veethi shoola is bad |

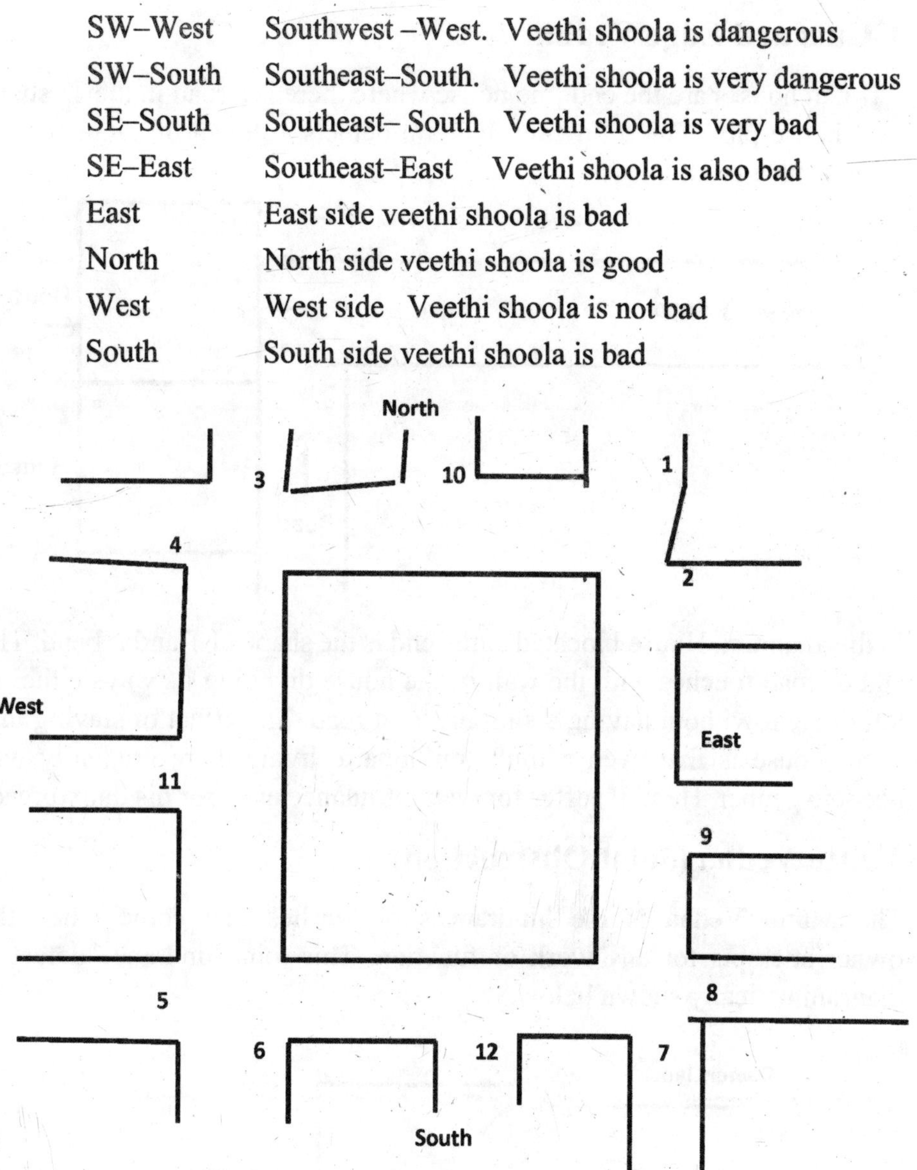

| | |
|---|---|
| SW–West | Southwest –West. Veethi shoola is dangerous |
| SW–South | Southeast–South. Veethi shoola is very dangerous |
| SE–South | Southeast– South Veethi shoola is very bad |
| SE–East | Southeast–East Veethi shoola is also bad |
| East | East side veethi shoola is bad |
| North | North side veethi shoola is good |
| West | West side Veethi shoola is not bad |
| South | South side veethi shoola is bad |



As regards the piercing of front door, the Veedhi Shoola is multiplied by the distance of objects twice the height. The Brihat Samhita identified these objects as dwara (Door) vedha, a road, a tree, the sinking soil, a corner edge, a wall, a water pool, or a pillar etc.

## T-Cuts and Edge Vedha

T–Cut houses are the end line house where there is a road in the T- shape with house plot. The following diagram depicts a model of T-cut section house with a road:-

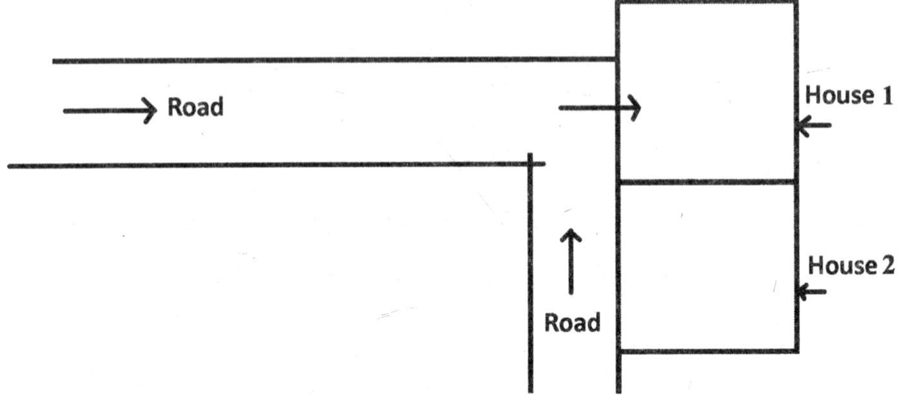


In this diagram, House I located at the end is the shape of T and L bend. The end of road touches with the wall of the house diverting its ways either to left or right without having a straight front road. The effect of staying in a T-cut house is that even a multi millionaire living there gradually will become pauper. He will suffer for want of finance even for his daily bread.

## Muttu Vedha (Joint Obstruction)

The Muttu Vedha is the hindrances or hurdles that come when the owner attempts for any work or function. This joint hindrance defect is diagrammatically shown below:

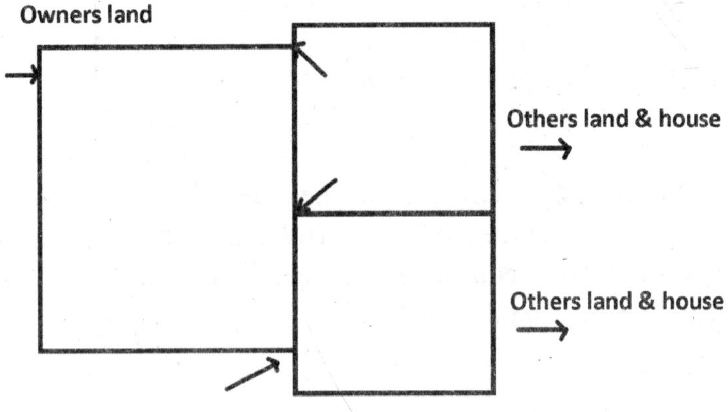


Muttu Vedha (Joint obstruction)

The Muttu Vedha is the wall touching owner's or other's plot either in the middle or anywhere. The plots need not be similar in all cases. In the above diagram, the big land owner gets Muttu Vedha in the centre whereas others get wall touch near their corner sides. Likewise, the others land touches centre of the plots. If such vedha occurs in the eastern side it is considered to be more serious than other sides. Any such dissimilar joint wall touch Vedhas are harmful for the plot owners and the occupants. It is suggested to plant trees in that adjoining junction or Thulasi plant for warding off muttu vedha bad effects. The Muttu Vedha is a simple matter but it always gives troubles at the entry level of job, profession or any good thing.

## Famous Vaastu purusha

- **Mythical View:** "The Vaastu Purusha" concept is linked with the Vaastu science, born as protégé of Asura Guru Sukracharya, during sacrificial rites to wipe off all Devas completely. A drop of perspiration of Guru Sukracharya fell in the yaaga fire, soon a skeptical dark combination of a cruel human wonder appeared. The sounds produced were very rough. It looked like a terrifying fire spitting demon. The appearance with horrible colour, sound, and spirit made everyone frightened. The Devas, Rishis, and others approached Lord Maha Devan for rescue.

The gigantic spirit threatened Heaven and the Earth to complete devastation. Lord Shiva directed all the Devas to Lord Brahma, the creater of all beings, for help and protection.

Lord Brahma suggested the Devas to occupy in his body and kick him to pull down to earth. As directed and desired by the Lord, the Devas occupied the rolling body and kicked him to push down to the earth.

The fallen spirit form had his Head at eshana, legs at nairuti, elbows at the Agni and vaayu corners, hands at East and North, thigh at West and South, stomach at brahma naabhi.

The helpless spirit besought Brahma for help, prayed and conveyed his worries. Being happy with Vaastu Purusha (demon), Lord Brahma gave him a boon that –

"He will exist in every plot. He is the presiding deity of the plot. He is supposed to rest his head on the Northeast"

The Viswakarma Prakasika describes the Brahma boon given to Vaastu Purusha as –

"You are the Vaastu Purusha created by me on Saturday, Kirthika asterism, Vyruth paada yoga, Vishti karanam in the middle of Bhadra on third lunar day of the dark half of Bhadrapada month. He who does not perform Vaastu pooja and does not offer Vaastu bali pooja gets disturbed with many obstacles of life and can be killed and even the dead becoming food to you."

• **Nitya Vaastu Purusha:** The Nitya Vaastu Purusha moves daily within every three hours, and each changes his position from one place to another. The sleeping hours is considered to be his resting time and will always be calm and quiet. This resting will be usually in the months of Meenam (Pisces), Midhunam (Gemini), Kanni (Virgo), Dhanu (Sagittarius). Usually these are very auspicious time to make construction work.

The time is the normal awake period in other months thus the date and time are given below:-

| | | | |
|---|---|---|---|
| Aries | Medam | 10th day | 9-15 to 9-30 AM |
| Taurus | Edavam | 21st | 10-28 to 10-45 AM |
| Cancer | Karthik | 11th | 8-12 to 8-30 AM |
| Leo | Chingam | 6th | 3-42 to 4-0 PM |
| Libra | Thulam | 11th | 8-10 to 8-30 AM |
| Scorpio | Vruchikam | 8th | 11-55 to 12-12 PM |
| Capricorn | Makaram | 12th | 11-05 to 11-15 AM |
| Aquarius | Kumbham | 20th | 11-05 to 11-17 AM |

The sleeping directions and months of Vaastu Purusha details are given below:-

| Month | Head | leg | Hands | Face |
|---|---|---|---|---|
| 1. Pisces (Meenam), Aries (Medam) Taurus (Edavam) | West | East | South | North |
| 2. Gemini (Midhunam),Cancer (Karkadak), Leo (Chingam) | North | South | West | East |
| 3. Virgo (Kanni), Libra (Thulam), Scorpio (Vruchikam) | East | West | North | South |
| 4. Sagittarius (Dhanu),Capricorn (Makaram), Acquarius (Kumbham) | South | North | East | West |

The change of movement of every three hours of Vaastu purusha is essential to fix the timings of house-construction functions.

1. Bhoomi puja, digging of sand, or digging of well or bore well has to be arranged first for pooja.
2. The foundation stone laying is done only after the earth pooja. It will be followed by well or bore well construction.
3. The process of construction of house walls will continue to lintel, then the front or main door, window frames will be fixed.
4. The milk boiling ceremony has to be performed at the house warming or Gruha pravesh.

In other words, the Vaastu Purusha is small in a little bottle but big in large plots. It is very significant point to remember that any construction on the ground covering his head, his legs, his hands and his posteriors will be fatal to self, father, wife and children. The most suitable section is on the ground covered by his stomach.

• **Vaastu Purusha Mandala**

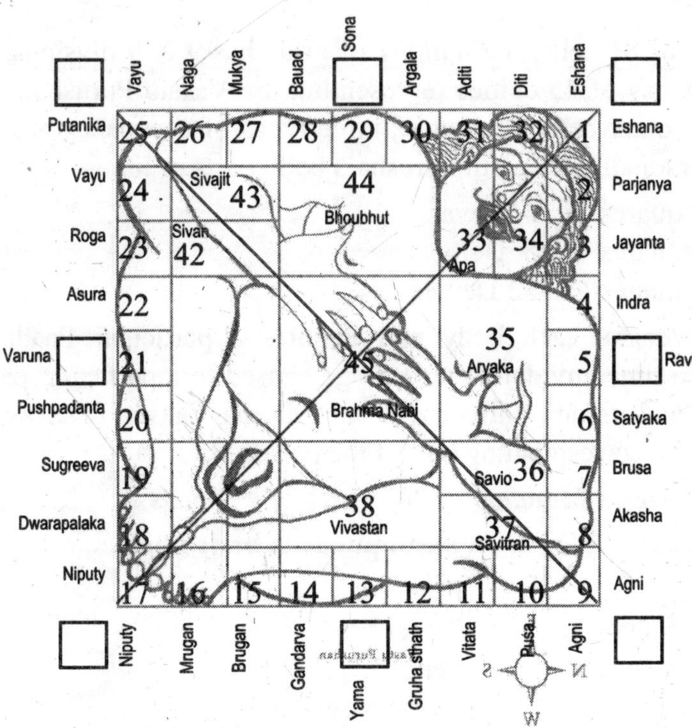


**The diagram of Vaastu Purusha**

After the Vaastu Bali Pooja a gold icon of Pancha Mrugasira (Five Animals Heads) will be kept on the Northeast wall or Northeast corner floor. The Pancha Mrugasirasus are Lion (Simha), Bison (Kaala), Boar (Karimpothu), Tortoise (Aama) and Elephant (Aana).

• **Paada Vaastu (Cells Profile):** Ekaseeti Paada Vaastu describes the number of deities occupied in each part of the Vaastu Purusha formed to identify the paadas. The Paada Devatas names are given in Paada Vaastu Mandala. The exposition of Ekaseeti paada Vaastu has been chiefly detailed in the Matsya Puraana.

In the body of Vaastu Purusha, a number of deities are occupied to push and kick to pull down to the earth. There are various kinds of grids developed by the ancients. The number of grids cells are paadas formulated conveniently to assess each paada mandala. The numbers of paadas are contained 7x7 = 49 grid cells, 8x8 = 64 grid cells, 9x9 = 81 grid cells and 10x10 =100 grid cells. If the damage, cut or defection happens to a particular paada during the time of construction, it is easy to trace it soon. The names of Padas and Paada Devatas are clearly shown in the Paada Limbs Chart of Vaastu Purusha.

In the case of 81 cells, the number of grids has 9 X 9 divsions, with the total occupancy of 45 deities representing the Vaastu Purusha's 45 limbs including 8 outer cells. Therefore, three types of occupancy are available with the personalized Vaastu Purusha's body parts or limbs.

| | | |
|---|---|---|
| 1. | 24 squares | 4 Devas |
| 2. | 16 squares | 8 Deities |
| 3. | 32 squares | 32 Deities |

In Paada Vaastu, each body part denotes a particular Paada. At the construction time any defect or damage caused to a particular part means that Paada and its deity directly hit the Marma Vaastu. (That will reflect damage to the corresponding part of the person) by:-

***I) Limbs Vaastu Mandala of 24 square of 4 Deities***

| | Devas | Vaastu purusha body parts |
|---|---|---|
| 1. | Apaka | Face |
| 2. | Savitraha | Finger base |
| 3. | Indra Jaya | Penis |
| 4. | Rudra | Finger base |

### *II) Vaastu Mandala of 16 square of 8 Deities*

| | Direction | Deities | Parts of Vaastu purusha |
|---|---|---|---|
| 1. | East | Aryama | Right breast |
| 2. | Southeast | Savita | Finger tips |
| 3. | South | Vivastan | Right stomach |
| 4. | Southwest | Vibhudha | Penis |
| 5. | West | Mitraka | Left stomach |
| 6. | Northwest | Rajayakshma | Finger tips |
| 7. | North | Pridwidhara | Left breast |
| 8. | Northeast | Apavats | Chest |

### *III) Paada Vaastu of 32 squares of 32 deities presided over the limbs of Vaastu Purusha*

| Devas name | Limbs parts | Devas name | Limbs parts |
|---|---|---|---|
| 1. Sikhi | Head | 17. Pitrugana | Feet |
| 2.Parjanya | Right eye | 18. Danvarika | Left hip |
| 3. Jayanta | Right ear | 19. Sugreeva | Left shank |
| 4. Indra | Right shoulder | 20. Pushpadanda | Left knee |
| 5. Surya | Right arm | 21. Jaladhipa | Left thigh |
| 6. Satya | Middle arm pit | 22. Asura | Left side |
| 7. Brusa | Middle arm | 23. Sosha | Left side |
| 8. Akasha | Right eye | 24. Papa | Left wrist |
| 9. Vaayu | Fore arm | 25. Roga | Left forearm |
| 10. Pusha | Right wrist | 26. Naga | Left elbow |
| 11. Vithata | Right side | 27. Mukya | Middle arm |
| 12. Gruhakshata | Right side | 28. Bhanta | Armpit |
| 13. Yama | Right thigh | 29. Soma | Left arm |
| 14. Gandhara | Right knee | 30. Sarpa | Left shoulder |
| 15. Bringa Raja | Right shank | 31. Aditi | Left ear |
| 16. Mriga | Right lip | 32. Diti | Left eye. |

If any dosha or vedha afflicted Mahasandhi (main) or Upa marma (sub-joints) through wall or window, pillar during construction on the limbs of the Vaastu purusha , it implies vulnerable points of the owner or the architect get disfigured. Under any circumstances, construction in the exterior part of 32 divisions and four paisacha cells ruled by Charaki, Vidhari, and Pootani and Paparakshasi should be avoided.

If any part of the constructed house is defective or the owner is injured due to that, it will also be affecting Vaastu Purusha. Usually women get trouble if Vaastu Purusha is weakened. If the head is weak, ill-health will prevail. Every thing clear and ok means the person becomes happy and prosperous.

The vedha blemish causes the death of family head in 6th year, loss of wealth in 9th year, loss of progeny in 4th year and ordinary evils in a year. "Vaastu Raja Vallabha" warns that

"Vaastu pooja vihinazcha
Sootradharae vinathadha
Sabra janma bhavethu kuzdhi
Sa karthru narak brajethu"

**Meaning:** "He, who does not perform Vaastu Bali Pooja during house warming ceremony and does not honour the architects, will suffer from leprosy for seven births and go to the Hell. He, who does the Vaastu Bali Pooja (homam) will live for 100 years and get free from grief or trouble and do well in heaven for a period of Kalpa."

# Bhaagam 4

## House Cell Divisions (Gruha Paada Vinyaasa)

Cell control deities are the Paada deities or gods occupied on the Vaastu Purusha's body to pull him down to the earth as per the permission or instructions of the Lord Brahma. Brahma Deva creates all human beings or creatures. The Vaastu Purusha is created in a special circumstance and the occupied number of Devas on Vaastu Purusha's body claimed the authority of cell. The Vaastu Shastra formulates a number of Paada Vinyaasa or cells division of land plots for the convenience and utilization rules.

The Cells Divisions or Paada Vinyaasa denotes the selection of grids and grid cells which are applicable to different houses. To suit the actual requirement of the owner's choice the land shape has to be decided by the Sthapati according to the house grids in consultation with the civil construction experts.

In each Grid cells division, the acceptance of Grid depends on the actual land space available and nature of house type decided by the owner. The details of various Vaastu Grid Cells divisions are given below as House Paada Vidhana Mandala:

- **Single Cell Grid or Eka- Paada Gruha Vinyaasa (Sakala Mandala):** This Sakala type of house has only one cell type in all grid portions. Calculations are based on 1X1cell, Eka Gruha varga division with outer eight paadas.
- **Two Cells Grid or Dwi-Padaa Gruha Vinyaasa (Pecaka Mandala) :** Pecaka House cells are two in numbers square varga divisions like 2X2 with eight outer cells.
- **Three Cells Grid or Thridhiya-Paada Gruha Vinyaasa (Pitha Mandala):** Pitha gruha cells divisions are thrice squares 3x3 along with eight outer padams.
- **Seven Cells Grid or Sapta Paada Gruha Vinyaasa (Sthandila Mandala):** Sthantila Gruha paadas 7X7 divisions are important for the construction of big palatial palaces and altars. The extreme eight paadas are included in this classification of House cells.
- **Eight Cells Grid or Ashta Paada Gruha Vinyaasa (Manduka Mandala):** Manduka Gruha paadas (Eight Cell Divisions) are very

useful for the construction of all types of buildings and residences. The Grid consists of 8X8 squares of 64 cells along with eight outer cells

- **Nine Cells Grid or Nava Paada Gruha Vinyaasa (Paramsayika Mandala):** Paramsayika Gruha classification is the most important and the best in all cases of residences and buildings with selected yonis. This will include 9X9 squares house 81 cells with outer eight cells.
- **Ten Cells Grid or Dasa Paada Gruha Vinyaasa (Asana Mandala):** Asana or ten into ten square divisions are also in use for the construction of all kinds of houses and buildings. Grid covers the total cells 108 cells including eight outer cells.
- **Elevan Cells Grid or Ekadasa Paada Gruha Vinyaasa (Sthaniya Mandala):** Sthaniya or eleven squares grid has 129 cells in total including the eight outer cells. Sthaniya Paada divisions are mainly used for construction of temples and garba gruhas around in temples in places of public importance.

The Gruha Paada division is quite necessary to assess the grid suitability to land. And if land is not in square or rectangular form, the Pada Vinyazsa (divisions) becomes difficult. Unless the land shape is corrected into square by rectification, the desired result will not be achieved definitely. So the need of Paada classification knowledge is very essential and significant.

## Nine Square (81) Cells Grid Division (Paramsayika Gruha Paadams)

Total fifty three numbers of Devas are present in the Eighty One Grid cells. 81 Grids (Squares) means 9 cells (paadas) of 9 times will make 81 cells with 53 deities. Names of Devas or Deities on all cells side wise details are given below:

***Side wise:***

a) East side starts with NE to SE: 1 Eshana, 2 Parjanya, 3 Jayanta, 4 Indra, 5 Ravi, 6 Satyaka, Brusa, 8 Andariksha, 9 Agni.

b) South side starts with SE to SW: 9 Agni, 10 Pusa, 11 Vithasta, 12 Gruhakshata, 13 Yama, 14 Gandharva, 15 Brunga, 16 Mruga, and 17 Nairuty.

c) West side starts with SW to NW: 17 Nairuti, 18 Dwarapala, 19 Sugreeva, 20 Pushpadanda, 21 Varuna, 22 Asura, 23 Sosa, 24 Roga.

d) North side starts with NW to NE: 25 Vaayu, 26 Naga, 27 Mukhya, 28 Bhallada, 29 Indu, 30 Argala, 31 Adhiti, 32 Dhiti.

The exact position of the numbered cells is located differently by above thirty two cells of 32 Devas who are situated at the forewalls of the grid. There are twelve Devatas positioned inner side of the grid with more cells. The following are the cell of multi combination having two/six cells each as given in the bracket.

e) Inside the grid: 33 Apa (2), 34 Apatvalsa (2), 35 Aryaka (6), 36 Savitavu (2), 37 Savitra (2) 38 Vivasta (6), 39 Indra (2), 40 Indrajit (2), 41 Mitra (6), 42 Shiva (2), 43 Shivajit (2), 44 Brubuth (6).

f) In the middle, Cell no 45 is Brahma naabhi or Brahmastan having nine cells.

g) Outermost cells in the grid are located around grid in side and corners:

1. 46 cell Sarvaskanda-------- East
2. 47 Aryamavu ----------- South
3. 48 Jerumbaka---------- West
4. 49 Pilipinchika--------- North
5. 50 Charaki----------- Northeast
6. 51 Paparakshasi------- Southeast
7. 52 Puttanika----------- Northwest
8. 53 Vithari-------------- Southwest

The total number of deities occupied in Vaastu purusha's body is as follows:

Middle Brahmastan----------------cell 1
Inner Devas----------------------cells 12
Grid forewalls Devas -------------cells 32
Outermost Devas -----------------cells 8

Grand total: a + b +c + d = 32 + e = 40 + f=9 + g= 8 = 89 cells and Fifty Three Deities.

## The Vaastu Mandala (Sectional Profile)–COSMOS VIEW

The ancients believed and practiced Vaastu as a way of life which is to compose the Vaastu Mandala as COSMOS, structure. The centre of the Cosmos is the brahmastaan consisting total twelve cells in combination with one Devata, the Sun. These twelve cells are considered as 12 Raasis. It has a clear mark that the sunrays, power and light should come from the ruling Raasi. Above the solar space, there are a number of stars crowded with or clubbed together, in which the numbers equate with 32 stars. Further eight stars acting as diks and vidiks guard similar as Ashta diks dwarapalas (knights). The outer space is known by paisacha zone (Demon Area).

All the twelve Raasis, the Sun, 32 Stars, 8 Ashta diks palakas are Fifty Three (53) deities of Vaastu Mandala.

• **House Profile Division (Gruha Mandala Vidhana)**: On the basis of occupancy of the paada deities, Paada division becomes an essential criterion to the constructions. The paada kalpana divisions enable to point out the specific cell, its deity occupied, and the Vaastu Purusha limb. Three types of paada vinyaasa are usually done, though there are several other divisions in force. The main paada classifications are given below:-

1. Ahta Paada Vinyaasa (Manduka or eight square Gruha paada).
2. Nava Paada Vinyaasa (Paramsayika or Nine square Gruha paada).
3. Dasa Paada Vinyaasa (Aasana or Ten square Gruha paada).

To find out the required paada and Vaastu limbs, a study of marma (key) points and details are necessary as per Vaastu science. Brief details are given below:

***Nine Cells Square Grid Divisions (Nava Gruha paada Vinyaasa) or Paramsayika:*** The paada squares of nine arriving a total of 81 (eight one) cells grid are very often taken as Paramsayika Gruha Paada Mandala. This can be drawn easily by making ten lines horizontally and within those lines are drawn another ten lines vertically to make the picture a square. Thus it will make 81 equal small squares of nine paada division contributing the occupancy of 53 deities. This will help the Sthapati to direct the masons or others to keep position and total perimeter of house or correct locating of the rooms, toilets, etc.

The detailed list of 81 squares with occupied 53 Devas with number cells is given below;

| S.No. | Paada Nos. | Deities Name | No. deity | Nos. Cells |
|---|---|---|---|---|
| 1. | 45 | Brahma Naabhi | 1 | 9 |
| 2. | 35 | Aryaka | 1 | 6 |
| 3. | 38 | Vivastha | 1 | 6 |
| 4. | 41 | Mitra | 1 | 6 |
| 5. | 44 | Bhubruth | 1 | 6 |
| 6. | 33 | Apa | 1 | 2 |

| | | | | |
|---|---|---|---|---|
| 7. | 34 | Apatvalsa | 1 | 2 |
| 8. | 36 | Savitavu | 1 | 2 |
| 9. | 37 | Savithr a | 1 | 2 |
| 10. | 39 | Indra | 1 | 2 |
| 11. | 40 | Indrajit | 1 | 2 |
| 12. | 42 | Shiva | 1 | 2 |
| 13. | 43 | Shivajit | 1 | 2 |
| 14. | 1 | Eshana | 1 | 1 |
| 15. | 2 | Parjanya | 1 | 1 |
| 16. | 3 | Jayanta | 1 | 1 |
| 17. | 4 | Indra | 1 | 1 |
| 18. | 5 | Aditya | 1 | 1 |
| 19. | 6 | Sathyaka | 1 | 1 |
| 20. | 7 | Brusha | 1 | 1 |
| 21. | 8 | Andhariska | 1 | 1 |
| 22. | 9 | Agni | 1 | 1 |
| 23. | 10 | Pushamavu | 1 | 1 |
| 24. | 11 | Vithasta | 1 | 1 |
| 25. | 12 | Gruhakshata | 1 | 1 |
| 26. | 13 | Yama | 1 | 1 |
| 27. | 14 | Gandharva | 1 | 1 |
| 28. | 15 | Brunga | 1 | 1 |
| 29. | 16 | Mruga | 1 | 1 |
| 30. | 17 | Nairuti (pithruvya) | 1 | 1 |
| 31. | 18 | Dwarapalaka (Pathihara) | 1 | 1 |
| 32. | 19 | Sugreeva | 1 | 1 |
| 33. | 20 | Puspadhidanta | 1 | 1 |
| 34. | 21 | Varuna | 1 | 1 |
| 35. | 22 | Asura | 1 | 1 |
| 36. | 23 | Dhrukovya (Sobhan) | 1 | 1 |
| 37. | 24 | Rogan (Bhogan) | 1 | 1 |
| 38. | 25 | Vaayu (Maruti) | 1 | 1 |
| 39. | 26 | Naagan | 1 | 1 |
| 40. | 27 | Mukhya | 1 | 1 |

| 41. | 28 | Bhallada | 1 | 1 |
|---|---|---|---|---|
| 42. | 29 | Soma(Indu | 1 | 1 |
| 43. | 30 | Argala | 1 | 1 |
| 44. | 31 | Adhiti | 1 | 1 |
| 45. | 32 | Diti | 1 | 1 |
| 46. | 46 | Sarvaskanda | 1 | 1 |
| 47. | 47 | Aryamavu | 1 | 1 |
| 48. | 48 | Jharambaka (Shunbaka) | 1 | 1 |
| 49. | 49 | Pili pinchuka | 1 | 1 |
| 50. | 50 | Charaki | 1 | 1 |
| 51. | 51 | Vidhari | 1 | 1 |
| 52. | 52 | Putanika | 1 | 1 |
| 53. | 53 | Paparakshasi | 1 | 1 |
| | | **Total** | **53 deities** | **89 cells.** |

Eighty nine cells include 81 cells in squares with external 8 cells.

1. The Gruha paadas starts from Eshana corner NE to Agni corner SE line; paada deities are serially numbered from one to nine. Area represents East side.
2. The paada deities starts from Agni moola to Nairuti moola and are serially numbered from 9 to 17. Area represents South side.
3. And the paada deities from Southwest corner to NorthwEst corner are numbered from 17 to 25. West area covers this side.
4. The Devas paada starts from 25 to 32 and are from the Northwest to Northeast line. North side will represent this area.
5. The centre deity is Brahma Deva, so it is called brahma naabhi. Cell No. is 45. Otherwise it is known as Brahmasthan.
6. The inner deities have more than one cell serially numbered from 33 to 44.
7. The outermost corner and sides are represented with eight cells touching boarder lines are serially numbered from 46 to 53.

In all diagrams only Paada numbers are provided. The above cell-wise information will give a clear picture of Paramsayika (Nine) Gruha mandala grids and its 53 deities occupied. The deformation of limbs is easily traceable and averted by avoiding such paada defects before construction begins.

## *Nava (Nine) Gruha (House) Paada (Cells) Vinyaasa (Division) Or Paramsayika*

(81 Cells grid diagram 53 deities 89 segments)

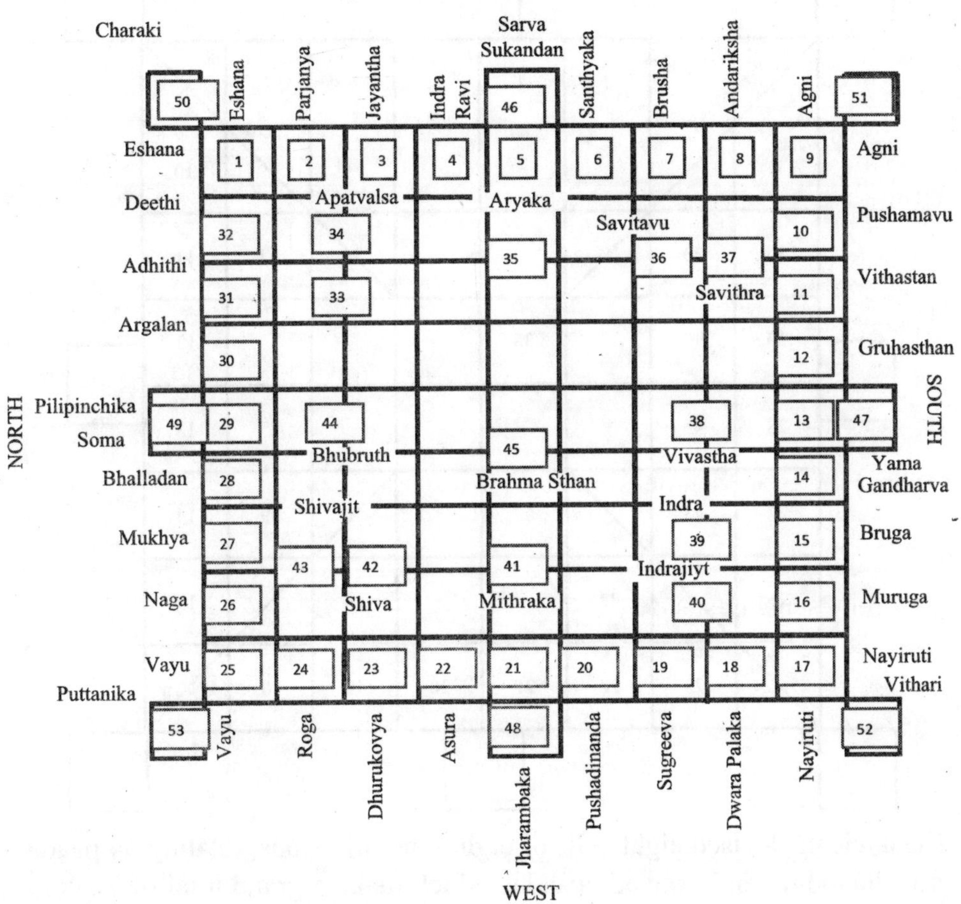


A perfect square of Nine Gruha mandala can be made by ten line each vertically or ten lines horizontally in combination grid consisting of:-

| | | |
|---|---|---|
| Brahmashtaan | 9 cells | 1 deity |
| Single cells paadas | 40 | 40 |
| Double cells of 8 | 16 | 8 |
| 6 paadas of 4 | 24 | 4 |

Total cells 89, deities 53

***Ashta (Eight) Gruha (House) Paada (Cell) Vinyaasa (Division) Or Manduka***

(64 Grid diagram 72 paadas 53 devas)

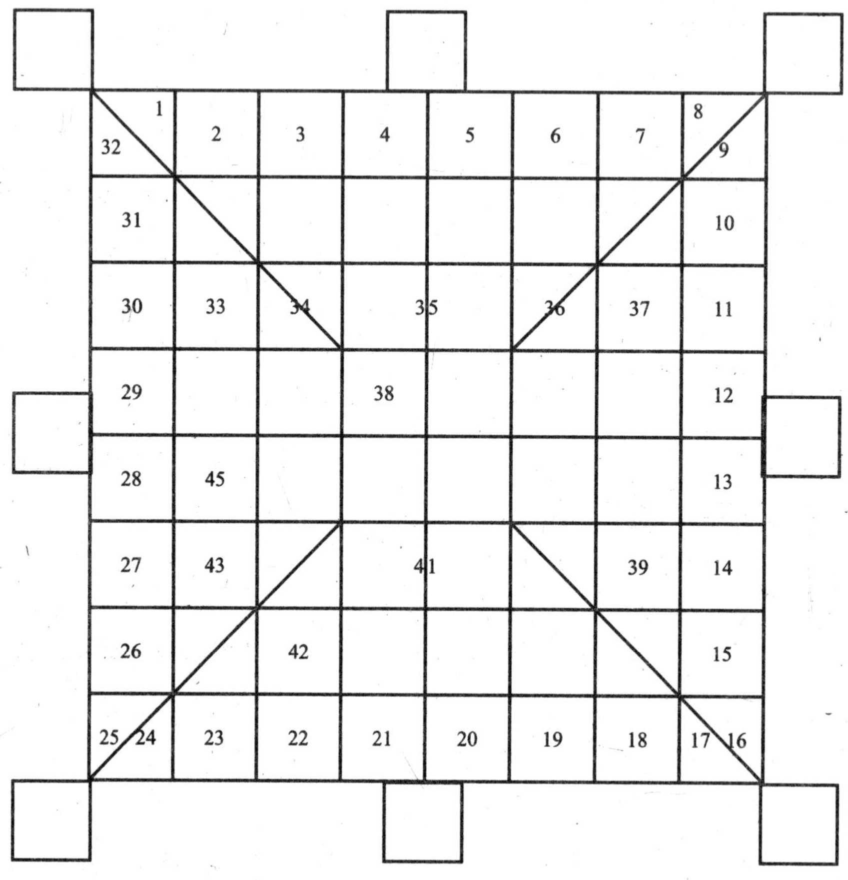


The ancients devised eight cells of eight inner divisions, totaling 64 paadas grid; including eight outside paadas which make a grand total of 72 cells. The numbers will represent the names of deities as provided in the above chart.

| | | |
|---|---|---|
| Brahma sthan | 4 cells | 1 deity |
| Half Cells 8 nos. | 4 | 8 |
| One Cells each 32 nos. | 32 | 32 |
| Two Cells of eight nos. | 16 | 8 |
| Four Cells of four nos. | 16 | 4 |
| Total | 72 cells | 53 deities |

***Dasa (Ten) Gruha (House) Paada (Cell) Vinyaasam (Division) Or Aasana***

(Grid diagram 108 padas 53 deities)

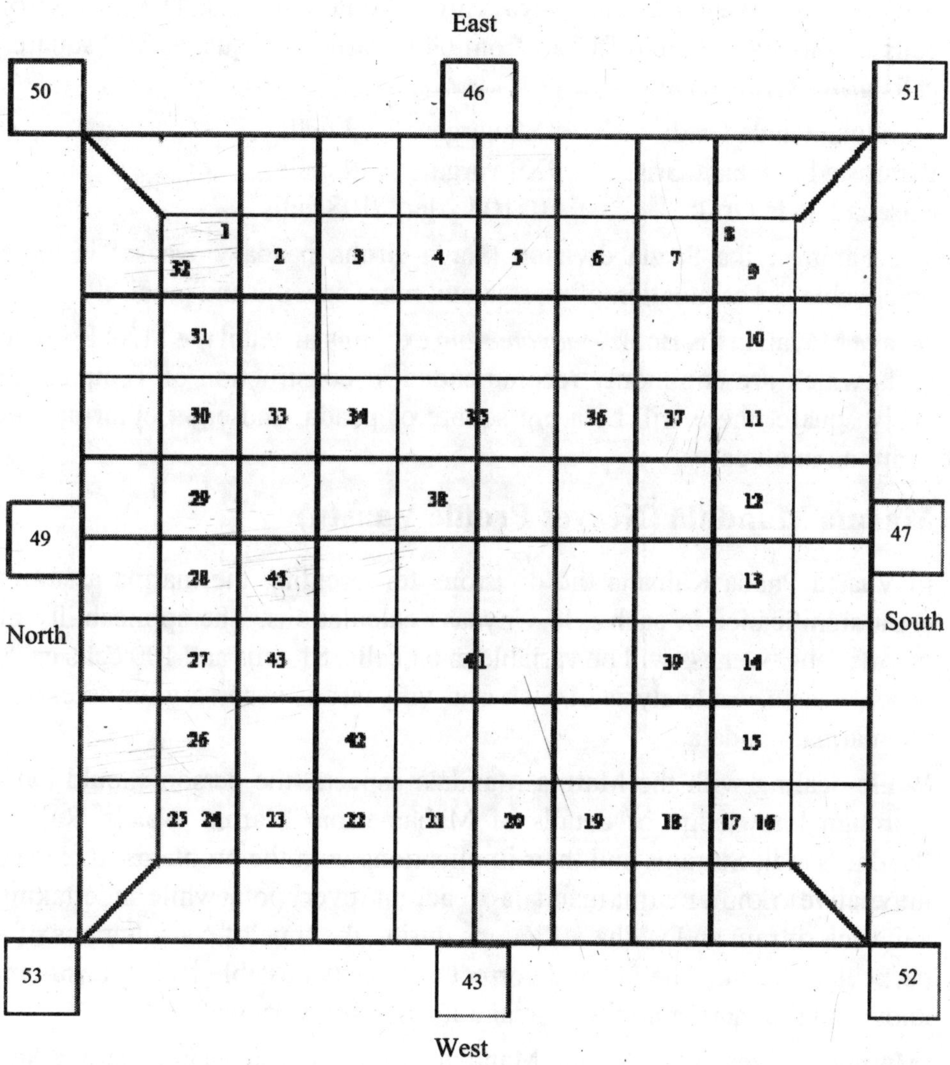

East

50 46 51

1 2 3 4 5 6 7 8 9 32

31 10

30 33 34 35 36 37 11

29 38 12

49 47

28 45 13

North South

27 43 41 39 14

26 42 15

25 24 23 22 21 20 19 18 17 16

53 43 52

West

| | | | | |
|---|---|---|---|---|
| Brahma Sthaan--- | cells | 16 | deities | 1 |
| Four deities 2 cells each | cells | 32 | deities | 4 |
| Eight deities 2 cells each | cells | 16 | deities | 8 |
| Eight deities of 1 ½ cells each | cells | 12 | deities | 8 |
| One cell each 32 deities | cells | 32 | deities | 32 |

Total Number of Cells in Dasa Varga

Vinyaasa cells 108 deities 53

In Ashta Varga division and Dasa Varga Vinyaasa, the names and numbers of Deities are the same with Nava Varga Paada Vinyaasa. The number of cells and its nature are different from 64 squares, 81 squares, 100 squares cells grids. Grids have:-

| | | |
|---|---|---|
| Manduka Paada Grid: | 8X8 varga | 72 cells |
| Paramsayika Paada Grid: | 9X9 varga | 89 cells |
| Aasana Paada Grid: | 10x10 varga | 108 cells |

The Paramsayika Paada division (Nava Gruha paada vinyaasa) is more practicable for calculation of marma and more specific and precise.

Maaya Mayan in his Book *Maayamatam* explains in detail the 11X11 square grids which are commonly recommended in construction of Temples. In every square, there will be a big square of paada, and eight outer paadas common in all cases.

## Marma Mandala (Nerves Profile Vaastu)

In Vaastu Paada Kalpana the divisions for deciding the marma assumes great significance in each grid vinyaasa calculations. The applicability of marma sensitiveness will be variable in 64 cells, 81 cells and 100 cells grids paada Vaastu. An analysis of each grid-vinyaasa is necessary for assessing the marma mandala.

While dealing with the Marma Mandala aspects, the person should have thorough knowledge of details of Mahamarma, Marma, Naadi, Rajjus, Sandhi Naadi, Sutrams and their implications with the problems. It is very imperative to know marma mandala of each and every point while undertaking a marma sutram and vedha afflictions during the time of consultations of a particular Vaastu. The apt and correct answer is possible if the consultant knows all the marma implication and its viability very well.

(Marma=Nerves intersection, Mandala=view profile, Maha marma=key nerves joints, Naadi=veins, Rajjus=circular intersection, Sandhi Naadi= Veins joinment, Sutrams= Thread line or formula theory)

- **Nava Paada Gruha Marma Mandala (Paramsayika Marma section)**

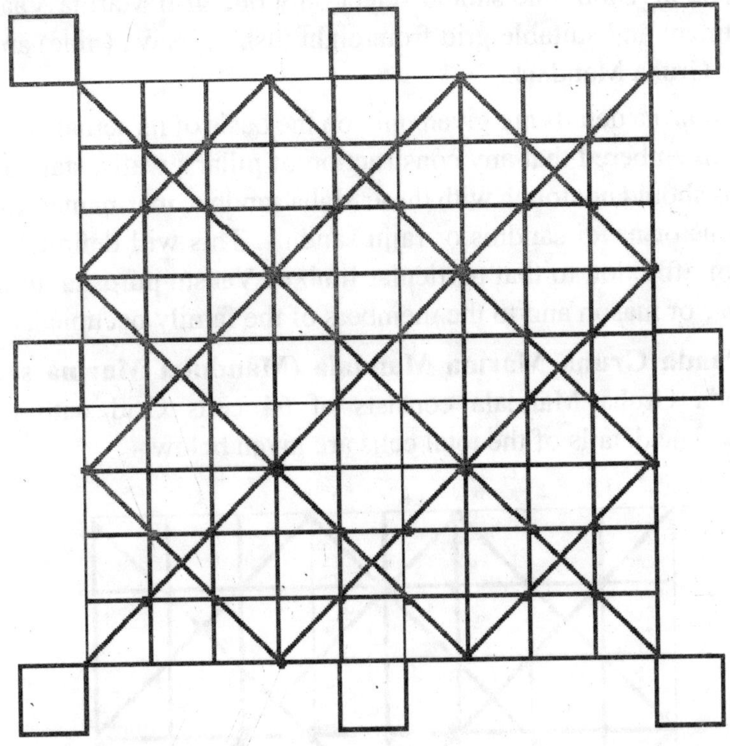

109 Sensitive points in Paramsayika Mandala
Nava Paada Gruha marma

| Maha Marma | ✳ | 1 |
|---|---|---|
| Naadi | ┬ | 24 |
| Naadi Sandhi | ┼ | 24 |
| Marmanta | ⇖ | 4 |
| Marma | ⋇ | 36 |
| Rajju Sandhi | ╳ | 9 |
| Rajju Marma Sandhi | ⇜ | 8 |
| Marmas | total | 109 nos. |

The Marma Vaastu is applicable to all grids joints and angles. In the Gruha cells vidhana division, one should select only one grid Marma Vaastu out of the pertinent and suitable grid from eight (ashta), Nava (nine) and Dasa (ten) Grids Gruha Mandala.

The above marma details are given only on the basis of its actual position. It has to be remembered that any construction of pillars, walls, staircase, and store rooms should not touch with these Maha sandhis, marmantas, marmas, naadis, rajjus or naadi sandhis or rajju sandhis. This will definitely create problems of affliction to that particular limb of Vaastu purusha, ultimately to the owner or mason and to the members of the family occupied.

• **Ashta Paada Gruha Marma Mandala (Manduka Marma section):** Ashta Paada Gruha Mandala consists of 64 cells Grid with total of 89 marmas. The details of the total cells are given below:-

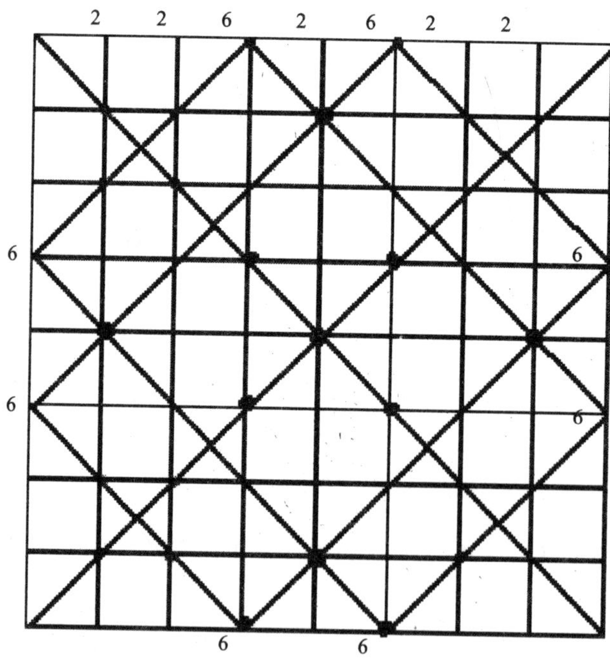


1. Maha Marma 5
2. Naadi 20
3. Naadi Sandhi 16
4. Marmanta 4
5. Marma 24
6. Rajju Sandhi 8
7. Rajju Marma 8

Marmas total 89 nos.

• **Dasa Paada Gruha Marma Mandala (Aasana Marma Mandala):** One Hundred Cells grid Dasa Marma Mandala has 129 marmas to be observed correctly while planning for a construction:

| | | |
|---|---|---|
| Maha Marma | | 5 |
| Naadi | | 28 |
| Naadi Sandhi | | 36 |
| Marmanta | | 4 |
| Marma | | 40 |
| Rajju Sandhi | | 8 |
| Rajju Marma | | 8 |
| **Marmas total** | | **129 nos.** |

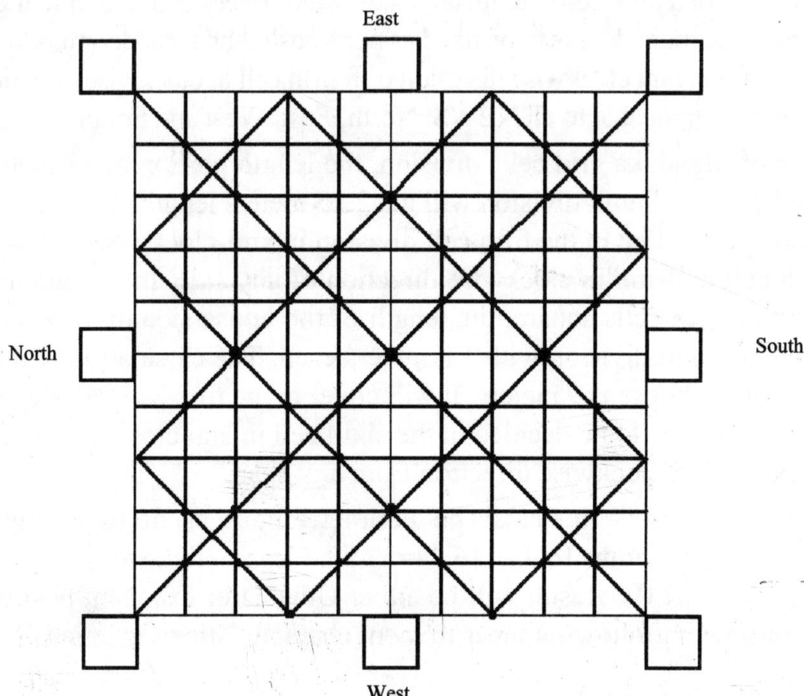

In brief, the marmas are occurring on the basis of paada gruha classification. The basis of the construction should follow the principles of 49 grids, 64 grids, 81 grids, 100 grids or 121 grids at the squares respectively of 7, 8, 9, 10, 11 numbers. These assumptions are purely done on the understanding and calculation of the best marma square in the available land area. Since the marma junctions differ from grids area selection; it is better to accept a common 9x9 grids squares Paada Vaastu Marma.

This marma part is considered to be the prime point to remember to avoid all the problems arising out of the construction. Hence, marma Vaastu in gruha mandala vinyaasam is the key point to study, to consult and to popularize its effectiveness to ensure correct Vaastu peace, prosperity and sanctity in one's life.

- **Practical analysis of Grids:** Among many Grids division, consideration is given only for three divisions of eight, nine and ten paada grids. Perimeter calculation is important to decide the progress and prosperity of the buildings. While commencing the contruction of the house, four sides perimeter measurement should be ascertained. That means the sum total of four sides i.e. measurement of two length and two width sides. In an example of measure of 18 meters length and 16.44 meters width, Perimeter is 68.88 or 95.16 hasta.

If the length portion is selected to suit the door face and gateways of the house, 18 meters is divided by 9 cells paramsayika division. Every cell length will get two meters. If the main door is to be fixed as per Vaastu, the front door has to be kept at sixth cell in anti clockwise direction or fourth cell in clockwise direction to any side. It is applicable to all NEWS: North, East, West and South.

In the case of Manduka grid cells division, the length portion of 18 meters is divided by 8; a cell unit division will get 2.25 meters length. The fixation of front door should be in the fifth cell division in anti-clockwise direction and fourth cell division in clockwise direction of any side. In Aasana grid cell division of ten cells square, the length of the house side of 18 meters has a small cell unit division with 1.8 meters each. The calculation will be half length of the house is 9 meters. It will cover in the fifth cell. Hence, the front door position is to be decided in the sixth cell in anti clockwise and is in the fourth cell in clockwise direction from any side.

The perimeter is 68.88 meters. The Perimeter consists of two lengths 18+18=36 with two widths 16.44 +16.44=32.88. Please refer to the perimeter measurement Chart IV. Result will be either Uthama or excellent position of Youth (age) with following measurement characteristic to mention:

1. Sapta Yoni
2. Measurement is 95 hasta 16 angulam or 68.88 meters

3. Age is youth
4. Ayam is 9.8
5. Vyaya is 7
6. Nakshatra is Maka

The house owner and inmates will be bestowed with peace, prosperity.

## Marma Sutrams (Nerve Centre)

A detailed analysis of marma roots, its main points and a cut portion of the paada marma classification of marma sutram is given below:

**A cut portion of Marma Mandala in 81 Cells Grid**

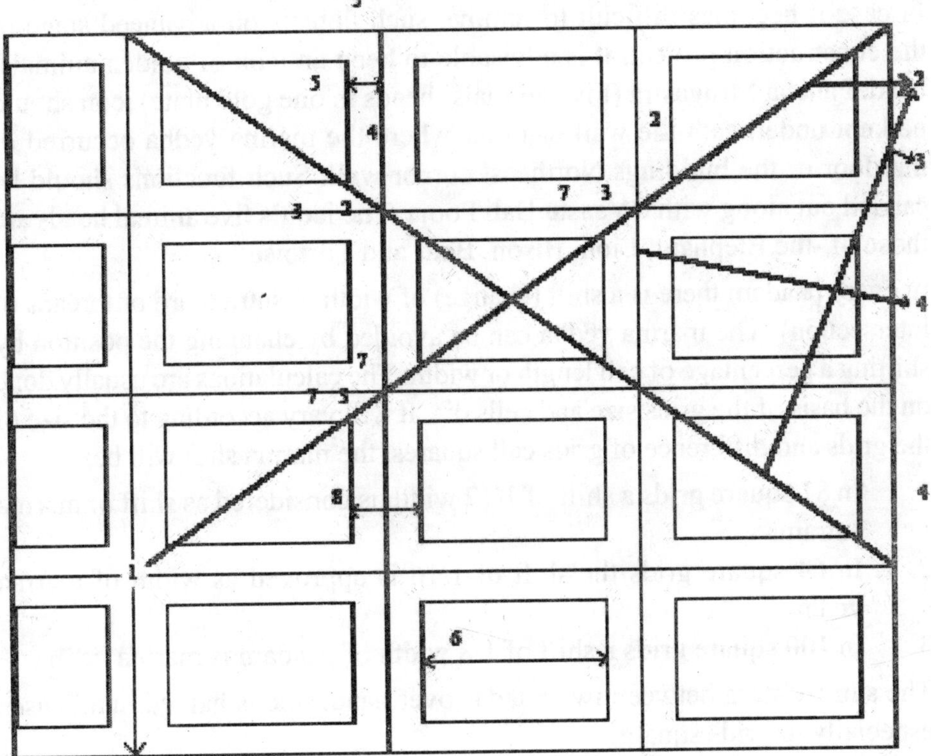

In this cut portion of the paada marma, sutra vistara and other details are:-

| | |
|---|---|
| Maha Marma | 1 |
| Rajju Line | 2 |
| Marmas | 3 |
| Naadi Line | 4 |
| Sutra Vistara | 5 |
| Paada | 6 |

| | |
|---|---|
| Karna Sutram | 7 |
| Paada Vistara | 8 |
| 1/12 Sutra Line | 9 |
| Brahma Sthaan | 10 |
| Rajju Sandhi | 11 |
| Naadi | 12 |

• **Marma Vedha ( Intersection Obstrucles) and its Shift:** Marma Vedha is a dangerous defect which occurs during the cross construction of pillars and walls over paadams. This will represent the personalized body parts of Vaastu purusha with his limbs. The limb pertains to the particular side, cell defects due to marma vedha (obstruction). That should be avoided.

In case it becomes difficult to remove such defects on advanced stage of the construction project, it is advisable to keep an icon of golden animals' head. Pancha Mrugasira (Five animals' heads in one gold plate) icon should be kept underneath the wall or pillar where the marma vedha occurred or the floor or the buildings Northeast corner wall. Such functions should be carried out along with a Vaastu Bali Pooja. The icon's five animal heads are those of -the Elephant, Lion, Bison, Boar and Tortoise.

In every paadam there is a shift (change) of width to sutra (cord or threads of intersection). The marma vedha can be avoided by changing the position by shifting a percentage of cell length or width. The calculations are usually done on the basis of the grids size and cells dia. It will vary according to the size of the grids and difference of grids cell squares; the marma shift will be:

1. In 81 square grids a shift of 1/12 width is considered as shift of marma sutram.
2. In 64 square grids the shift of 1/16 is approved as width of marma vedha.
3. In 100 square grids a shift of 1/8 width of paadam is marma vedha.

The sutra-vistara between two paadas over naadi line is halved in all cases especially to grids squares.

A Chart showing the shift of sutrams, sutra-vistaras is given below:-

| | | | |
|---|---|---|---|
| 1. | 81 square grid | 1/12 | 1/24 |
| 2. | 64 square grid | 1/16 | 1/32 |
| 3. | 100 square grid | 1/8 | 1/16 |

The gap should be maintained for marma safety measures.

The marma sutra length or width is decided individually in all cells. If these sutra vistaras (gap) between one cell to another is touching during construction of a house, sub-house, anganam, well, pond, etc. it is known by sutra vedha.

• **Effects of Sutra vedha (Thread Obstrucles):** If sutra occurs in eastern side, it will end in the husband deserting that house. The Southeast sutra vedha will result in leprosy to all house members. Likewise, South side sutra side sutravedha causes enmity. Nairuti (SW) is fatal for the progeny. West side goes to the loss of wealth. NW vaayu kon also attempts to attract veins diseases. The North side creates vamsa (lineage) destruction and Northeast eshana will definitely bring a loss of food grains etc.

## House Construction Parameter (Views on House Vaastu)

Various levels of Vaastu Rules are applied to foundation, platform thara (basement), paadamana (height between (shoe and Uthara), anganam (House frontage), antaralam (Corridors), patramana (offset) , shoe (base), upapidam, paduka (Footing), jaya thara (flower platform), malli thara (Jasmine platform), veranda (Alinda), Thara (floor), Bhithi (wall), vedika, Thunnu (pillars), pothika (support bracket) etc. Requirement has to be scrutinized before drawing a plan.

There are certain house parts (like utharam, varotharam, machu (staires) puram, kolayam, mondayam, avichil, kazhukolu, vaamada, vala, mangala palaka, amaraputtu, saksha, sutra pattika, etc.) which are irrevelant in this modern era. Modern houses are built in RCC with iron and steel combination with modern art work or architectural design and modified marine wood, plywood or laminated decolum. However materials like sand, stone, cement, wood etc. are in use along with modern items for the house construction.

• **Foundation (Garbha Vinyaasa):** The foundation and heavy structure below the ground level assume great importance in *Maayamatam* and *Manasaara* in chapter 12. The level of the site should not cause any stagnation of water and difficulty in drainage. According to the soil conditions, the depth of the foundation shall be equal to:

- The kaayam (body height) of a man
- The height of the basement
- The land surface or water level
- The one-third width of the house
- But it is not less than 1H8A or 96 cms.
- The entire plinth area earmarked for the building under construction should be raised by 24 cms, 36cms, Or 48 cms with sand (charal) soil, stone or red earth.

Given below is a basic adhishtana form of shoe, paduka and complete details of depth of the foundation. An ornamental elevation "the upapidam", the seat above basement an additional pedestal sitting or sockle (Pedestal) may be made for royal vision, safety, beauty and height. This upapidam is an optional platform projection with a height of 144cms and may be preferred for dwaja or virshaba yoni.

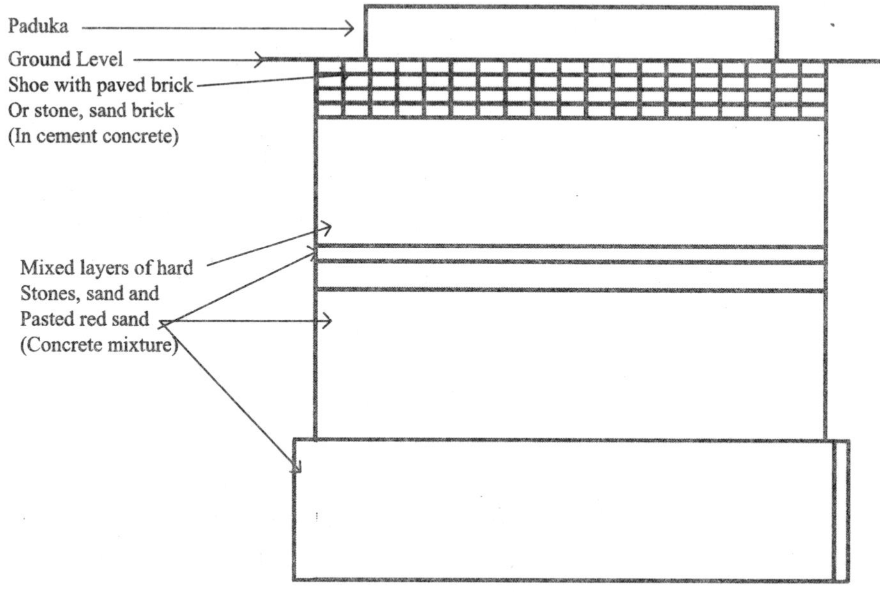


**Picture of the Foundation**

• **Length Breadth Theory:** There are four types of length breadth theory in Vaastu science. They are:

1. Samata Thayatikam (Equal Square)
2. Paadhadikam (More Length and Less width)
3. Ardhaadikam (Half extra length and width)
4. Paadhonam (More length and width)

***Samata Thayatikam (Square) Ratio 1:1:*** If the length and breadth are equal in all four sides it is known by the name Samata Thayatikam. The perimeter half is divided by 12,16,20,24,28,32,36 etc. numbers and four bhaagam are kept as width, the balance will be treated as length.

For example: 4 hasta lengths X 4 hasta widths equals to a square. Otherwise it is 4 hasta widths within the length of 12 hasta, 16 hasta, 20 hasta, 24 hasta etc. is also permitted. These are called full Samata Thayatikam.This measure is best suited to Manusyaalams (houses).

***Paadadhikam (More Length Less Width) Ratio 5:4:*** If the perimeter half 9 is divided by keeping 4 bhaagams for width, 5 bhaagams for length, it is known by Paadadhikam. Another method of Paadadhikam is to calculate the half perimeter divided by any of the following figures 13, 17, 21, 25, 29, 33 etc. In this 4 bhaagam will be considered as width and the remaining the length bhaagam.

***Ardhaadhikam (Half more length to width) Ratio 6:4:*** The perimeter 20, half is denoted by 4 sections of breadth and 6 sections of length will be considered as Ardhaadhikam. In other words, it is also applicable by perimeter half divided by any of the following figures 14, 18, 22, 26, 30, 34 etc. consider 6 length and 4 breadth. This Ardhaadhikam is also equates with paadhonam, and is good for human occupation.

***Paadhonam (More Length To Width) Ratio 7:4:*** The perimeter 22 half is denoted by length 7 bhaagam breadth 4 bhaagam and is called Paadhonam. An another way of considering perimeter half is divided by any of the numbers 15, 19, 23, 27, 31, 35 etc. keeping 4 sections as width, the remaining sections will be of length. The measure of Paadhonam is destructive in nature and therefore it has to be rejected in all measurements.

These measurements are very useful for Devaalayams (Temples) more than the manushyaalayams (Residential houses).

• **Gamanam (House Middle Section):** The angana (Frontage) madhya (Centre) sutram (Nerves) and gruha (House) Madhya (Middle) sutram (nerves) should not touch each other. Some space gap or distance should be maintained to avoid vedha or obstruction. It will result in vamsa naasam (destruction of generation). The distance shift between angana (Frontage) sutram and gruha madhya sutram (house middle section) is known as Gamanam. The Gamanam should be arranged clock-wise from gruha madhya sutram distance. It operates from –

- East House 9 cms to move towards South
- West House 21 cms to move towards North
- South House 3 cms to move towards West
- North House 15 cms to move towards East

• **Anganam (Frontage):** Anganam is the house's open frontage where the entry or exit of the house is. This will differ with single, double or triple and four sided houses. According to the size, nature of the house anganam will be large and spacious. In a four sided chatu saala houses, the common court yard is called Anganam. The frontage of all four sided dhik houses is either in rectangular or in square shape. The length stretches from South to North and the width extends from West to East. The perimeter of anganam should be in dwaja (ketu) yoni.

The difference between the length and breadth will be 1, 2, 4, 8, 9, 12 angulams of ayam or vyayam or gunamsa. Canons of gunamsa stipulated are to be applied. The Anganam is the yard outside the yard bhagyanganam and middle one is known as madhyanganam. It is also possible to make kuzhimuttam (Open frontage) at eshana corner making the way for passage of drainage water flow either to East or North or/Northeast.

Anganam placed at the middle of the Four Dik house is as below:

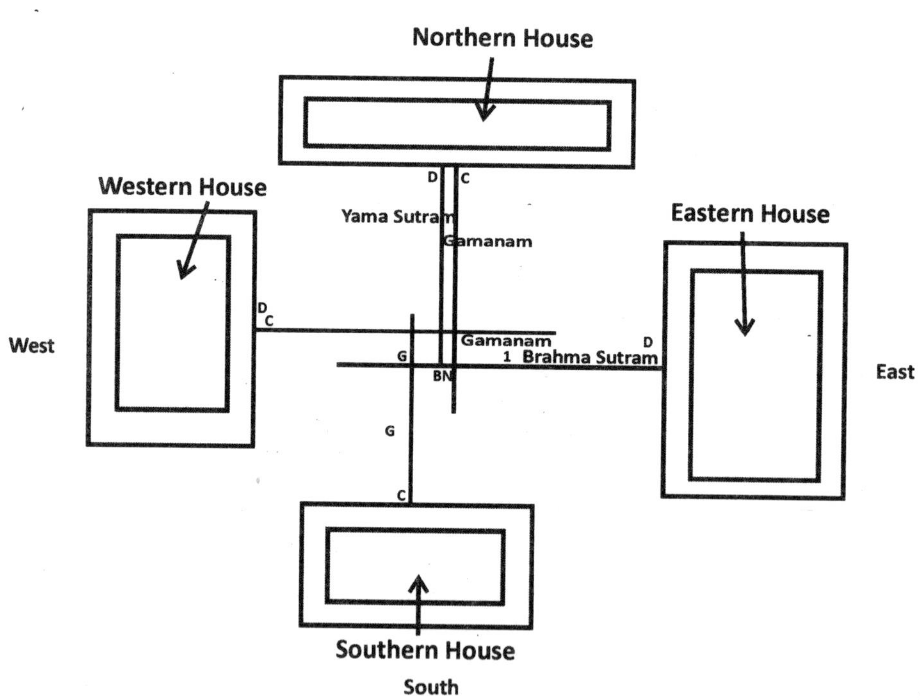


BN. Brahma Nabhi

1. Brahma sthan
2. Yama sutram

D. Door
G. Gamanam
C. Middle of the house

• **Mulla Thara (Platform for Jasmine Or Sacred Basil):** The Platform for Jasmine or Mulla Thara, constructed as per Vaastu norms, consists of five main factors starting from down to upwards padukam, jagati, kumudam, galam and prati.

The plant should be grown at the Northeast sector of Apan and Apatvalsan cells of the pada classification. The shape of malli or thulasi thara (platform) may be a combination of square and octogen 16 sided polygons or a circle. The height is equal or less to adhisthana divisible by six to eleven. However diagonally crossing i.e. Karna sutram of the site should be avoided to select the platform.

A mention is made in ancient texts regarding the importance of Thulasi (sacred basil) as a 'Divine Plant' to be planted in the Northeast side of the house anganam. It is an Ayurvedic medicine, worshipped by all in India. The ancient texts mentioned that the malli thara was also used for Thulasi in the anganam.

The model thara is given below:

1. Prati
2. Galam
3. Kumudam
5. Padukam

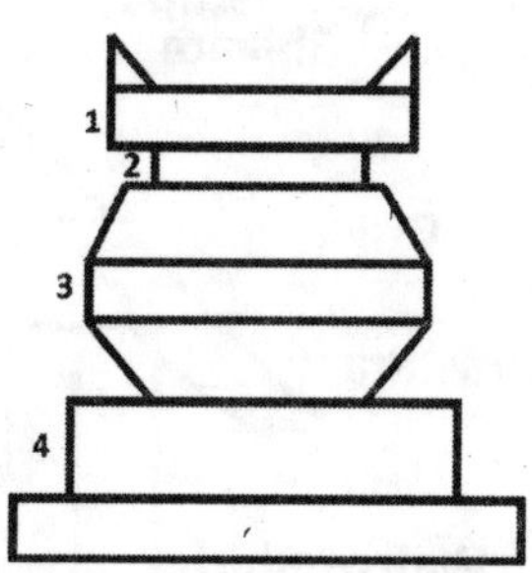


**Malli/ Thulasi platform in an artist's view**

• **Patramanam (offset):** Patramanam is a term used for the offset of space between outer Utharam (Wood wall plate) vertical edge to the edge of the plinth (external) purapad which may measure of eight angulam or its multiples thereof.This Patramanam will usually apply to the chatu salas (Four sided houses) expecially to the frontage anganam side. The same yoni of the house will have to be maintained in patramanam which will be 18 (6A) cms to South or North sides, and 36 (12A)cms to West side. Means 3cms=1A.

• **Shoe (Underground Basement):** Shoe is the bottom level basement at the ground for laying foundation for the construction. The base of shoe will be made more firm and strong below the foundation. In certain cases an extra length Upapidam (additional basement) shoes are made. The portions of foundation commence from padukam, jagati, kumudam and they will be placed above the shoe. This is the lowest course of adhisthana at the ground level and will elongate to the level of patramana height.

• **Antaralams (Corridors):** The vidik houses conjoin with four dik houses with a separation by antaralams also known as Corridors. Every corner requires two corridors each usually available with all chatu salas as passage which cannot be so wide or narrow. The corridor rule says that too narrow attracts diseases to inmates, too wide provides loss of wealth and no gap (only a wall separation) results in death. An ideal corridor has the size of 96cms width (1H8A) if the house length is 8H (576cms) i.e.1/6 of the house length will be considered as corridor.

• **House Parts (Above the basement):** Above the ground level of the land basement the ancient version is having the following parts as detailed.

A cross-section of the house is given below:

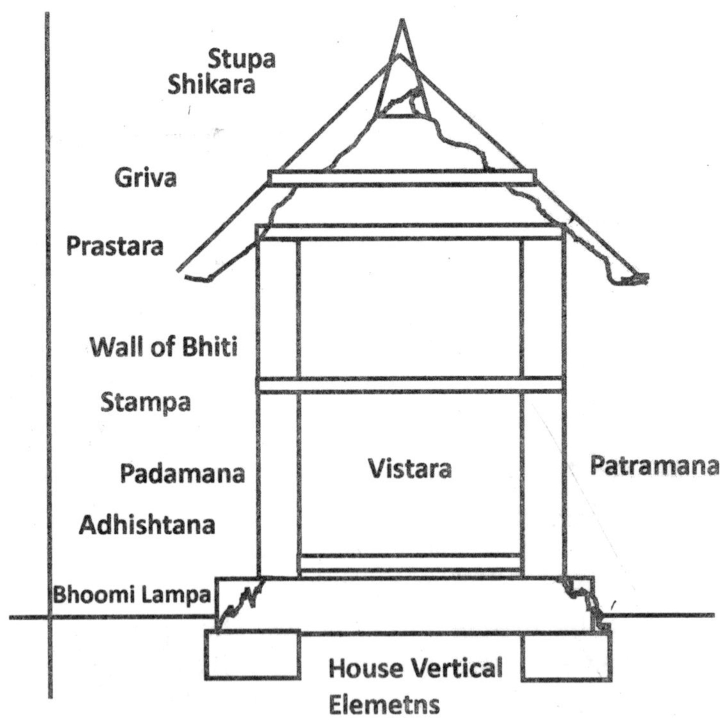


In this diagram, the earth level is visible upto bhumi lamba. Above the bhoomi lamba adhishtana, padamanam, ptramanam, stampa wall, prastara, griva, shikara, stupa etc. are visible in the diagram.

a) Out of the nine total height, one–third parts of the basement of adhisthana is paduka. Two-third height is Jagati. The ratio can be made by 2:7 (or 1:2). This basement is called Manchaka with Paduka and Jagati. The outward shift of paduka will be ¾, 1/2, 1/3, or 3/5 part.

b) Likewise the height of the basement is divided by 5/6

   1 part paduka height
   2/3 parts Jagati height
   1 part gala height
   1 part prati height

c) When the height of the basement is divided by 14, then the height of 2 parts paduka is

   6 parts jagati
   1 part lower vanchana of gala
   2 parts gala
   1 part upper vachana of gala
   2 parts height prati

This division is known as Galamanchaka, the outward offset prati will be equal to that of jagati. The inward shift of gala with those of galamanchaka should be decisively one-fourth of the height of the gala.

• **Pillars:** Pillars and walls are constructed to support the uttaram from the basement. On the basis of padamana the height of the pillar can be raised upto utharam by reducing pedestal seating called oma and the thickness of pothika (pillar supporting bracket). Different types of hard stones and wood are used to make pillars of square, octagonal, circular or 16 sided with varied designs.

According to Mayamatam square pillars are called Brahma Kanta

Octogonal pillars are known in the name of Vishnu Kanta

Circular pillars are called Rudra Kanta

16 -sided pillars are usually called Saumya Kanta; and the combinations of all variety of pillars are Rudra Chandra.

The pillar base is oma, while the top is Pothika. The peetham oma has strength if made with stones or hardwood. All pillars should have tenons of width equal to 1/3 of its own width. The width is equal to the diagonal base of the pillar and the height is equal to half diagonal or 1/3, ¼, or ½, or less than that, resembling the lotus flower or fillets.

The width is called danda. The proportionate system of dandamana is used for pillars and curvings. According to the load bearing capacity of the pillars, the ratio is mentioned as 1/11 and ¼. The wood used for pillars has the ratio 1/10 or 1/11. For stone pillars, the ratio may be between 1/8 and 1/9. The pillars are made with mud for which the ratio will be 1/5 or1/4. This ratio is used in the design of columns of modern engineering practice.

Certain parts of the house are governed with very extensive ancient methods of making details, which are rarely used nowadays. Hence only the names are mentioned below:

1. Wall (Bhithi)
2. Pothika (Support bracket)
3. Varotharam (Wall plate for small houses)
4. Arudotharam (Wall plate for big houses)
5. Chututharam (Around Utharam reapers)
6. Dwara Madhya sutram kazhukole (Reapers)

To avoid vedha while fixing the nails (wooden nails) in all madhya sutra points a yavam measure of gamanam has to be provided.

# Bhaagam 5

## Perimeter (Chutalavu)

The perimeter is the main key for all Vaastu calculations. This is the actual basis for the calculations for age, yoni, ayam, vyayam, nakshatra, tithi, karanam weeks etc. while considering the various aspects of a progressive house's perimeter that will lead to a happy, contented and prosperous long life. Refer to calculation of Table 4 for ready Perimeter both in meters and in kolu measurement.

The total length and width of a house are considered for perimeter on running metre calculations. Two lengths and two breadths are the perimeter value. The architects or planners make house drawing and measurement on meters or hasta/kolu basis. The Perimeter is calculated on foundation with projection and padukam.

• **Calculation of Age of The Buildings:** There are Shadvargas or six types of yardsticks to measure the efficiency or longevity of constructions i.e Aya, Vyaya, Yoni, Vaara, Nakshatra and tithi. The calculation of the Sadvargas of Vaara, Nakshatra and Tithis will determine the structure and the age of the buildings. These calculations will enable the architect for the correct orientation and dimensions. The methods of ascertaining in these Aya, Vyaya, Yoni, Tithi, Nakshatra or Vaara are based on the remainders obtained to make the construction good and auspicious. In each case, remainders will have different results. All the other factors are important and emphasized for the building stability along with Shadvargas.

Full information and explanations are provided to ascertain the longevity of the proposed building in Vaastu texts on the basis of perimeter.

| | | | |
|---|---|---|---|
| 1. Aya (Promotive) | (Length X 8)/12 | = Remainder | = Aya |
| 2. Vyaya (Depreciative) | (Breadth X 9)/10 | = Remainder | = Vyaya |
| 3. Yoni (Cumulative) | (BreadthX3)/8 | = Remainder | = Yoni |
| 4. Vaara (Week) | (Height X 9)/7 | = Remainder | = Vaara |
| 5. Nakshatra (Star) | (LengthX 8)/27 | = Remainder | = Star |
| 6. Tithi (Lunar day) | (Height X 9)/30 | = Remainder | = Thithi |

***Age (Ayus):*** Several phases are involved in calculations phenomena in a building process and the information is necessary for ascertaining the age and the longevity. The perimeter of the constructed structure multiplied by eight and divided by twenty seven will be equal to the quotient age up to 5 to be accounted. Above five quotients arrived will have to be divided again by 5 to limit the age to denote the numbers 1 to 5 as below:

| | | | |
|---|---|---|---|
| 1. | Number 1 | Childhood | (C) |
| 2. | Number 2 | Adolescent | (A) |
| 3. | Number 3 | Youth | (Y) |
| 4. | Number 4 | old | (O) |
| 5. | Number 5 | Death | (D) |

The planner calculator, the shilpi, the Acharya, the mason and the Architect have to avoid number 5 of death while calculating the age of the building.

**For example: The perimeter of a building is 29 hasta 16 angulam. Find out the age of the building:-**

H=Hasta. A=Angulam.

The perimeter 29 Hasta 16 Angulam one hasta is 72 centimeters and angulam 3 cms 29X72+16X3 = 2088 = 48 = 2136 Formula = 2136X8=17088 (PX8 divide by 27 = Q = 1 to 5 = Age)

17088 divided by 27 =632.888 divided by 72=8.8

Quotient= 8 divided by 5 is equal to 1 and 3/5= 3 = Y= Youth.

The Age of the building is Youth. It is excellent combination for construction.

***Yoni (Origin):*** The Yoni is the soul, the most pivotal organ of the building measurement for Vaastu. There are eight kinds of Yonis available according to dik vidik conditions. The eight yonis are Dwaja yoni, Dhuma yoni, Simha yoni, Kakura yoni, Vrushabha yoni, Khara yoni, Vyaya yoni and Vayasa Yoni. The Yoni calculations are done by adding double length and double width of the building (perimeter) multiplied by 3 and divided by 8 and the remainder is the Yoni.

**For example: The perimeter 57 hasta 16 angulam. Answer is 21.65. Here quotient is not applicable.**

Remainder: 0.625X8 (57X72 = 4104 = 48 = 4152X3 = 12456-:8 = 1557 and divided by72 = 21.625). 625X8 = 5.

It will be Vrushabha yoni in western directions. No. 5 is good.

**a) <u>Dwaja Yoni (Yoni Number 1):</u>** The first and foremost Dwaja Yoni or Ketu Yoni is controlled by Jupiter (Guru) having satwa guna which bestows natural goodness and fortune. East direction prevails to enter towards West.

This yoni has apt use in all ventures of house, boats, vehicles, ships, boxes, nests, wells, ponds etc.

This yoni also called "Kizhakini".

For example: The perimeter is 29 Hasta, 16 Angulam multiplied by 3 and divided by 8, the remainder will be No.1. That means Dwaja yoni or Kizhakini.

**b) Dhuma Yoni (Yoni Number 2)**: If the perimeter is multiplied by 3 and divided by 8, and the remainder is two, it is Dhuma Yoni. The direction of the yoni is towards Southeast. It has neecham (ugly) and adhama credentials which are totally unsuitable yoni for any good construction results.

**c) Simha Yoni (Yoni Number 3)**: The Simha Yoni or thrioyoni is arrived when the perimeter of the house multiplied by 3 and divided by 8, the reminder becomes 3. This Yoni is controlled by Mars with thamo guna and South direction which lead to good health and prosperity. This yoni is useful for West or North directions. The throne (Simhasanam) or Aavani Palaka, Peedam are curved and made with this yoni.

For example: Perimeter 27 Hasta 16 Angulam multiplied by 3 and divided by 8= 10.3 Remainder is 3 which stands for Simha Yoni or Thekini.

**d) Kakuram Yoni (Yoni Number 4)**: The yoni number four becomes the remainder from perimeter multiplied by 3 and divided by 8. The yoni will prevail over South and West regions of the house. This yoni is neecham and adhamam which is unsuitable for any good work. It will result only in quarrels and fight.

**e) Vrushabha Yoni (Yoni Number 5)**: The perimeter of the house multiplied by 3 and divided by 8 will give rise to number 5. The Vrushabha Yoni has the direction of West with deity of Saturn which is considered to be the thamo guna quality. The Pancha Yoni or Vrushabha Yoni is famous for dhanyalayams (Grain Storage houses) and good for prosperity. This Yoni specification is also used in ponds, wells, nests, etc. like ketu Yoni.

**f) Khara Yoni (Yoni Number 6)**: The Khara Yoni has 6 number as remainder with Northwest direction. The Sixth Number Khara yoni is not at all good for any work. It may create mental disturbance and other dangers. Therefore, Khara Yoni is not advisable to use for yoni of perimeter calculations.

**g) Gaja Yoni (Yoni Number 7)**: The Gaja Yoni or sapta yoni has North direction with the deity of mercury and rajo Guna qualities. The Vyshyas are considered very prosperous and wealthy due to the use of Number seven

Gaja yoni. This Yoni is also derived from the perimeter multiplied by 3 and divided by 8, the remainder comes to 7. The Sapta Yoni is quite commonly used for sleeping materials like cots; beds, etc.

**h) Vayasa Yoni (Yoni Number 8)**: The Vayasa Yoni prevails upon the Northeast direction. The Vayasa Yoni with 8 numbers is not applied for any good work since it causes the destruction of the hereditary edifice.

***Ayam (Income):*** Ayam means inflow of income. Calculations are made with perimeter multiplied by 8 (eight) and divided by 12 (twelve).

For example: The perimeter is 57 Hasta 16 Angulam. Multiplied by 8 and divided by 12 = 57X72+16X3 = 48X8 divided by 12 = 38.5. More clearly it is 4104+48 = 4152 X 8 = 33216 divided by 12 = 2768 again divided by 72 = 38.5. Remainder is 5.

There is a chart of 12 types of Ayams accrues. The ouput is clearly shown in each remainder from 1 to 12. Here No. 5 remainder depicts the availability of food grains in abundance.

**Chart of Ayams**

| Ayam No. | Remainder | Result of Numbers |
|---|---|---|
| 1 | Yogam | Accrued Benefits |
| 2 | Bhoga | Sensual Pleasure |
| 3 | Samthrupti | Fame and popular |
| 4 | Veeryam | Courageous |
| 5 | Dhanyam | Food Grains in abundance |
| 6 | Dhanam | Wealth Amass |
| 7 | Sukham | Spiritual happiness |
| 8 | Dharma | Sanatan mind |
| 9 | Gjanam | Knowledge and wisdom |
| 10 | Yoga | Meditation in solitude |
| 11 | Siddhi | Enlightment to Virtues |
| 12 | Ardha | Purusharth fulfilment |

***Vyayam (Expenditure)***: It means loss or expenses. The perimeter is multiplied by 3 and divided by 14, the remainder is Vyayam.

For example:

The quotient is less than 14. The remainder will be any number within 1 to 10. The vyayam has a ten number chart having a result for each number. In remainder 5, the reault is shown as "sampathi" and it means abundant wealth. It is good vyayam number.

The Vyayam Chart has ten types of remainders and its results 1 to 10 are given below:

| Vyayam No. | Remainder | Results |
|---|---|---|
| 1 | Bhukhti | Pleasure, Achievement |
| 2 | Mukhti | Relief from troubles |
| 3 | Subham | Well-being, auspicious |
| 4 | Samvrudhi | Prosperity |
| 5 | Sampathi | Increase in wealth |
| 6 | Dhanam | Financial benefit |
| 7 | Mahima | Famous and Popular |
| 8 | Nashaka | Destruction |
| 9 | Kalaham | Quarrel and fight |
| 10 | Sneham | Love in all meanings (Sarvadha) |

The Vyayam is good if it is controllable and is to be kept less than ayam. Otherwise more expenses and hardships will follow.

***Astrological Shastra Relatios With Vaastu*** : The Vaastu Science and Astrology will move together to work and co-ordinate with the functions for mutual help. Some common functions involve time and space aspects which are to be reconkoned with the following considerations:-

**a) Nakshatras (Constellations)**: The Nakshatras are obtained when the perimeter is multiplied by 8 and divided by 27, for finding out the constellations starting from Aswathi to Revathi. The balance (remainder) is to be noted after division in angulams; again it will be multiplied by 60 and divided by 24. (Equivalent to One hasta is = 0.72 centimeters, one hour =60 nazhikae and one day = 24 hours).

For example: Perimeter is 29 Hasta 16Angulam. 29 H 16A x8 divided by 27 = 21H8A, Quotient is 21. The remainder is 8. That means 22nd star Thiruvonam (sravana), 8 Angulamx 60 divided by 24 = means 20 nazhikae. (29X72+16X3 = 2088+48 = 2136 X 8 = 16832 divided by 27 = 632.88 divided by 72 = 8.8)

The calculation result is in Thruvonam star at 20 nazhika time. (The calculation is done on the basis of a day time = 24 hours, one hour 60 nazhika and one minute is equal to 60 vinazhikae).

The merits and demerits of the constellations are to be consulted while selecting an auspicious time or job.

**b) Tide Progression:** When one suggests timings of a good construction to start, it should be at the tide progression time. During this tide progression time, water level in canals, rivers, seas, or ocean will be at a high level. Usually, the tide progression occurs during the day time 12 to 1 PM. This happens when Moon occupies raasi.

There are twelve raasis or signs in a raasi chakram. The names of raasis are the same names of 12 months starting from Aries to Pisces or months from Chaitram to Phalgunam). For three raasi time of seven and half hours, the tide progression will remain. And the tide regression will commence in force after passing three moon raasis. It occurs both during the day and the night. Consultaion with an expert is necessary for ascertaining good time for pooja or good construction work.

**c) Gannantham Dosham:** Gannantham is a particular type of hindrance, not auspicious for starting any good work. During the Gannantha Sandhi any good function or work is found very dangerous for the people involved in the construction work. Gannantham will fortify in three ways:

Firstly, by Nakshatra Gannantham: first fifteen nazhika time (6 hours) of three stars Aswathi, Makam, Moolam and last fifteen nazhikae of three stars Aayilyam, Triketa or Revati.

Secondly, by Tithi Gannantham: One nazhika time (24 minutes) starting tithis of Pradhama, Shasshti and Ekaadasi or ending tithis of Panchami, Dasami and Poornima or Amavaasi.

Thirdly, by Raasi Gannantham: Half nazhika time (12 minutes) each starting Aries, Leo and Sagitarius or ending Raasis of Cancer, Scorpio and Pisces. This inauspicious bad timing has to be avoided under any circumstances.

**d) Ushnam Vedha**: Ushnam is an inauspicious dosha (defect) which is very bad for conducting good functions. This Ushnam is a peculiar type of heat emit from Ushna dosha rebounding with time in certain constellations. All the stars have 24 hours or 60 nazhikae to function in a day. The name of stars and timings of affliction details of Ushnam are as follows:

1. In the case of Aswathi, Rohini, Makam, Atham (hasta), punartham (punarvasu) stars have ushnam for a duration of 71/2 nazhika or 3 hours after start of the 71/2 nazhika of the stars.
2. In Bharani, Makayiram (Mrigasira), Pooyam (Pushyami), Pooram, and Chithira (Chitta) stars have 5 nazhika times after 55 nazhika of the start of the stars.
3. 9 nazhika times after 21 nazhika to the constellations of Karthika, Thiruvathira (Aridra), Aayilyam (Aslesha), Uthram, and Chothi (Swathi) have ushnam time.

4. For first eight nazhika time to Moolam, Vishaka, Thiruvonam (Sravana), Pururuthati (Purvabhadra) stars have ushna dosham.
5. Last eight nazhika times for the stars of Anizham (Anuradha), Pooradam (Poorvashada), Avittam (Dhanishta), Uthratati (Uthara bhadra) have ushnam heat.
6. Ten nazhika after 20 nazhika for the constellations to Triketa (Jyeshta), Uthradam (Uttarashada), Chadayam (Satabhista) and Revati have ushnam.

This has to be avoided under any circumstances.

e) **Visham Vedha**: The Visha dosham is another bad time to be looked into while considering the timing of auspicious activities. The Visha dosham is applicable to one hour thirty six seconds for certain constellations during small duration of 4 (four) nazhika time (1 hour 36 minutes). The following are Visha dosha times in each star.

| Stars name | after nazhika |
|---|---|
| 1. Aswathi | 50 |
| 2. Bharani, Pooradam, Uthratathi | 24 |
| 3. Karthika, Punartham, Makam, Revati | 30 |
| 4. Rohini | 40 |
| 5. Makayiram, Swati, Vishaka, Chitta | 14 |
| 6. Thiruvathira | 11 |
| 7. Pooyam, Pooram,Triketa, Moolam, Uthradam | 20 |
| 8. Aayilyam | 32 |
| 9. Uthram, Chadayam | 18 |
| 10. Atham | 22 |
| 11. Anizham, Thiruvonam, Avittam | 10 |
| 12. Pururuthati | 16 |

The Visha dosham exists only for the duration of four nazhikae after the time mentioned above for each constellation.

The Nakshatra, Gannantha and Visha doshas are strictly avoided. According to Thara (Star) Rule on deriving the perimeter luck position found good and very auspicious for the Thara Bhala (Star power) are the numbers 1, 2, 4, 6, 8, 9 and 3, 5, 7 are very bad and unlucky to the house owner.

***Tithi (Lunar Days):*** The Tithi is calculated on the basis of house perimeter formula multiplied by 8 and divided by 30. The balance remainder in angulams is multiplied by 60 and divided by 24 nazhikae, the Tithi is also ascertainable.

For example: Perimeter is 29H16A i.e. 29-16X8 divided by 30. Tithi will be extended to 27 days. Reduce 15 days of shukla paksha beyond 12 days

Thriodasi in Krishna Paksha. Balance 8X60 divided by 24 = 20 nazhikae. That is Thriodasi with 20 nazhikae.

There are some Tithi doshas persisting like Pradhama, Dwidhiya, and Thridhiya-----upto Pournima or Amavasi. Thithis have names like Nanda, Bhadra, Jaya, Riktha, Poorna, etc. The Chaturthy, Navami, Chaturdhasi in both Sukla Paksha and Krishna Paksha are Riktha Tithis which are not auspicious for good functions. However Full Moon and New Moon and Tithis Panchami, Dasami or Pancha Dasis are excellent for good for all functions.

**Karanams:** In each tithi, there are two karanams

1) Purvardh 15 karanams and

2) Uthararth 15 karanams.

This will make 30 days in a full month having share in Krishna Paksha (wane days) and Shukla Paksha (wax days).

The details of Karanams and tithis occurrence are given below:

| **Shukla Paksha** | | | **Krishna Paksha** | | |
|---|---|---|---|---|---|
| **Tithi** | **Purvarth Karanams** | **Uthararth Karanams** | **Tithi** | **Purvarth Karanams** | **Uthararth Karanams** |
| Pradhama | worm | Lion | 1st | Tiger | Pig |
| Dwidhiya | Tiger | Panni | 2nd | Donkey | Elephant |
| Thrithiya | Donkey | Elephant | 3rd | Cow | Vrushti |
| Chaturty | Cow | Vrushti | 4th | Lion | Tiger |
| Panchamy | Lion | Tiger | 5th | Panni | Donkey |
| Shashti | Pig | Donkey | 6th | Elephant | Cow |
| Saptami | Elephant | Cow | 7th | Vrushti | Lion |
| Ashtami | Vrushti | Lion | 8th | Tiger | Pig |
| Navami | Tiger | Panni | 9th | Donkey | Elephant |
| Dasami | Donkey | Elephant | 10th | Cow | Vrushti |
| Ekadasi | Cow | Vrushti | 11th | Lion | Tiger |
| Dwadasi | Lion | Tiger | 12th | Pig | Donkey |
| Thriodasi | Pig | Donkey | 13th | Vrushti | Tiger |
| Chturdhasi | Elephant | Cow | 14th | Vrushti | Pullu |
| Poornima | Vrushti | Lion | 15thNew Moon | Four legs | Snakes |
| Full Moon | | | Amavaasi | Animals | |
| | | | Black Moon | | |

Karnam as per Krishna Paksha Thriodasi 20 nazhika tithi will be Elephant. However, Vrushti Karanam in Krishna Paksha Chaturvasi at utharayam pullu, four legged animals, snakes, puzhus are supposed to give bad doshas. Hence, it has to be rejected from the construction measurement of house, temples etc.

**Vaara (Weeks):** Weekdays start from Sunday to Saturday. The reminder will be obtained by multiplying the perimeter by 8 and divided by 7. The Papis (evils) controlled by Sunday (Sun), Tuesday (Mars), Saturday (Saturn) are not good for auspicious functions. The remaining week days duly controlled by planets are good, i.e. Monday (Moon), Wednesday (Mercury), Thursday (Jupiter), and Friday (Venus).

For Example: The perimeter 5H16A multiplied by 8 and divided by 7 will be 6H3A. The week day will be after 6th day, i.e. seventh day Saturday.

• **Mruthyu Yogam:** The following combinations are considered as Mruthyu Yogam. That means ill-luck for death. The combinations of Mruthyu Yogam are as follows:-

- Makam (Maka) with Sunday
- Vishakham (Vishakha) with Monday
- Thiruvathira (Aridra) with Tuesday
- Moolam (Moola) with Wednesday
- Chadayam (Satabhisha) with Thursday
- Rohini (Rohini) with Friday
- Uthradam (Utharashada) with Saturday

Omit this Mruthyu Yogam for all measurement house construction.

***Dhakdha Yogam:*** While making house measurements Dhakdha Yogam has to be avoided.The following combinations of thithis and week days will have:-

- Sunday & Dwadhasi
- Monday & Ekadhasi
- Tuesday & Panchami
- Wednesday & Dwidhiya
- Thursday & Shashti
- Friday & Ashtami
- Saturday & Navami

***Pakshantara Yoni:*** The Pakshantara Yoni is calculated from the perimeter multiplied by the length and breadth area and divided by 8. The remainder is yoni number. In some places calculations are done on the basis of carpet area or plinth area instead of perimeter.

***Pakshantara Vyaya:*** The Pakshantara Vyaya can be arrived with perimeter is multiplied by 9 and divided by 8.

For example: 57H16A perimeter is multiplied by 9 divided by 8. The remainder is Vyaya and it is always less than the ayam.

***Pakshantara Week:*** The perimeter is multiplied by 3 and divided by 7. The remainder is also divided by week number only.

***Pakshantara Ayam:*** Add one-third of the perimeter with double perimeter divided by 8. The remainder number will be Ayam Number.

***Pakshantara Age (Ayus):*** The perimeter is multiplied by 27 and divided by 20, the result of quotient will be pakshantara Age. In North India this method is more prevalent and practicable.

***Pakshantara Tithis:*** The perimeter is multiplied by 9 and divided by 30, the reminder is tithi number.

***Raasi:*** The perimeter is multiplied by 4 or 8 separately and divided by 12; the remainder will be 12 Raasi Numbers starting from Aries to Pisces.

***Brahmadhi Colours:*** When perimeter is multiplied by 3 or 9 separately and divided by 4, the reminder will be Varna group's colours, i.e. Brahmins, Kshetriyas, Vaishyas and Shudras. The remainder 1 denotes the caste Brahmin, 2 kshetriyas, 3 Vaishyas and 4 Shudras.

**Dhruvadhis:** It means quality or stability. The perimeter is multiplied by 3 or 2 separately and divided by16, the remainder is the following Dhruvadhis. The perimeter is multiplied by 8 and divided by 7, the Nakshatra Number again divided by 8, the vyaya, both nakshatra and vyaya number divided by 13, the remainder number also denotes Dhruvadhis.

Dhruvadhis are classified into sixteen Dhruvadhis qualities as per Manushyaalaya Chandrika stanza 42 & 43.

| | | |
|---|---|---|
| 1. | Dhruva | Stability |
| 2. | Dhanya | Grains |
| 3. | Jaya | Success |
| 4. | Vinaasa | Calamity |
| 5. | Khara | Hardness |
| 6. | Kanta | Attractiveness |
| 7. | Mana Prasada | Cheerfulness of mind |
| 8. | Sumukhatva | Attractive Face |
| 9. | Vaimukhya | Aversion |
| 10. | Asaumyatva | Roughness |

11. Viroda — Enmity
12. Vithod bhava — Amassment of wealth
13. Kshaya — Consumption
14. Akranda — Crying
15. Vrudhi — progress
16. Jayam — success

**Computation Formulae:** In brief the combination group of computation formulae is given below:

P= Perimeter, Q= Quotient, R= Remainders, B= Balance.

| | | | |
|---|---|---|---|
| 1. | Yoni (origin) | PX3 divided by 8 | R=1 to 8 |
| 2. | Vyaya (Expenditure) | PX3 divided by 14 | R=1 to 10 |
| 3. | Ayam (Income | PX8 divided by 12 | R= 1 to 12 |
| 4. | Nakshatra (star) | PX8 divided by 27 | R= 1 to 27 |
| 5. | Age (Aayus) | PX8 divided by 7 | Q= 1 to 15 |
| 6. | Thithi (Moon Paksha) | PX8 divided by 30 | R=1 to 15 |
| 7. | Dhruva (Stability) | PX2 divided by 16 | B= 1 to 16 |
| 8. | Raasi (Month) | PX4 divided by 12 | B=1 to 12 |
| 9. | Vaara (week) | PX8 divided by 7 | R= 1 to 7 |

**Applicable Yoni For Houses:** The applicable yoni of a house is given below:-

| S. No. | Direction Diks | Yoni No. | Dik Yoni Side houses | Vidik Yoni Corner Houses |
|---|---|---|---|---|
| 1 | Eastern House (Kizhakini) | 1 | Dwaja 1 | Dwaja 1 NE |
| 2 | Southern House (Thekini) | 3 | Simha 3<br>Dwaja 1 | Simha 3 SE |
| 3 | Northern House (Vadakini) | 5 | Gaja 7<br>Dwaja 1 | Gaja 7 NW<br>Simha 3 |
| 4 | Western House (Paschimkini) | 7 | Vrushabha 5<br>Dwaja 1<br>Gaja 7 | Vrushabha 5<br>SW Simha 3 |

**Placement of jeeva sthan, yoni, caste & result:**

| Yoni | Colour | Diks | Result of Aarudam (Central Point) |
|---|---|---|---|
| Dhajam | Brahmin | East | Wealthy (Success) Swathyikam |
| Dhumam | Neecham | SE | Danger (Death) Adhamam |

| Simham | Kshetriaya | South | Wealthy (Prosperity) Thamogunam |
|---|---|---|---|
| Kakuram | Neecham | SW | Danger (Quarrel) Adhamam |
| Vrushabham | Shudram | West | Wealthy (Food Grains) Thamogunam |
| Kharam | Neecham | NW | Danger (Childless) Adhamam |
| Gajam | Vaishya | North | Wealthy (Well Being) Rajoguna |
| Vayasam | Neecham | NE | Danger (Childless) Adhamam |

The beneficial Aarudam (beneficial point) determination is important among Shilpakala Experts. The Jeeva Sthan (Living point) has to be find out from the following four Sides:-

North Facing In South Side (Simha Yoni) Prosperity
East Facing In West Side (Vrushabha Yoni) Grain Gain
South Facing In North Side (Gaja Yoni) Well-to-do
West Facing In East Side (Dwaja Yoni) Wish Fulfilment

**Age of the building veethi-wise**

The approximate life of the buiding based on Ploting Schedule of the land has been standardized in Vaastu Tests.

Goveethi – 500 years prosperity
Agni Veethi – 10 years, poverty
Andhaka Veethi – 8 years, death (owner)
Bhuta Veethi – 6 years, loss of finance
Jala Veethi – 10 years, loss of children
Naga Veethi – 100 years, life
Gaja Veethi – prosperity forever
Dhanya Veethi – Happy life for 1000 years.

# Bhaagam 6

## Vivid Salas (Different types of Houses)

Various types of houses are in the purview of Vaastu texts as it purely depends on the owners' financial capability and availability of land plot for construction. People prefer dik or vidik houses as recommended by Sages where four kinds of houses are in use.

1. Ekasaala (Single House)
2. Dwisaala (Double House)
3. Trisaala (Three Sided Houses)
4. Chatu Saala (Four Sided House)
5. Chatu Saala (Four Sided House with Corner House)

• **Ekasaala (Single House)**: An Ekaasala house is a single roomed accommodation which is made by one side direction, single door with varandahs in one side or around the house. This has been explicitly mentioned in the following ancient Vaastu texts:-

1. Aparajitha priocha
2. Bhojas Samarangana Sootradhaara
3. Maayamatam
4. Vishwakarma Vaastu Shastra.

These authorities have arrived over 104 different kinds of single room type house patterns which were in use in ancient time. Out of the known available Ekasaalas, Sixteen (16) models are worth mentioning. The rest of the models were not suited for the living conditions prevailed then.

Sixteen house types shown below are in the rough sketch form. These houses have fence for earmarking the boundary of the plot. The house is situated at South means the location or direction of the house within the premises. The details of the single roomed houses with alindahs are given below:

***Dhruva Eka Saala***: Dhruva single room accommodation has a door at the North side. There is no verandah in any side of house. This rectangular or square size shaped, single cabin house is generally used for granary or storage purposes.

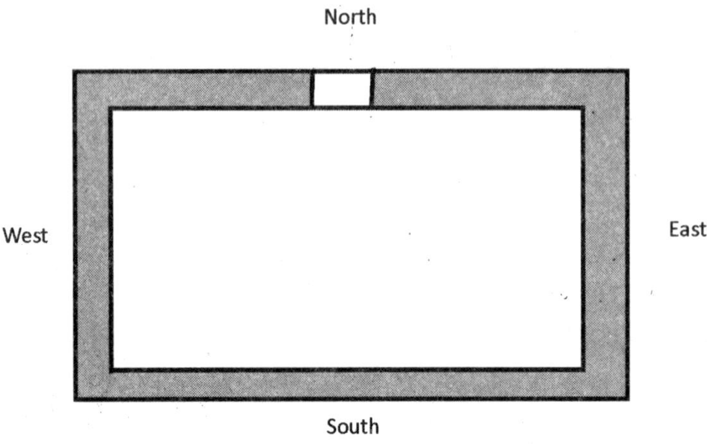


**A Model House of Dhruva Saala**

***Dhanya Eka Saala***: Dhanya single cabin house has two doors, main in the West and the other in the East side. In the front, there is a verandah on the West. This single roomed house is also used as a store house of food grains.

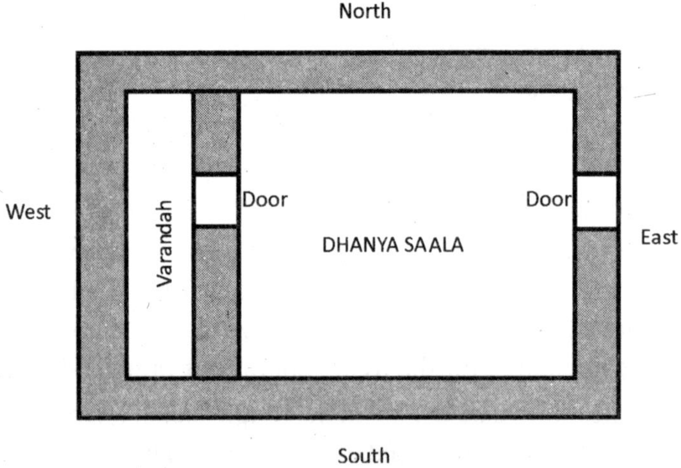


***Jaya Eka Saala:*** Jaya single room house is built on the North side. The door is situated at South and there is a front varandah. This house brings luck and success.

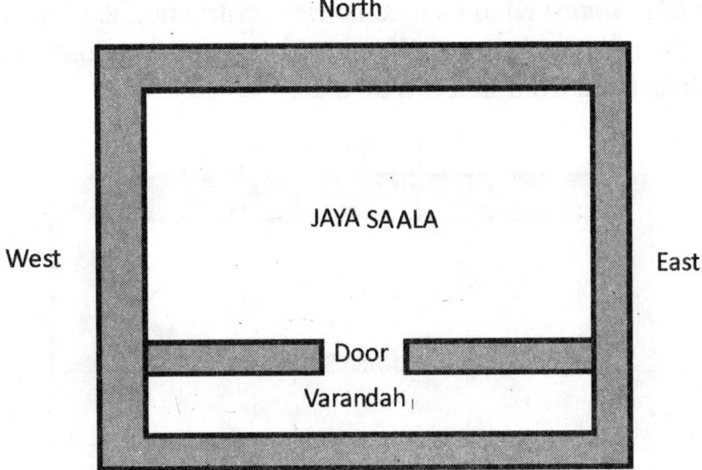


**A Model One-room House Of Jaya Saala**

***Nanda Eka Saala:*** In Nanda single house, the main door is placed in the East and another door in the South. Verandahs are situated in front and on the right side. This house will always give inmates happiness.

The diagram is given below with doors situated in East and South.

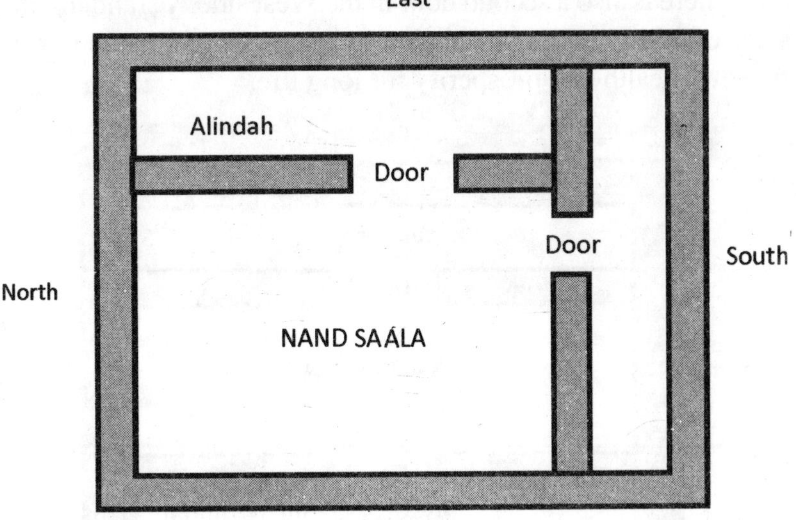


**A Model House Of Nanda Saala**

***Khara Eka Saala:*** Khara single house construction is in the eastern side with the main door placed at West. This house brings only sorrow if the alinda is placed in front in the West side.

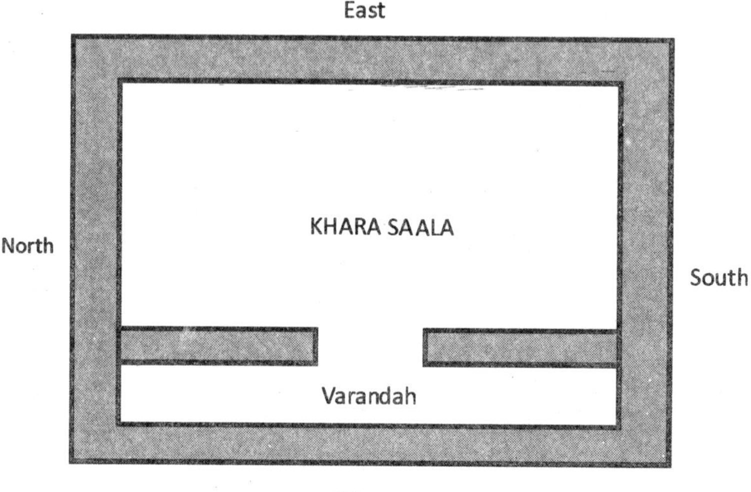


**A Model Khara Ekasaala**

***Kanta Eka Saala***: In Kanta single house, the main door is placed in the East side. There is also a second door in the West side. Verandahs are placed both sides of West and East. This house brings more amassed or inherited wealth, better health and prosperity for long life.

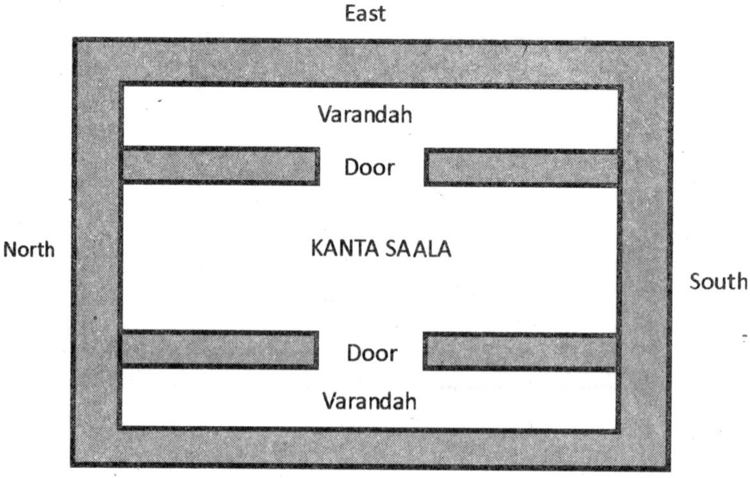


**A Model House Of Kanta Ekasaala**

***Manorama Eka Saala***: The main door of Manorama single room house is located at South. Another door is placed at West. Verandahs are situated both at East and West sides. This house will give more satisfaction and mental peace to the inmates.

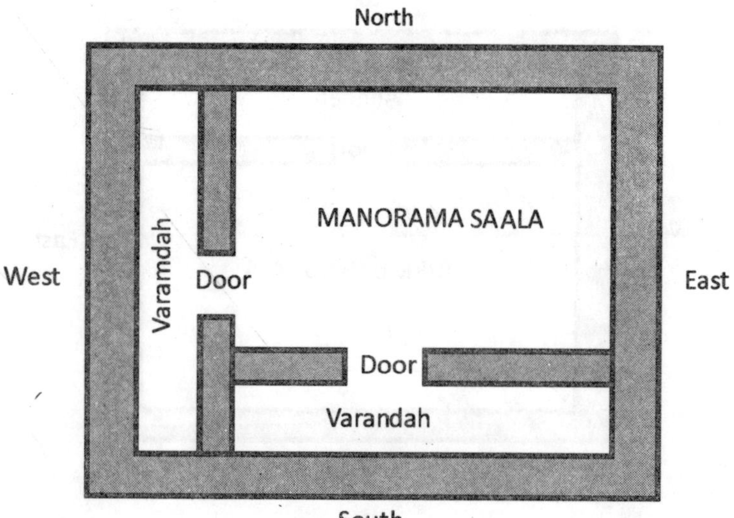


***Sumukha Eka Saala***: This ideal single room accommodation Sumukha saala has a gate in front of the main door placed in the East. Verandahs and doors are placed in all the three directions, i.e. East; West and South. This house will bring many favours and honours from all associates or well-wishers especially from rulers.

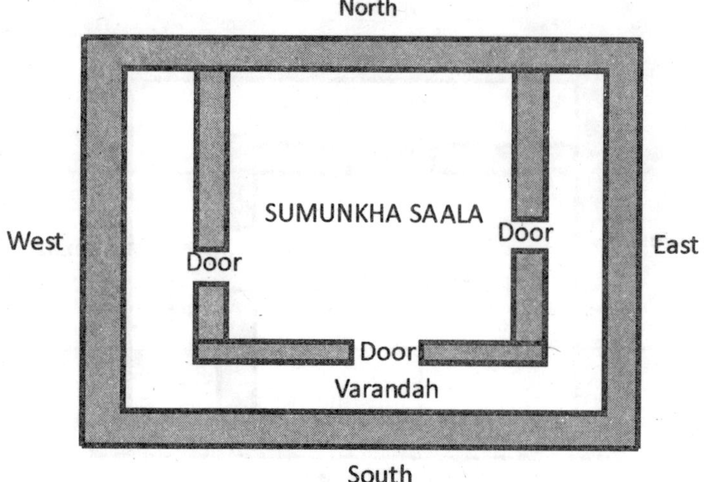


**A Model House Sumukha Ekasaala**

***Durmukha Eka Saala***: The Durmukha single house accommodation has a door and an alinda at North side. This house is constructed at South side. The house will stimulate quarrel and frequent travels.

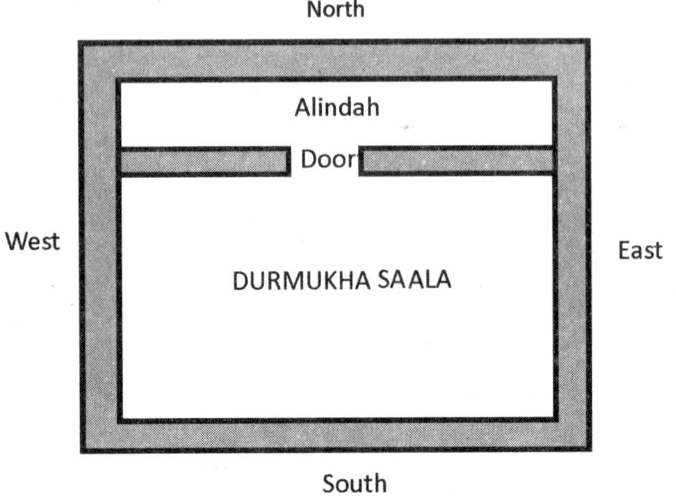


**A Model Durmuka Eka Saala**

***Krura Eka Saala:*** Usually Krura single houses are constructed on the West side. The main door is located at East and another door at North. Verandahs also can be had both at East and North sides. This house will create fatally incurable diseases. The word Krura itself means cruel.

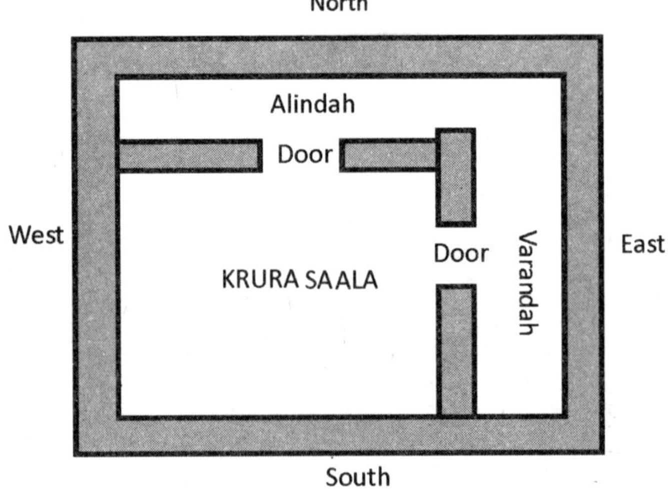


**A Model of Krura Ekasaala**

***Supaksha Eka Saala***: The Supaksha single room house is placed at South. The main door is located at North. The next door is also placed at South. Sage Garga's view is that this supaksha saala house augurs well for prosperity and good luck to the occupants. But some hold the view that this will produce fear of foes.

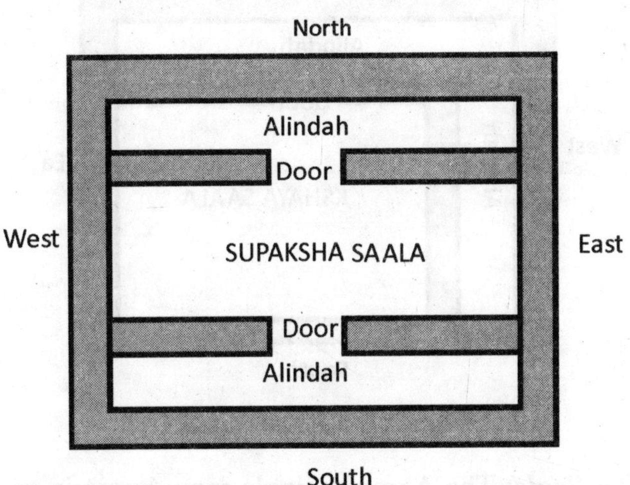


**A Model House Supaksha Ekasaala**

***Dhanda Eka Saala***: The Dhandas House is constructed on the West side. All the three sides have alinda or verandahs and doors except the West side. The main door is situated at the East side. This house will bestow good luck of money, increase in cattles or gain of gold and silver.

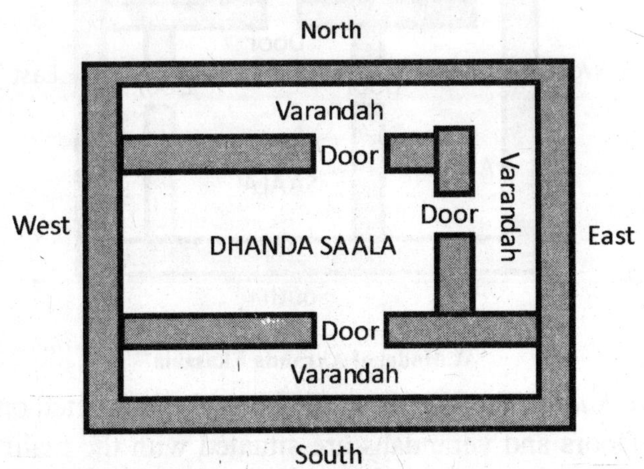


**A Model House of Dhanda Ekasaala**

***Kshya Eka Saala***: Kshya single cabin house is always built on the East side. The main door is on West with another door at the North side. Both East and North sides have alindahs or verandahs. This house will destroy all prospects of health, wealth, progeny or finance.

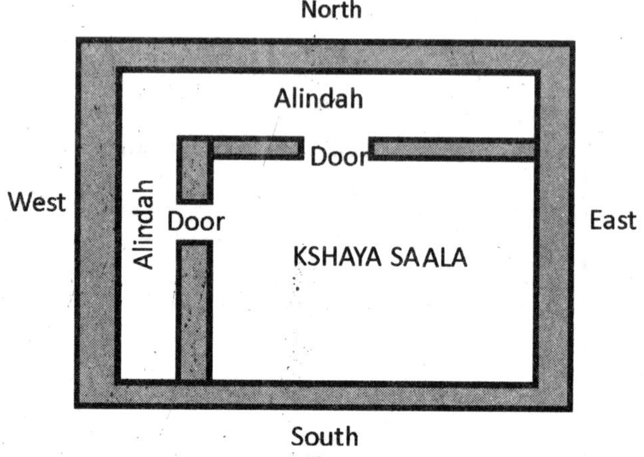


**A Model of Kshaya Ekasaala**

***Akranda Eka Saala***: The Akranda single room house is constructed on the West side. The main door is situated on the East side. It has doors and verandahs on three sides except the South side. This house will invite frequent sorrows and death of kith and kin.

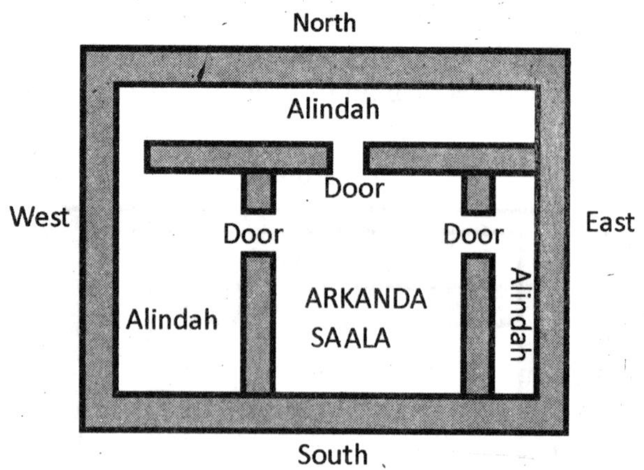


**A Model of Akranda Ekasaala**

***Vipula Eka Saala***: The Vipula single house is contructed on the East side of the plot. Doors and verandahs are situated with the main in South and others in West and North sides. This house will ensure happiness and good health to all inmates or associates. No provision for a door or an alindah is allowed at the East side.

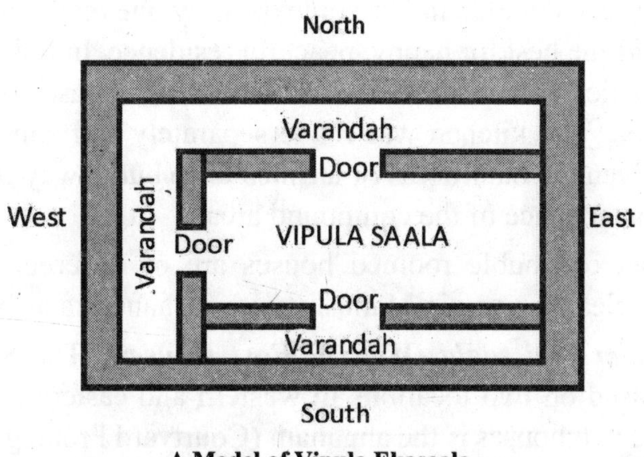


**A Model of Vipula Ekasaala**

***Vijaya Eka Saala***: The Vijaya house is constructed in a single room provision with full coverage of verandahs around. The doors are situated in all four sides of which any one can be used or considered as the main door according to the choice of the house owner. Since the alindahs are at a full length around the house, it will give good health and abundance of wealth to the inmates.

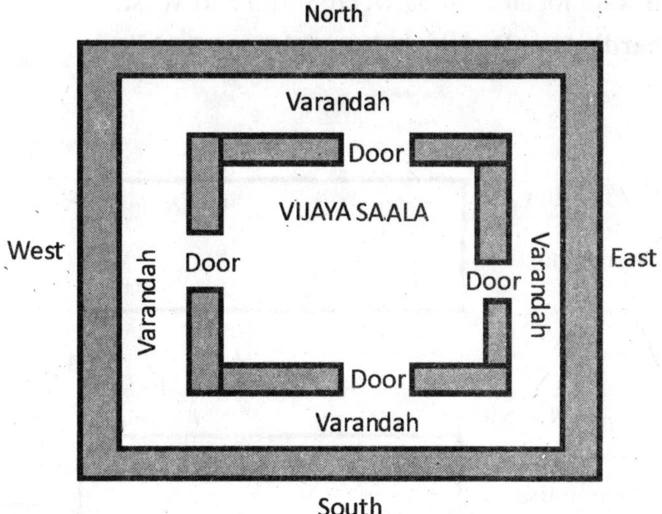


**A Model of Vijaya Ekasaala**

The ancients have shown the sixteen models of Ekasaala (Single Roomed House) out of the total varieties explained in the Vaastu texts. If any one ventures to construct an Ekasaala house, the best combination can be designed for betterment and happiness.

• **Dwi Saalas (Double Houses Types)**: Though several Dwi (two) saalas (houses) have been detailed in Vaastu texts, only one model Sidhardhakam is considered as the best for happy, peaceful residence. In India, there was a customary practice to have at least two rooms space house without kitchen accommodation. The kitchen was made separately and annexed with the main house. Even the bathrooms or latrines were built away from the main house in the outer space of the compound area.

Two house set or double roomed houses are of different kinds. Some references are clearly given in Manushyaalaya Chandrika as below:

***Sidhardhakam Dwi saala (West & East Houses)***: The Sidhardhakam Houses are based on two locations in western and eastern sectors. At the centre of these two houses is the anganam (Courtyard Frontage). The house plot is to be fenced on four sides with one main gate.

This double house is very prospective and a model for good double sided residential accommodation. The meaning of Sidhardhakam itself is something accrued for the good virtues.

Two house models are given below.

1) Sidhardhakam located in between West and East.

2) Sidhardhakam located in between South and West.

**Type 1 Sidhardhakam Dwi Saala Located West And East**

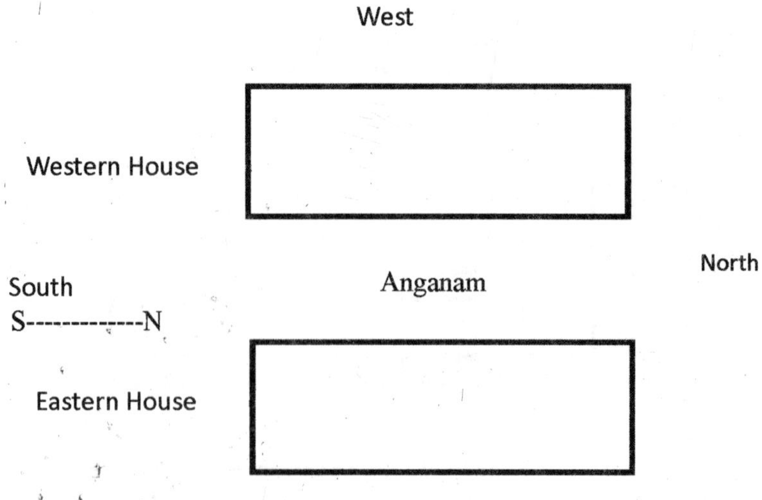


**A model of West & East located Sidhardhakam**

**Type 2. Sidhardhakam Dwi Saala Located South And West**

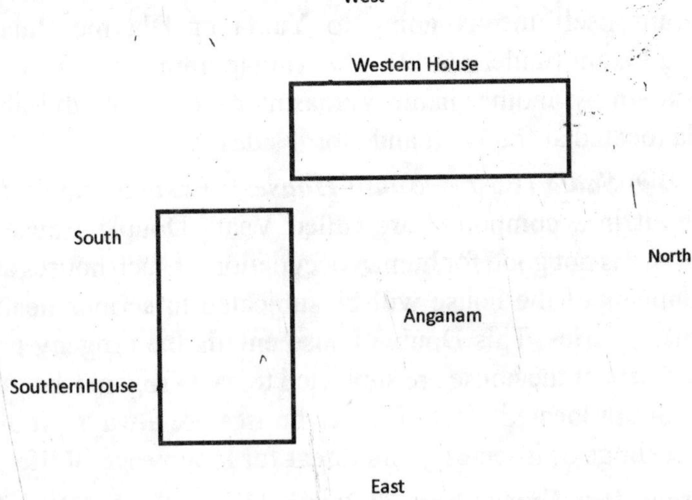


**A model of West & South located Sidhardhakam Dwi Saala**

***Kacham Dwi Saala (South & North Houses)***: Two sided houses at Southern and Northern houses are located in a compound with anganam at the centre. This Kacham Houses are not good for occupation and stay. The stay in it will cause quarrel and fear in all inmates.

Nobody will recommend constructing a building like the kacham Double house for a stay.

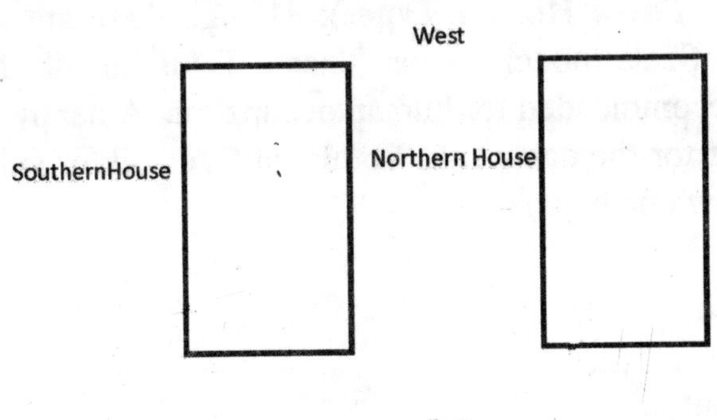


**A model house Kacham Dwi saala**

***Yamapuram Dwi Saala (West & North Houses)***: The Yamapuram Dwi saalas have two dik houses at western and northern sides. The name Yamapuram itself means going to Yama or Dharma Raja's kingdom Yamapura lokam (under world). The Yamapuram the two sided dwi saala, is also known by another name Yamasupam. It is not advisable to have a dwi saala located at the West and North sides.

***Vaata Dwi Saala (East & South Houses):*** East and South Sides of two houses built in a compound are called Vaata Double House. The Vaata double house is not good for human occupation. If such houses are occupied, all the inmates of the house will be subjected to serious health problems and mental worries. This Double house entails the progeny prospects and some members of the house are subjected to vaata rogam (rheumatism). The East and South located Vaata Double houses are always problematic, and produce feelings of insecurity and threat for long peaceful life.

***Dhandam Dwi Saala (East & North Houses):*** The Dhandam Double houses are usually constructed at northern and eastern sectors of the compound. In the centre there will be an anganam. The ancients have advised not to construct Dhandam Dwi Saalas on account of the forthcoming quarrels and infighting between the inmates and external foes. This type of houses encourages litigation and court cases that will promote moral degradation and melancholic conditions.

The Dhandam Dwi saala also creates unnecessary fear and diseases. Hence, Sidhardhakam Dwi Saalas models are good for human happiness and long stay.

• **Triple Saalas (Three Houses Types)**: Though there are several kinds of houses in Tri Saala models as per Vaastu Texts, mainly four types of dik houses are recommended for human occupation. A happy and peaceful stay is important for the occupant. Prominent three dik or side houses are enumerated below one by one:

1. Sukshetram
2. Hiranya naabhi
3. Chulli
4. Damsam tri saalas.

*Sukshetram Tri Saala (North, South And West Houses)*

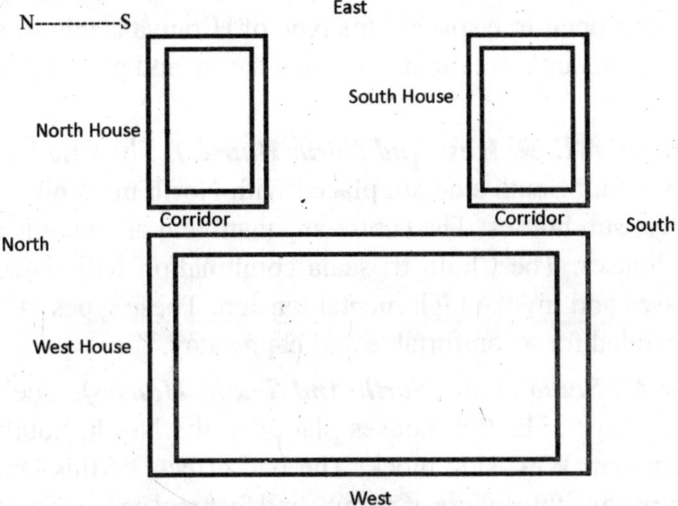


**A model Tri saala: Sukshetram House.**

The Sukshetram Tri saala house consists of three sided dik houses placed at West (Main House), North and South side's houses leaving free space at the East. There is a passage area or corridor in between the houses. This type of tri saalas will foster wealth, progeny and prosperity.

*Hiranyanaabhi Tri Saalas (South, West And East Houses)*

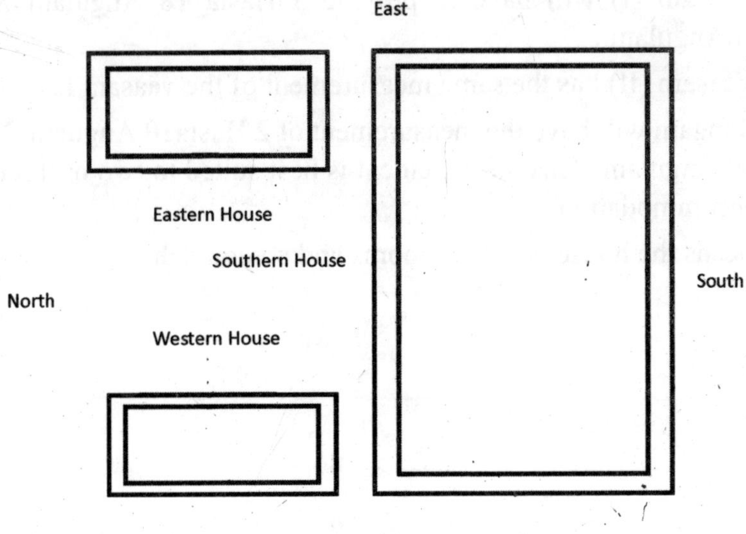


**A model Hiranyanaabhi Tri saala**

Hiranyanaabhi tri saala dik gruhas are situated on the South main house with West and East sub-houses. No house is around on the North side which is kept as open free space. This type of Hiranyanaabhi tri saalas will multiply the occupant's wealth and bring a happy and peaceful long life to all inmates.

***Chulli Tri Sala (East, West And North Houses)***: The Chulli three sided dik houses without South side are placed with North main house and with East and West sub houses. The centre anganam and antaralams are placed in between houses. The Chulli tri saala combination will result in heavy financial losses and invoke high mental tension. These types of houses are not recommended for a comfortable and happy stay.

***Dhamsam Tri Saala (East, North And South) Houses):*** The Dhamsam Tri Saala has three side dhik houses placed in the North, South and East regions other than West side block. The bad effects of this Dhamsam tri saala will create an atmosphere of enmity and fear and cause loss of children. These types of tri saalas are not advisable for occupation. The main house is placed at the East block.

Partitioning the saalas into convenient rooms is important i.e., Vaasam, Rangam and verandahs or alindah are to be considered. The measurement of alindahs or verandahs are given as 10H 22A. The wall thickness will be 10 Angulam,

a) Vaasam (I) will have to provide 3 Hasta 18 Angulam X 4Hasta 10Angulam

b) Vaasam (II) has the same measurement of the vaasam I,

c) Rangam will have the measurement of 2 Hasta10 Angulam X 4 Hasta 10 Angulam. This measurement is best suited to two or three roomed accommodation.

That means the house has three rooms and a verandah.

# Bhaagam 7

## Chatu Saalas (Four Houses Types)

Chatu Saala means Naalu Kettu Pura having four sided dik houses on all sides North, East, West and South. The centre of dik sided houses has courtyard with the gamanam. Specifications will suit best yoni to the house and the anganam by avoiding vedha. Shifts of vedha will be removed to free from all troubles. These types of Chatu Saalas are the symbol of the rich and noble families. Their reputation is highlighted with eminent personalities of the family in different walks of life.

The four sided houses are a special phenomenon along with four cornered houses, corridors or antaralams attached with care and scrutiny. The age old practice and its greatness still survive with prominence. It will take more years to grasp the in-depth of age old elegance and excellence of designs. The ultra modern, artificial style and architectural attraction are considered the ostentation of the financial abundance with certain groups or individuals.

There are several kinds of vidik houses attached with side houses in different parts of India in varied forms: thatched, made of bamboo or different timbers like teak, aanjili, jackwood tree. Wood of some trees like teak, venteak or irrumullu types are used for construction work as reapers, plank for making doors, window frames and shutters. Palm and coconut trees leaves are used for thatching the roof cover of house instead of using tiles. Some of the houses are built with mud, clay limestone or available materials. These sorts of houses physically exist even nowadays, in rural areas. Certain houses have storage facilities inside the house as kalavara and underground secret chambers.

According to the location and nature, the Chatu Saalas houses have different kinds of classifications per:

- **Brihat Samhita**

The Vaastu Book Brihat Samhita mentions the dik houses division as:

1. Sarvatobhadra Chatu Saala
2. Nandya Varta (Pin wheel flower or Crape Jasmine) Chatu Saala
3. Vardhamana Chatu Saala
4. Swastika Chatu Saala
5. Ruchaka Chatu Saala

The Maayamatam explains the same types of chatu saalas classifications.

However, the Manushyaalaya Chandrika moves a step forward to a classification of Sarvatobhadra into seven kinds of Vardhamana Chatu Saalas. The following model sketch of houses in all case is surrounded by wall or fencing.

The Brihat Samhita's classifications of five kinds of Chatu Saalas are given below:

***Sarvatobhadra Chatu Saalas (Four Sided Houses)***

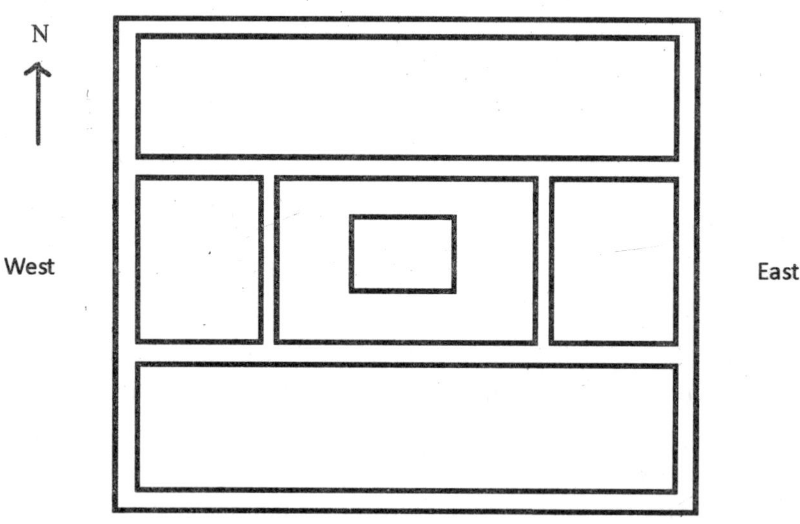


**A Model of Sarvobhadra Chatu**

Sarvatobhadra Chatu Saala has internal alindah without exit passage. But it has entrance to four sides. Four Dik houses, four sided entrance and central anganam are the speciality of Sarvobhadra four sided house.

***Nandya Varta Chatu Saala (Pin Wheel Flower Or Crape Jasmine) Type***

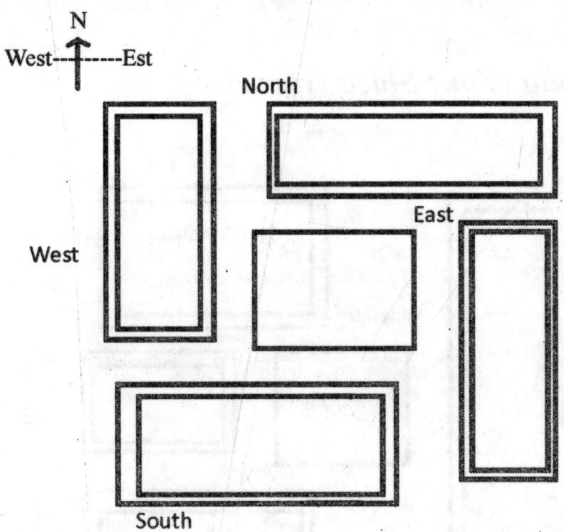


**A Model of Nandya Varta or Pin Wheel flower Chatu Saala**

The Nandya Varta Chatu Saala has three entrances, having four internal alindahs with four exit points. No provision is made for East side entrance. The four sided house has corridors in between houses and its internal central anganam is the attraction to this Nandya Varta (crape jasmine) flower type Chatu Saala.

***Vardhamana Chatu Saala (Four Sided House)***

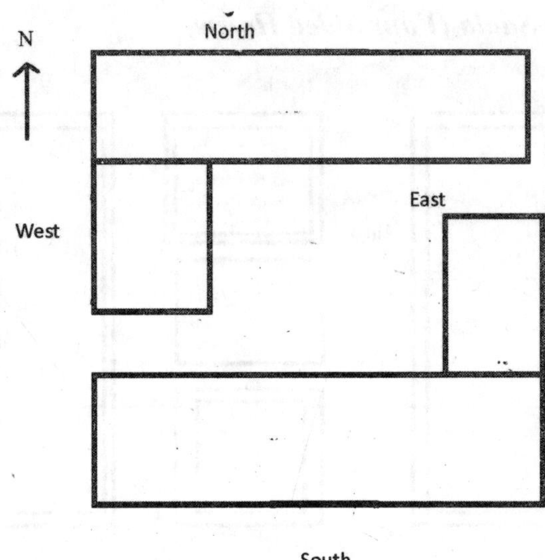


**A Model of Vardhamana Chatu Saala**

Vardhamana Chatu Saala has three sides entrance at East, North and West. This Chatu Saala has two exit points, four internal alindah and four gateways with middle anganam.

***Swastika Chatu Sala (Four Sided House)***

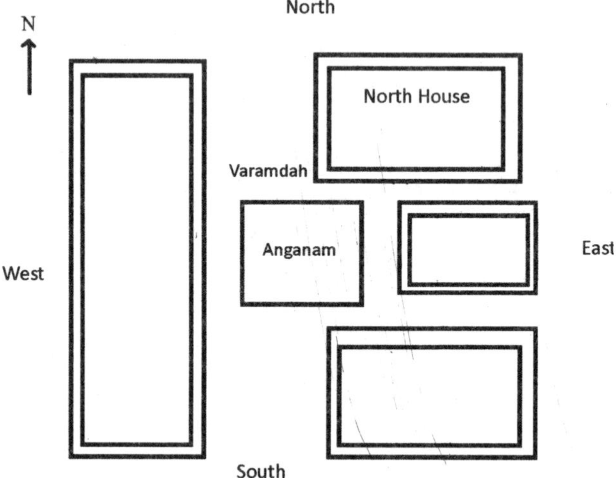


**A Model Swastika Chatu Saala**

The Swastika Chatu Saala has only one entrance with four exit points and having three internal alindahs. The side houses are dissimilar in shape. The middle anganam is adjusted with the shape of the direction houses.

***Ruchika Chatu Saala (Four Sided House)***

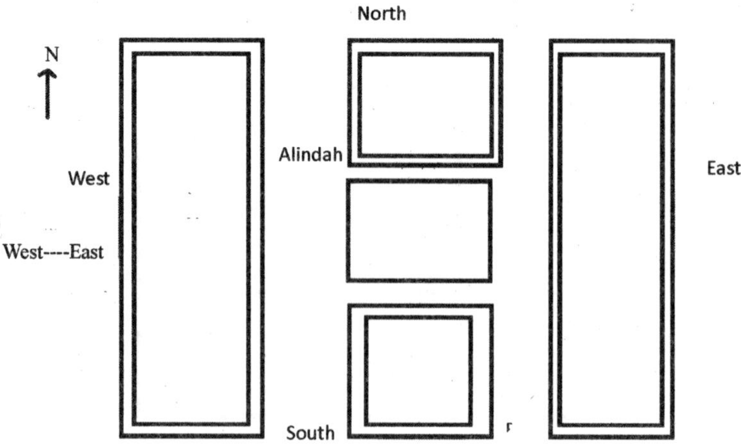


**A Model Ruchika Chatu Saala**

Ruchika Chatu Saala has three side entrances in the East, West or South zone except the North. Two houses of West and East are very big whereas the South and North houses are small in size. Four alindahs and four exit points give the peculiarity of the Ruchika Chatu Saala.

• **Manushyaalaya Chandrika:** According to "Manushyaalaya Chandrika" there are two groups of Chatu Saalas which mention nine categories:

a) Specially designed Chatu Saalas like Bhinna (variety) Four Sided dik Houses without corner houses.

b) Integrated Chatu Saalas like the houses which have both dik (sided) and vidik (corner) conjoined.

The details of Chatu Saalas in Manushyaalaya Chandrika are:

1. Vishudha Bhinna Saala: Separate four side houses (Dik Gruhas) without konalayams (corner gruhas)
2. Slishta Bhinna Saala: Like houses conjoining four side houses with two corner gruhas.
3. Samslishta Bhinna Saala: Complete varieties of houses that are also called Nandya Vartha (Crape Jasmine or Pin Wheel flower) type Saala having full range of four dik and four vidik houses.
4. Vishishtha Bhinna Saala: These are eight direction gruhas with divisions also known by Slishta Bhinnashta Saala.
5. Mishra Bhinna Saala: Means mixed separate houses in all four sides.
6. Sammishra Bhinna Saala: Means totally joined as one in look but very different due to keeping the anganam, gamanam and antaralam passages.
7. Misraka Chatu Saala: This is known as Kshetriya Chatu Saala which is totally square in nature.
8. Chatu Saala: This has four sided house in square shape.
9. Madhya Praruda Saala: Have 4 dik and 4 vidik houses look separate but totally combined.

***Vishudha Bhinna Saala (Distinctive Different Houses):*** Details of the side houses of Distinctive Different Gruhas are given below:

<u>Details of measurement</u>

North house: size 5.94x2.58mts.
East house: size 6.66x2.10 mts.
South house: size 6.96x2.70 mts.
West house: size 7.26x2.94 mts.

M—middle, A—Anganam, P---padukam
North to South length----8.58 mts
East to West width-------7.86 mts

Four separate houses are included in the Vishudha Bhinna Saala as follows:

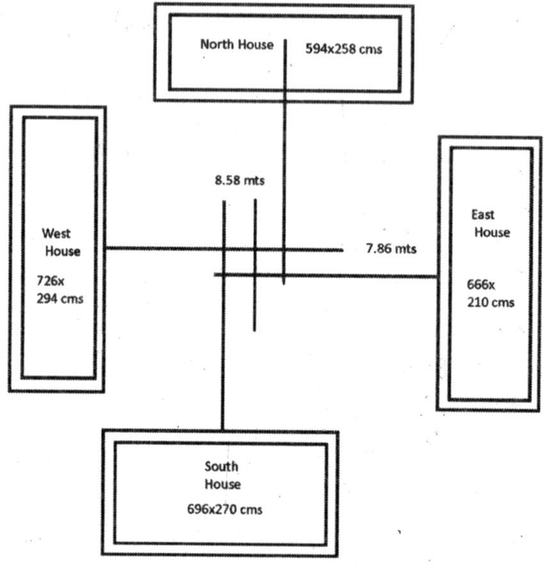


**1. A Model of Vishudha Bhinna Saala**

Vishudha Bhinna Saalas are four direction houses with anganam at the centre. The centre part of the house should not collide with the middle of the courtyard by keeping gamanagulam bit distance to dislocate the marmas on the pillars or walls touch each house.

For the Vishudha Bhinna saala, the yoni of the direction should be selected i.e. Simha Yoni to South house, virshabha yoni to West house, gaja yoni to North house and dwaja yoni to the direction house. The anganam – the common middle courtyard inside the padukam takes dwaja yoni. There should not have any vedha touch between the space of Madhya sutram frontage and the houses.

The main house is to be located either in the West side or in the South side, depending upon the environmental factors like hills, roads, canal, river, paddy field etc. Breadth is bigger for main house than for other saalas. The West side house is made as main house; the width of the South house will be lesser than that of West, lesser towards to North and East side houses in order. Likewise, the South house is to be made as the main house, width of the West, North and East should be reduced in order in each case. Width measurement factor is the decisive consideration for making the main house.

Such types of saalas are suitable for all sections of the people. However, it is noted that Brahmins, as a group of pooja oriented folk, will prefer this type of gruhas.

The top utharam and its wood structural rules are not applicable as the modern architectural or structural roofs and floors are made with RCC top and brick walls. The difference between ancient and the modern designs should be noted by observing the two, by customary practice and by traditional construction nomenclature.

***Slishta Bhinna Saala (Conjoining Houses)***

Details of measurement are:

North House: 474X378cms
West House: 606X414 cms
South House: 651X402 cms
East House: 726X342 cms.
Anganam: East to West 14.94 mts,
South to North: 18.30 mts.

Other corner houses: not on scale

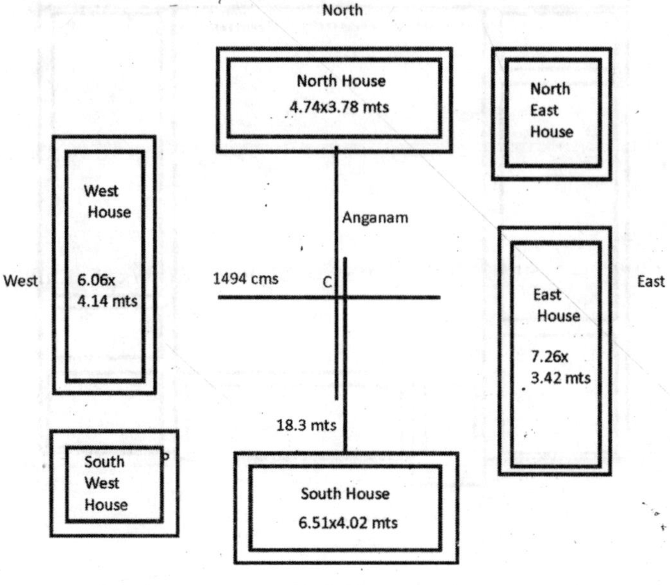


**2. A Model House of Slishta Bhinna Saala**

This Slistha Bhinna Saalas have four dik houses and two corner houses at Southwest and Northeast vidiks. The conjoining gruhas have link with two kon houses leaving free vaayu and Agni corner space. Free passage is provided in between saalas, and that will enable the suthikas or shudras entrance to the house. This type of Gruhas will suit to all kinds of Varna group's communities allowing reserved rooms for suthikas (house maids or servants) or ladies during periods and delivery time. And the word suthikam means mutual conjunction.

The friendship between southern and western houses is firm, so also that of the northern and eastern houses. By conjoining two or more corner houses naturally a connection is obtained called slistha. The gap provided in between the houses is meant for entry or exit of shudras, workers or ladies during periods and houses separation.

***Samslishta Binna Saala (Complete Different Houses) :*** Like Crap Jasmine Or Pin Wheel Type

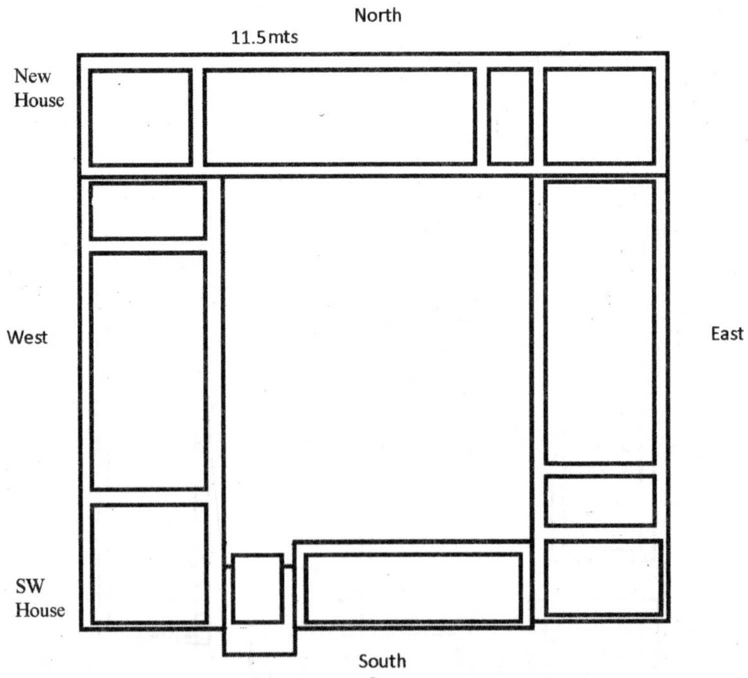


**3. A Model House of Samslishta Bhinna Saala**

Details of Completely Different Houses measurement are:

West house: 558X240 cms
North house: 522X234 cms
East house: 582X198 cms
South house: 546X258 cms
Anganam: South to North: 7.62 mts, West to East: 6.60 mts.
Corridor: NW 81cms, SW 69cms, NE 69 cms, & SE 81cms
Total: South to North length 12.54 mts and West to East width 11.58mts.

Samslishta Bhinna Saala is a different house form with the entire coverage of diks and vidiks sections. This house looks like Nandyavarta (crap jasmine) flower combinations.

The corridor or antaralam inner wall is constructed in between corner and direction houses. So this kind of houses is called "Janya Janakatya Bhavanam".

***Slishta Binnashta Saala (Eight Direction Houses):*** The Direction and Corner Gruhas combined with a number of varieties will make common phenomena for Slishta Binnashta Saala. The wall plate is extended to the corridor or antaralams without making sandhi-joints between konalayams and dik side houses. Thereby, these houses remain separately and the exit is along with their mutual contact (Slishtatya). Though the houses are connected visibly by each other, the separation and independence assume great importance to Slishta Binnastha saalas. The varothara chuttu (perimeter) and aganothara chuttu must be calculated in dwaja yoni. In corner houses, the separation walls are made on the side of the corridors. A model of Slishta Bhinnastha Chatu Saala is given below:

Details of measurement

North house: 10.02X4.26 mts
West house: 13.41X4.62 mts
South house: 10.26X4.5 mts
East house: 10.62X4.5 mts
Corner NW: 5.22X4.26 mts
Corner SW: 4.62X4.62 mts
Corner SE: 4.50X4.50 mts
Corner NE: 4.71X3.90mts
CorridorNW: 4.62X0.99 mts
Corridor SW: 4.62X1.41 mts

Corridor SE: 4.5X1.23 mts
Corridor NE: 3.90X1.41 mts
Anganam: North to South: 13.86 mts
Anganam: East to West: 13.14 mts
East side length: 22.62 mts

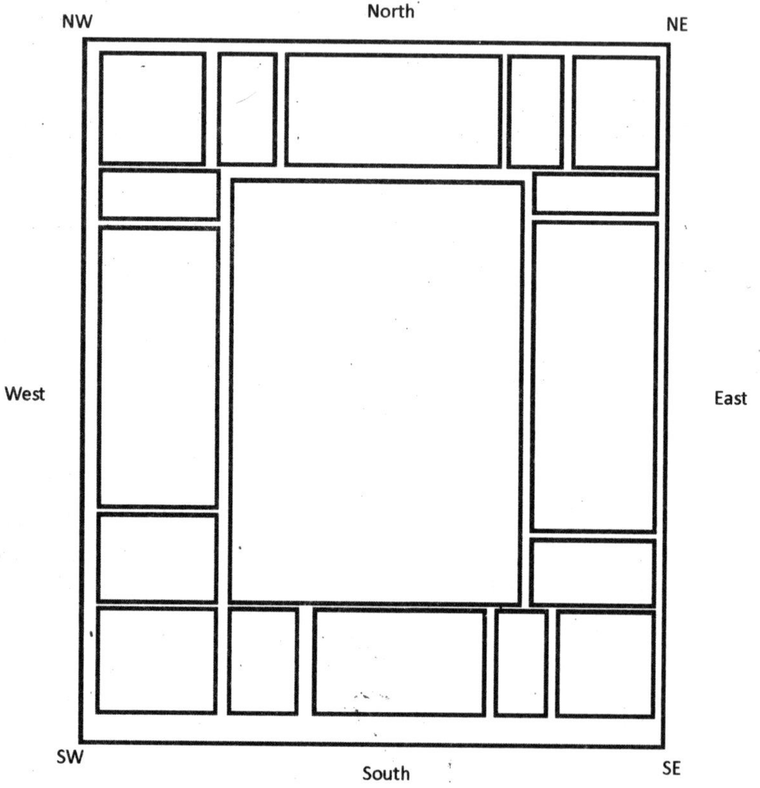


**4. A Model House of Slishta Bhinnashta Saala**

The dik house-wise yoni should be used for the side houses. Fix yoni for corner gruhas with dwaja yoni, eshana or agni gruhas with simha yoni, nairuti gruha with virshabha yoni and vaayu gruha with gaja yoni.

The dik relationship between all side houses is maintained with corner houses by keeping individual identity by not touching or joining each other.

***Mishra Bhinna Saala (Mixed Separate Houses):*** Prime specification for Mishra Bhinna Chatu Saala must be calculated on the perimeter of dwaja yoni along with the perimeter of varotharachuttu and anganachuttu. There is no need to keep the wall plate on the top of the corner houses.

Given below is a plan of corner house fixation with side houses and corridors joining.

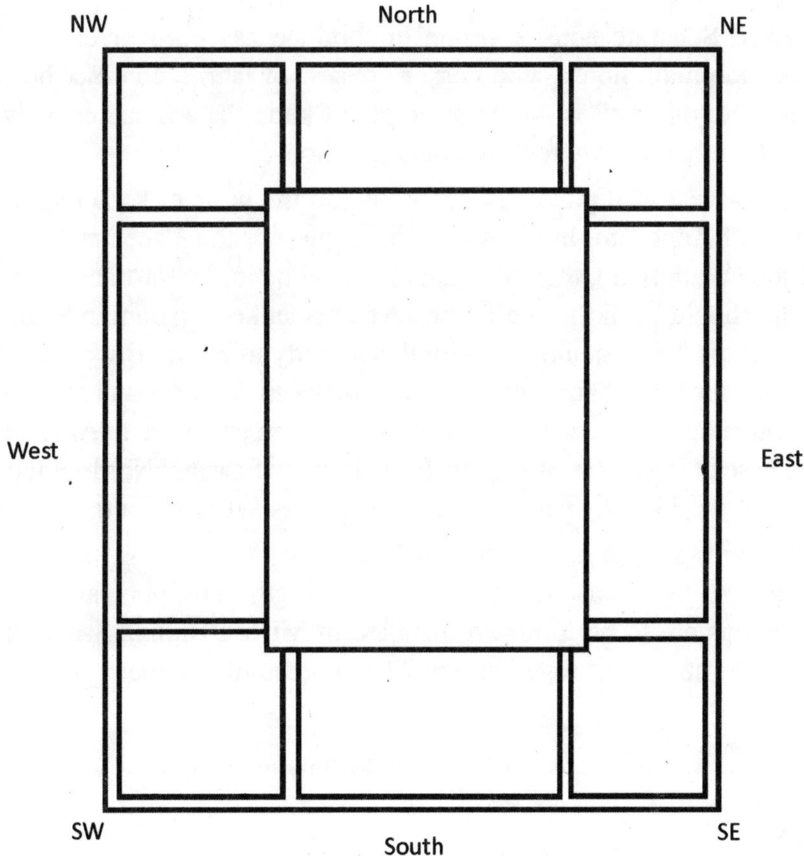


**5. A Model House of Mishra Bhinna Saala**

Details of measurement

North House: 6.18X2.34 mts
West House: 6.54X2.70 mts
South House: 6.42X2.58 mts
East House: 6.51X1.98 mts
House width: 11.58 mts.
Anganam: West to East: 6.90mts, North to South: 7.53 mts
Corner houses not scale.

In Mixed Separate houses, prime importance has been given for mixing yoni of the main house with corner houses. In fact, the corner houses are linked with dik houses on the principle of kada thala (head & body rules) where no utharams are required in corner houses.

The East-West wall plates are connected on the basis of kada thala rules or the rule of Adheyam. In Kada thala principle, for the placement of utharam position (Wall plate), the body (kada) should be in the East and the position of head should be in the West. For the placement of utharam in South-North direction the head should be in South and body in North. But as per Rule of Aadhara, for the utharam placement in between the East and the West, the position of head should be in the East and body in the West. In Aadhara basis; in the case of East-West wall plate Head is in the East and North–South plates in the North. The body part automatically comes West or South respectively.

While joining or fixing the wall plates, if any shortage is seen in length, sandhis are to be inserted to adjust the length. The yoni and gamanam stipulations are to be followed for diks. In Mishra Bhinna Saala all house wall plates are joined together, one different from the other.

***Sammishra Bhinna Saala (Completely Mixed And Different Houses):*** Dwaja (Ketu) yoni is recommended for Sammishra Bhinna saalas varotharam, anganotharam, padhukam both external and internal and wall plates for all side and corner gruhas. Certain formulae are used to find out the breadth of the wall plate.

This type of houses is also called Malla pandhal (Jasmin make-shift vidhan). The idols of Lord Ayyappan and Bhagavathi Bhadra Kaali are often kept in anganam. A sketch of a Sammishra Bhinna Saala is given below:

Details of measurement:

North House: 7.74X2.94 mts
Northwest house: 2.94X2.94 mts
The same measurement is applicable to side houses: 7.74X2.94 mts
And corner house has the same measurement: 2.94X2.94 mts
Dimensions are also same in all sides: 15.08X15.08 mts.

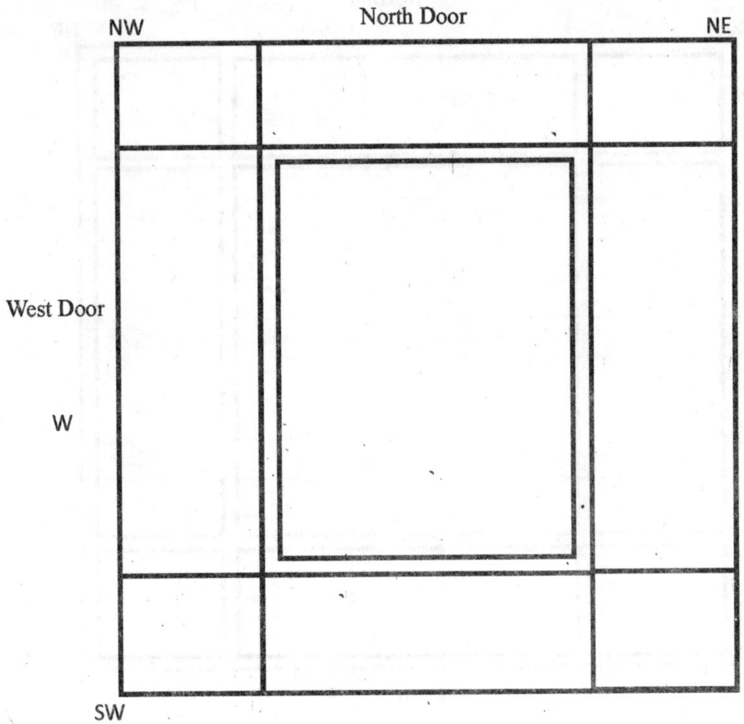


**A Model House of Sammishra Bhinna Sala.**

All dimensions of diks and vidiks houses in all angles and measurements are same. All four sides have doors at the centre. In East and West, inside doors are also available.

***Misraka Chatu Saala (Mixed and Square eight houses):*** Misraka Chatu Saala is not exactly of the square size, but it has a different appearance with four sided and four corner houses. Misraka saalas have dwaja yoni for the basis of perimeter to all houses, anganam and padukam. The yoni and gamanam will be as per its diks prescribed whether diks or corner houses are divided internally by walls. These types of Chatu saalas are very special to kshetriyas. However, it will be used by Varna communities according to their choice and will. These Misraka Chatu Saalas are the most suitable choice for Royal Palaces.

Details of measurement:

All eight houses have width of 3.90 mts and length of 7.74 mts. The total one side length of the house is 15.08 mts. with equal measurements in all sides. Likewise all corner houses have 3.90mtsX3.90 mts. Anganam length is also 7.74X7.74 mts.

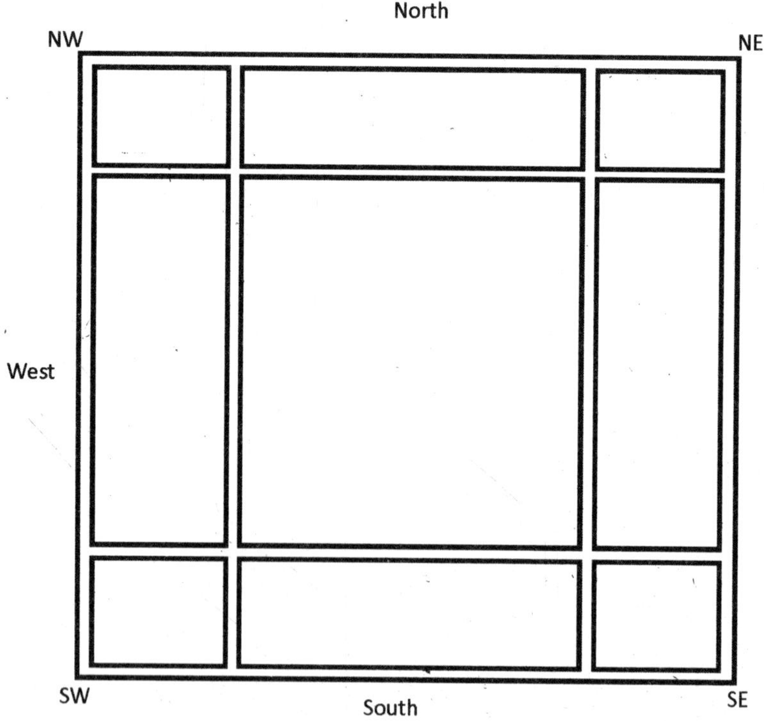


**A Model Sketch of Misraka Chatu Saala**

***Chatu Saala (Nalukettu Veedu):*** This Chatu Saala is not different from other types except that it has a perfect square size and also equal dik houses and four corner houses. Dwaja yoni is selected for wall plate, padukam, perimeter of side and corner houses. It is very particular to keep the middle anganam and house doors in the sutram. Hence vedha dosha will not affect these chatu saala house formations. No gamanam is involved in side houses and no walls are required around the corner houses. The kshetriya Varna community prefers this kind of Chatu Saala.

Details of measurements:

Measurements of Chatu or Four Sides Houses and Misraka Chatu Saala are the same and they are almost square in form and in size.

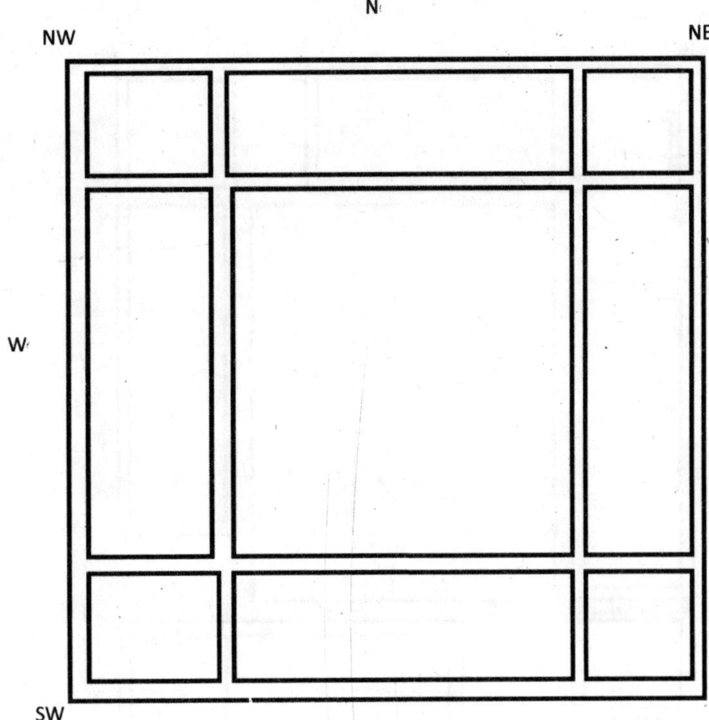


**8. A Model of House Chatu Saala**

***Madhya Praruda Saala (Middle Elevated House):*** All Chatu Saalas prescribed are to maintain the breadth of the wall plate at the centre to be a Madhya Praruda Saala.

This type of corner houses has a slight difference from other kinds of chatu Saalas in middle breadth measure. However, the anganothara and varothara perimeters will be accounted with either dwaja yoni or virshabha yoni.

The corridors, main or corner halls make the type more complex. In some areas, the name used for this kind of four side houses is Samslishta Bhinna Saala.

The method is not similar in all Indian states. Hence variations are possible but the principles followed are within the purview of Vaastu Norms.

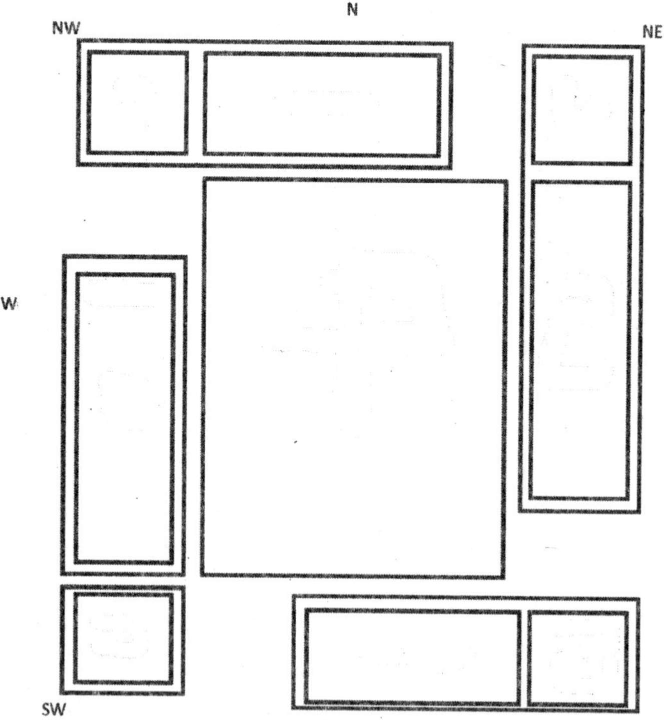


**A Model House of Madhya Praruda Chatu saala**

Basing the centre point, the perimeter is computed on wall plates for all four sided houses.

The Wall Plate problem will crop up if the House is thatched or tiled at roof top of the house or bulding. Nowadays concrete mixture is used for making roof with iron and steel, and coloured tiles are used for beautification.

The Sided Houses construction is easier if roof structure is done in concrete mixture than the olden methods with leaves, tiled roof with head and tail rule of wooden planks. Reinforce cement concrete roof structure can be moulded in any shape or fashion. The old fashioned structural designs stand everlasting and admirable as they do not affect any marma vedha.

# Bhaagam 8

## Gateways (Padipura)

A Gateway or Padipura is an entrance to the land plot. That point of entry should herald the good luck and fortune of the owner of the house or occupants.

The land area may be large enough to construct a specious bungalow or an accommodation needed in future for the comfortable stay of many. But the Vaastu norms are the same for all types, big or small.

The entry gate depends on the factors like entrance road facility, others plots, compound wall or fence etc. Gateway means not only an opening entrance into the house compound but also an exit passage. Gateway or padipura is provided to each house according to style and size of the house and the area of the plot. The best cell or paada is selected for the progress to all inmates. A brief of actual results in particular cell is summarized and given below for each side paadas in selecting the owner's choice. Out of such detail in chart, the best gateway cell selection is as follows:

| | | Name of cell | Cell Number |
|---|---|---|---|
| 1. EAST SIDE | : | Parjanya | 2 |
| | | Jayanta | 3 |
| | | Indra | 4 |
| | | Brusha | 7 |
| 2. NORTH SIDE | : | Mukhya | 27 |
| | | Bhallada | 28 |
| | | Soma (Indu) | 29 |
| 3. WEST SIDE | : | Dwarapalaka | 18 |
| | | Pushpadinanda | 20 |
| | | Varuna | 21 |
| | | Asura | 22 |
| 4. SOUTH SIDE | : | Pushamavu | 10 |
| | | Gruhakshata | 12 |
| | | Brunga | 15 |

1. The entire area is covered under the nine grid eighty one paramsayika cells division with 53 deities.
2. Karna, Mruthyu sutrams cross starts from corner to another corner.
3. Brahma, Yama Sutrams divide diagram vertically or horizontally, and start from one side to another side.
4. Rajju, Paryanata, Naaga, Shoola sutrams will act as circulator of blood or veins.
5. Sandhis will connect all joints and diversions.
6. Brahma naabhi at centre stimulates the entire marma Vaastu paadas or cells.

It is necessary to consider all these before fixing a point to make a gateway into residence as entry or exit. According to the results of each paada, the Gateway cell should be selected as follows:

| Cells No. | | |
|---|---|---|
| | 2 | Success and more female folk |
| | 3 | Wealth and prosperity |
| | 4 | Royal Status and life |
| | 7 | Cruelty and luck |
| | 10 | Common life and struggle |
| | 12 | Prosperity and Good life |
| | 15 | Agriculture and farming life |
| | 18 | Success and Prosperity |
| | 20 | Unexpected rise and prosperity |
| | 21 | Sudden inflow of wealth |
| | 22 | Successful life |
| | 27 | Good karma and children |
| | 28 | Wealth and prosperity |
| | 29 | Good Children |

The gross output value and actual results are given below as per chart 32; Cells external line divisions are numbered from cells 1 to 32. This chart of 32 cells gateway placement result will be very useful in choosing the land plot especially in Metros, Corporations and Municipal areas.

Select the best entrance for the house gate. There should be total nine cells in each side and the best paada should be chosen out of the noted cell details with number.

Divide by 9 in each side per nine grid cell division. Keep the Gate ways in sixth paadam or cells in anti-clockwise direction. In clockwise, fix the gate at the fourth cell position on any side. Both ways, the point will be one and the same.

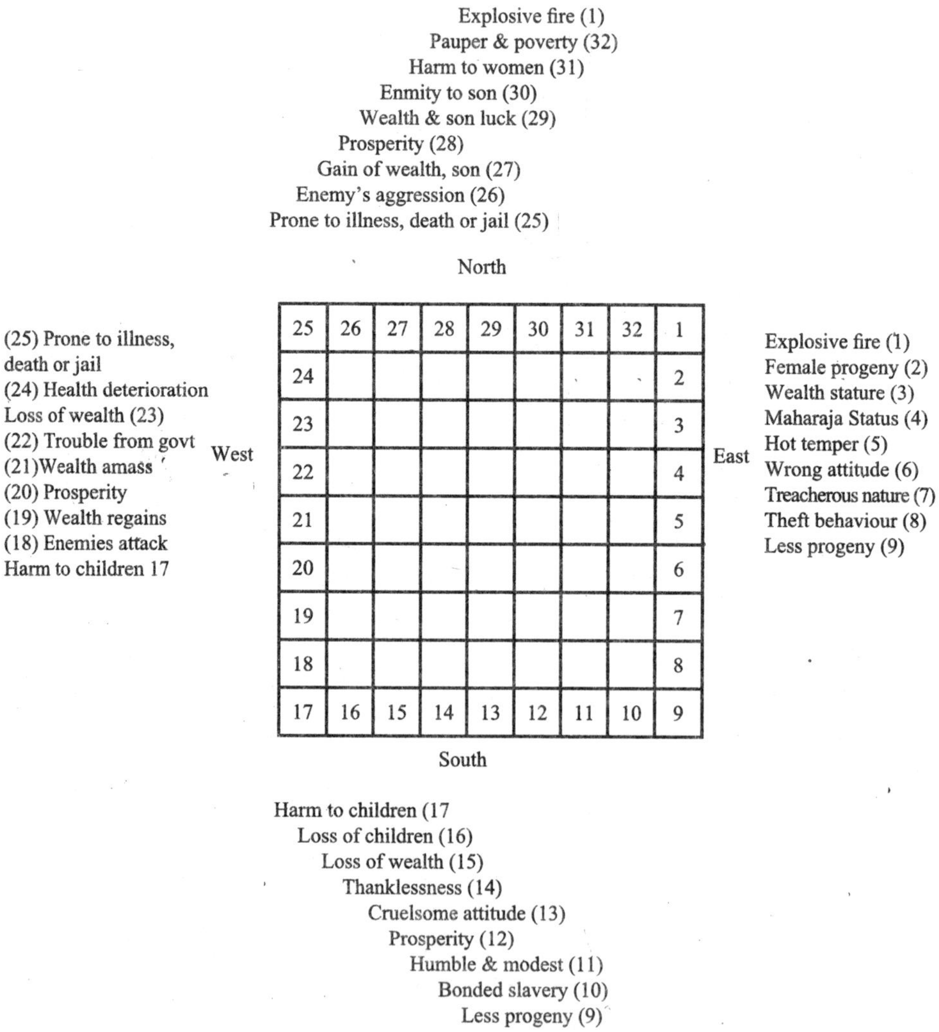

Explosive fire (1)
Pauper & poverty (32)
Harm to women (31)
Enmity to son (30)
Wealth & son luck (29)
Prosperity (28)
Gain of wealth, son (27)
Enemy's aggression (26)
Prone to illness, death or jail (25)

North

(25) Prone to illness, death or jail
(24) Health deterioration
Loss of wealth (23)
(22) Trouble from govt
(21)Wealth amass
(20) Prosperity
(19) Wealth regains
(18) Enemies attack
Harm to children 17

West

| 25 | 26 | 27 | 28 | 29 | 30 | 31 | 32 | 1 |
|---|---|---|---|---|---|---|---|---|
| 24 | | | | | | | | 2 |
| 23 | | | | | | | | 3 |
| 22 | | | | | | | | 4 |
| 21 | | | | | | | | 5 |
| 20 | | | | | | | | 6 |
| 19 | | | | | | | | 7 |
| 18 | | | | | | | | 8 |
| 17 | 16 | 15 | 14 | 13 | 12 | 11 | 10 | 9 |

East

Explosive fire (1)
Female progeny (2)
Wealth stature (3)
Maharaja Status (4)
Hot temper (5)
Wrong attitude (6)
Treacherous nature (7)
Theft behaviour (8)
Less progeny (9)

South

Harm to children (17
Loss of children (16)
Loss of wealth (15)
Thanklessness (14)
Cruelsome attitude (13)
Prosperity (12)
Humble & modest (11)
Bonded slavery (10)
Less progeny (9)

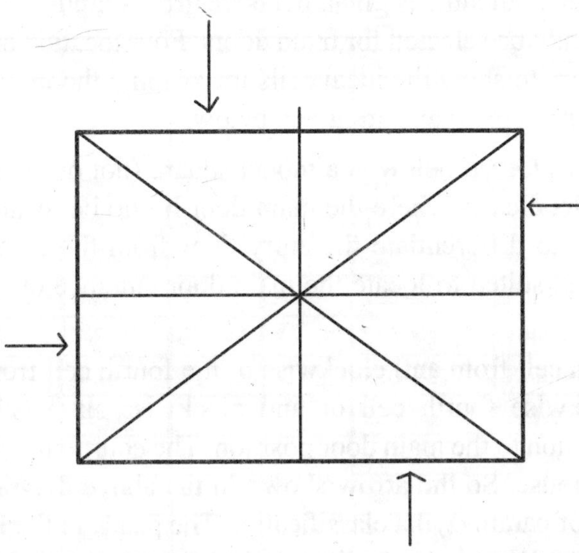

In the above diagram the arrow marking will depict the cell position for keeping the main Gate. The best number should be selected for Main Gate and for Main Doors.

## Dwaram (Doors)

Doors called dwarams should be placed to enter the house from the courtyard. According to the road location, house main door will face the side convenient in entering. The door should be located at the centre midway between the courtyard and the house. Direction should be in placing the main door on any convenient side for one door entrance.

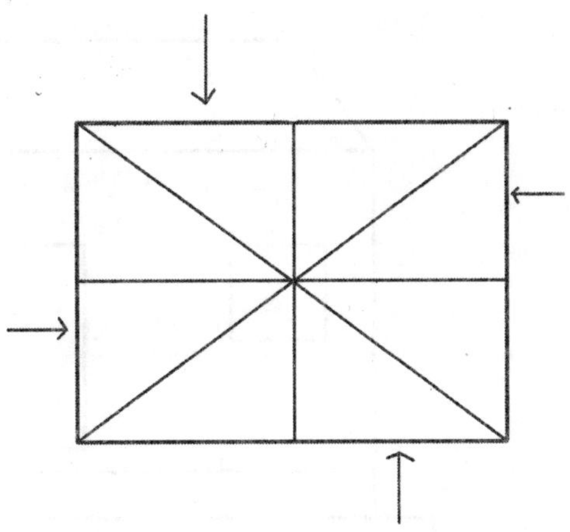

**Position of Location of Door: Main Entrance**

In the selected side, the total length is divided by nine. Keep the main door straight to gate ways in sixth paada or cell on anti-clockwise direction. In clockwise direction, fix the front door in a line of main gate at the fourth cell position on any side.

The entire cells net outcome is given in above gross output value chart. The best number should be selected for main doors. Four location arrows shown in the diagram are to show the ideal cells for keeping the main entrance of the house. The paadam details are given below:

• **Doors Position:** Given below is a model square (not on scale) with nine columns to depict clearly where the main door has to be located. The nine square is drawn to differentiate the entry door from the courtyard to the house. Cells, best suited to locate the main door entrance on any side, are as follows:

Base is the sixth cell from anti clockwise or the fourth cell from clockwise direction. Clockwise fourth cell or anti clockwise sixth cell should be selected as direction to the main door position. The courtyard will be always in front of the house. So the arrow shown in the above diagram points on the square grid of paramsayika classification.The paada in the East is Indra, North is bhallada, West is pushadinanda and South is gruhakshata. In the rectangular houses also, the rule will be applied to locate the main door. The cells size might differ in length and in width. The sill, head and posts should be fixed in the correct location.

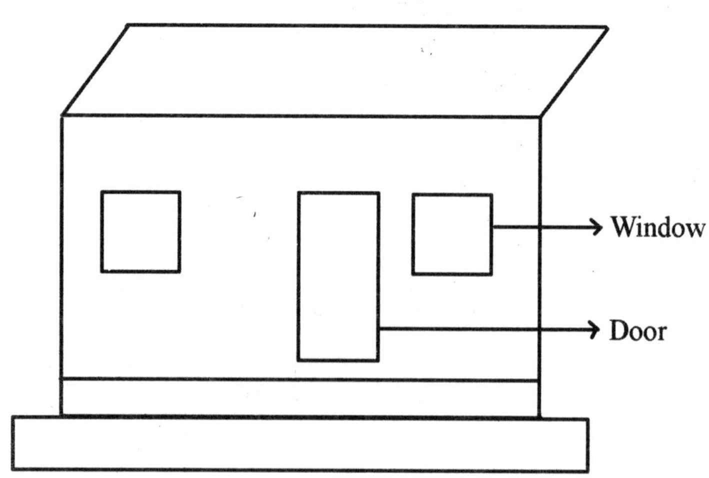


**Front Door and Window position**

***Size of the Doors:*** The size of the doors has been clearly mentioned in the book Manushyaalaya Chandrika with its inside dimensions:

| | | | |
|---|---|---|---|
| 1. | Main door | 192 cms height | 84 cms width |
| | Other doors | 186 cms - | 90 cms - |
| | Small doors | 174 cms - | 78 cms - |
| 2. | Window large | 120 cms - | 156 cms - |
| | Window medium | 138 cms - | 114 cms - |
| | Window small | 126 cms - | 78 cms - |
| | Window tiny | 102 cms - | 78 cms - |
| 3. | Ventilators big | 42 cms - | 90 cms - |
| | Ventilators small | 36 cms - | 72 cms - |

• **Shutters:** There are two shutters for a door as per the rule mentioned in the book Manushyaalaya Chandrika. Some will prefer two planks of equal length or width instead of one. The thickness provision should be made 10 cms to 12 cms or equals to 2 ½ to 4 matrangulams.

The sill thickness should be more than the posts and head. The top beam should be akin to the posts. Nowadays top beam and uttarams are made in concrete; hence no such complications are involved. All measurements are prescribed in angulam base of ayam (income), vyayam (expenditure), and the age is either youth (3) or Adolescent (2). But death age is not recommended with the dwaja yoni, and of perimeter, ishta dhirga or gunamsa.

At present, solid one single shutter plank is used with embossing or carving artistically for beautification.

• **Mangala palaka (Plank):** The Mangala palaka is fixed above the head of the door plank on a wooden frame palaka. While constructing the wall, the

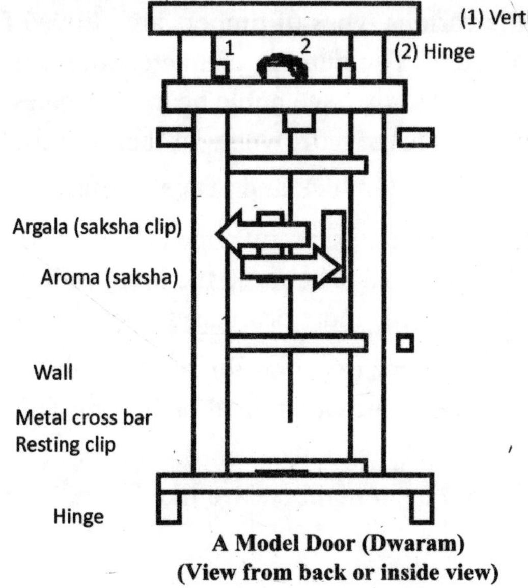


**A Model Door (Dwaram)**
**(View from back or inside view)**

gap will be covered with the door head. This Mangala palaka is also known as kurum palaka. Images of birds, animals, god/goddess are beautifully carved on this door plank. The Managala palaka has the double purpose of closing the gap above the head of the door and having a storage space behind it.

The door hinges are provided at the top and bottom. Aroma 'saksha' (latch) is made with strong wood and strap tips attached to restrict the movements by argala (wooden reaper clips) allowing pass through the holes provided within the saksha.

In front of the door, the following curvings or embossing is common:

1. Nila vilaku (Lighted lamp).
2. Birds, peacock with spread feathers.
3. Animals usually elephant with trunk downward leaning to right.
4. Lord Ganesh with blessing hand and trunk leaning to right.
5. Bhagawati Saraswathi with lotus flower.
6. Lord Krishna with murali (flute).
7. Maha Lakshmi blessing with money dropping hand etc.

The main door will be always large in size. The other doors are smaller than the main. Small size doors are usually used for stores or bathrooms. Each room must have doors in even numbers like 2, 4, 6 etc. the door numbers in a room should not be in odd numbers like 3, 5. However room provided with an arch entry will compensate the odd number problem.

It is also observed that the various types of timbers are utilized for making sill, top-head, posts or shutters. The number characteristics will affect the inmates. Big doors means the family have noble hearted inmates of helping nature. Small doors entry reveals the narrowness of their minds.

Big doors of the main house bring in luck and peaceful life.

• **Windows:** The French style windows, pretty wide and the base at the floor level, are the fashion of the day. That is believed the best symbol of luck and prosperity and children may become more prosperous than their parents.

• **Ventilators:** Ventilators are very essential for the sunlight and fresh air into the house and they should be provided in all bathrooms and toilets.

In a house, the number of doors, wndows, ventilators should be counted separately, the best ideal total even numbers are like 2, 4, 6, 8, 11, 13, 15, 17, 19, 22 etc.

• **Position Of The Main Door With Back Door:** The position of back door with the Main Door is drawn clearly as below. The entry point of front door should not be in straight with the back door point. That means the front and back doors must not be in the same alignment. They must not be exactly in back to back position. Placement of any room in between the front and the back doors will solve such problem. Please see the diagram.

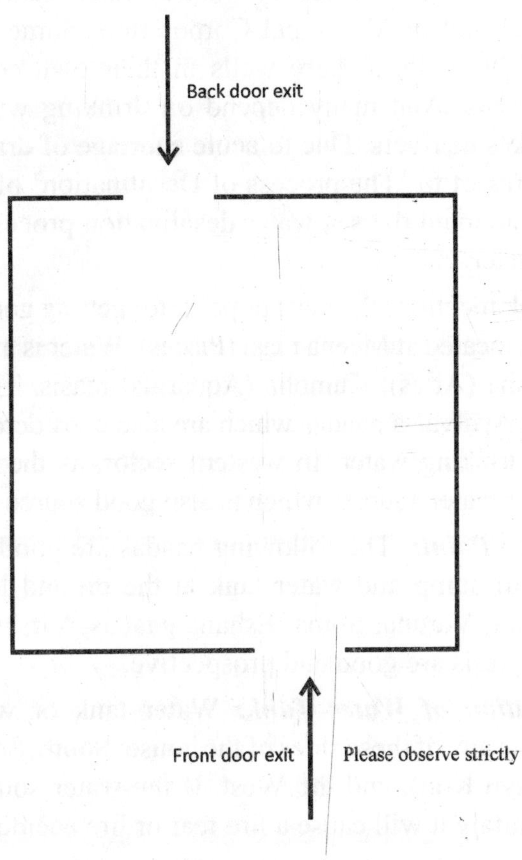


• **Water (Jhalam):** Human beings cannot survive without water like other living beings. In Vaastu Shastra, water is associated with "dhan" or money. Man badly needs water for his existence; he uses it for a variety of purposes or functions. A study of Water source is needed to find out whether it is drawn from well, bore well, river, lake, canal, and pond. The provision for sump or other underground pipe line the storage of water should be made and located at point of luck and prosperity. The distribution channels from overhead storage water tank or other water distribution pipe line connections to various rooms kitchen and bath rooms are carefully scrutinized. The water storage, usage, distribution and treatment point are very pivotal for regular free inflow of money or for good luck in cash or kind. The source of water and its receiving point assume great prominence for prosperity and progress to its inmates and optimistic atmosphere at home.

Nowadays, many inhabitants living in urban or rural areas depend up on Colony group sharing schemes of public water distribution system of concerned Panchayat or Municipal Corporation. Some are lucky to have fresh water in the wells or bore wells in their own compound for their water requirements. And many depend on drinking water largely drawn from ponds, lakes or rivers. Due to acute shortage of drinking water many countries now resort to 'The process of Desalination' of sea water. Some countries have adopted the sea water desalination process by converting it into drinking water.

The Vaastu book mentions the raasi or point for getting good water. A well or borewell can be located at Meena raasi (Pisces). Water is available from other points like Mesha (Aries), Kumbha (Aquarius) raasis. There are two other names Apa and Apatvalsa paadas which are also considered good for getting good and soft drinking water. In western sector, as the last resort, varuna paada is used for water sources which is also good source of drinking water.

***Water Storage Point:*** The following paadas are good and advisable for the placement of sump and water tank at the ground level. Antariksha, Indra, Mahidhara, Varuna, Soma, Eshana paadas, Virshabha (Taurus) and Mesha (Aries) raasis are good and prospective.

***Ban on Position of Water Tank:*** Water tank or water sump is not recommended on any of these sides of the house: South, Southwest (Nairuti), Northwest (vaayu Kon), and the West. If the water sources are placed at Southeast, definitely it will cause a fire fear or fire accident or accident.

The Southwest well is promoter of accidents, either by road or by other means, family separation, litigation or quarrel within six years on completion of a year of occupation.

In Northeast, well, bore well, sump, or water storage tanks should be kept at a little distance away from karna sutra marma line in order not to have any vedha touch. If the karna sutra touches such water storage sump, tanks, or well naturally involve loss, unnatural heavy expenditure, loss of profession and even demotion will be the result. So be very careful in not touching the karna sutra line through the NE water sources areas. This marma (Nerves intersection) effect will be a perennial problem for the entire family and all inmates.

• **Septic Tank**: A Septic tank, into which sewage flows, is an important factor in building plan. Its location and maintenance are of great concern to the health of inmates and neighbours. The provision of Septic tank located at an undesirable place will affect the inmates badly. The house owner or house wife will have to face dangerous consequences soon after six months of the completion or its use. If septic tank is placed at wrong position, the multiple bad effects will prevail throughout a period of 12 years. Both social status and financial stability of the owner or inmates position will gradually lose their lustre and power.

The Septic tank manufacture and its use have had revolusionary changes since the rooms were attached with toilets. The septic tank should be placed at a correct location so that it may not emit any foul smell. The best suitable place for keeping the septic tank is in the areas of Yama khanda or Asura khanda of the plot. In the Northwest Asura khanda area portion is very delicate in digging the land in the ground level. This will lead to heavy infliction to women folk and complete destruction of ladies (naari naasham). Therefore, it is better to avoid Northwest septic tank position exactly on the corner. Digging for any kind at NW will cause the lady destruction one by one or all at a time in various forms. This bad effect will follow if the digging is done for drinking water purpose also. This has been pointed out very specifically in all Vaastu texts especially in Manushyaalaya Chandrika, Maayamatam, Brihat Samhita, or Manasaara.

• **Overhead Water Tank**: Wherever water sources are good, ground level storage facilities are permissible in locations of North, Northeast, East or West. Such locations have to be avoided in keeping the overhead tanks on the top or terrace of the buildings. That means no overhead tanks shall be installed in such areas over the house. It is advisable to keep South, Southeast, Southwest and Northwest overhead tanks on top or terrace of the building. It is better to keep overhead tank on the Northwest as it proves more beneficial than other recommended sides. This opinion is formed from the feed back results which the author has received in many places.

On the top of the terrace, cemented overhead tank or readymade one available in the market can be installed at the Northwest side. It should not be exactly at the corner but a little space should be left for the sutram cord lines i.e. Mruthyu Sutra line from Southeast to Northwest corners.

• **Kitchen:** In a house, the position of a kitchen assumes much importance as per norms of Vaastu books. The Southeast portion of the house is suited for kitchen area. However in Kerala, due to the Southwest monsoon winds and Northwest summer winds, a kitchen at northeastern sector of the house is preferred. The head of the Vaastu Purusha was on the Northeast when he had fallen. The Southeast portion of the house is very good for the kitchen. Given here are some opinions on kitchen expressed in Vaastu Tests :-

***Brihat Samhita:*** says the Agni paada Southeast, Parjanya Northeast and Jayanta cell, Indra cell are good cells for the best use of kitchen and allied functions.

***Maayamatam:*** Cells of Indra, Adhitya, Sathyaka, Brusha, and Argala are best suited for kitchen work. The text Maayamatam recommends that the area of kitchen is situated around East or Southeast portions of the house.

***Manushyaalaya Chandrika:*** Southeast Agni, Northeast Eshana and Northwest Vaayu corner are good for kitchen placement. Any pooja or ritual homa functions are to be performed in the eshana portion; it suggests to use the paishacha paada in Agni corner Southeast for kitchen purposes.

The common tendency found in the business people is to construct any house, villa or flat, with the kitchen at any point wherever free space is available on Nairuti, Agni, Eshana or Vaayu corners. The inmates will experience bad/ good effects according to the place of the kitchen. The Southwest kitchen placement will result badly at a later stage. The other corner areas will result in a slow work process and ending to a deformity and loss.

An important point to be observed is that no kitchen should be placed at the centre of the houses, the Brahma naabhi will be activated to bad results to all family members from the day occupied. The kitchen platform should be placed at eastern side if the kitchen is provisioned at SE or NE. The Southwest kitchens are not advisable as one cannot stand facing either East or West and North sides while preparing food.

For example, at NW side kitchen platform, the cook faces West and at SE or NE side kitchen platform the cook faces towards East side. In NW or NE kitchen, sometimes platforms arranged at North side will force the cook to face towards North. The facing towards the East while preparing food is always good and preferable.

The same is expressed in all Vaastu books and confirmed from one's own experience after having a feedback.

• **Toilets And Latrines**: In olden days toilets or latrines are kept away from the main house. Nowadays, it becomes a fashion to keep it 'attached'. That has created a serious problem to the inmates. Even now, it is not good to keep toilets inside the main house. But nobody is interested in going outside for its use, perhaps due to privacy, proximity and safety reasons.

One has to remember the Vaastu purusha's position when he fell to the earth: his head at eshana, legs at nairuti, elbows at agni or vaayu corner, hands at East and North, thigh at West and South and stomach at Brahmasthan i.e. Brahma naabhi.

Hence latrines or toilets are not permitted in the following zones of the house.

***Northeast:*** If someone places latrine or toilets at the Northeast region, the following bad effects will appear:

a) Vein pain, blood clotted pain, blood circulation disorder. Fluid of the body becomes anti septic. First, such symptoms will appear in ladies, then children, subsequently in male members of the family within a short span of three years.

b) Even after rectification, minimum one year is required to coup up from its bad effects and three years or more up to six years to normalcy. Latrines or toilets are not permissible at SOUTH WEST and NORTH EAST corners.

***Southwest:*** In the Southwest corner, it is also not permitted to have latrines or toilets at the kanni moola. In Such cases, the latrines and toilets should be removed from the Southwest corners. The Southwest latrines and toilets will give troubles to all the male members starting from head of the family. They may turn dullards over a period of six years. If no rectification or removal of latrines is done, the male members will become inactive or face death. In other words, after the correct rectification and removal of latrine or toilets from the Southwest region corner, a minimum of three years will be taken to get back to normalcy. In the meantime, the lost life cannot be retrieved and it should be therefore remembered not to construct Southwest corner latrines or toilets. Avoid Karna sutra lines running between the Northeast to Southwest corners for any constructions.

The marriage of the children will not take place in the proper time by creating a complete blockade or stoppage for marriage. Inordinate delay or even no consummation of the marriage is also possible.

• **Bathrooms**: Bathrooms are permissible in all directions or in any of the direction North, East, West or South and corners SW, SE, NE or NW. However, no restriction is attached in keeping the bathrooms in parts of the house but no permission is granted to provide the same in the Brahma naabhi or centre part of the house.

Latrines are permitted at the Southeast or Northwest regions or any other in between places of directions but not Southwest or Northeast corners.

• **Staircase (Sopanam):** Staircases are made normally in clock-wise directions. The architectural designs of various kinds are used for structural beauty. The modern trend is to make the staircase more attractive and elegant. Various kinds of staircases constructed are worth mentioning. This will differ in buildings, residences and its usuage. Some staircase has different straight steps in a line or diverted lines. Some stairs have folded type or round steps in spiral directions. There are four models of sopanams available in Vaastu shastra books:

1. Three Khanda
2. Sanka Mandaka
3. Vallimandaka
4. Artha Gomuthra

These Sopanams are made in square, rectangular, circular, geometrical and spiral types; their models are available. The staircases are allowed to be made in all directions especially Southwest, Northwest, Southeast, West and South sides. No Sopanam or staircase may be made at Northeast of the house.

The Northeast staircase will affect the children's mental health badly especially starting from the first born. Children's wisdom or intelligence will not develop to that of the age group. The mental balance of the inmates and associates will get disturbed and they will confront with many problems. This phenomenon is observed in several popular cases

• **Master Bedroom:** The house owner and his spouse should use the Master Bed-room located at the Southwest room. The other bed-rooms have to be different from the master bedroom.

• **Pooja Room:** Pooja room is a room earmarked for the spiritual needs of the inmates, arranged as per their tradition and culture. The middle portion or brahmastan and the Southwest section of the house should be used as pooja room. For convenience, sides of West, Southwest, South, North or Northeast locations are allowable for pooja space or room. Some people prefer to have kanni moola Southwest corner for prayer. Temple like structure made for pooja should be provided at convenient locations as specified any where inside the house but under no circumstance it should be kept under the staircase or beams or pillars.

• **Work Area:** The work area should be separate from the kitchen and kept at least one meter away from the main house or kitchen. The work area requires separate construction partition, passage and distance for progress and ingenuity. This separate work area will solve the problems of sutra vedha obstructions and difficulties.

• **Measurements Of Rooms:** While measuring the length and width of the house rooms, it is better to keep the length of the rooms in even or double numbers.

For Example: Feet-wise measurements are 6, 8, 11, 13,15,17,19, 22, 24, 26, 31 etc. so that no odd number or zero number is permitted.

• **Vaastu Rules for Room Length:** The Vaastu Shastra has prescribed some rules regarding room length which bestows good and beneficial aspects to the inmates. This rule should be applied at the time of drawing a house plan for the approval of the authorities, for achieving the best and royal life. This applicability is not only to residential houses but also to all industries, factories, and offices.

The FEET-WISE details are given below:

**Favourable length (in feet)**

| No. of feet | Result |
|---|---|
| 6 | Lucky life |
| 8 | Good luck and success |
| 10 | Plenty of cattle |
| 11 | Good and plenty of milk |
| 16 | Good and promotive |
| 17 | Royal life |
| 20 | Royal and happy life |
| 21 | Plenty of cattle |
| 22 | Happy life |
| 26 | Good royal life |

**Unfavourable length (in feet)**

| No. of feet | Result |
|---|---|
| 7 | Bad result and poverty |
| 9 | Misery and unhappy |
| 12 | Loss and heart burn |
| 13 | Bad and wavering |
| 14 | Bad, enemies predominance |
| 15 | Bad, obstacle at every step |
| 18 | Bad, loss in dealings |
| 19 | Poverty and death |
| 23 | Diseases and sufferings |
| 24 | Ordinary life. |

| | | | |
|---|---|---|---|
| 27 | Wealthy and God's grace | 25 | No God's grace |
| 28 | God's grace | 34 | Bad, vacate soon |
| 29 | Plenty of cattle and wealthy | 40 | Sad, miserable life |
| 30 | Sri Lakshmi's grace | 43 | Evil, unhappy |
| 32 | Grace of Vishnu and Murugan | 44 | Loss of sight |
| 33 | Good favours from all | 46 | Extreme unlucky |
| 35 | Sri Lakshmi's grace | 49 | Poverty and sufferings |
| 36 | Good encouragement | 51 | Loss and get cheated |
| 41 | Royal life | 53 | Wavering, feel insecurity |
| 42 | Sri Lakshmi's grace | 55 | Bad, loss of everything |
| 45 | Gain and profits | 58 | Hurdles, obstructions to life |
| 50 | Good luck favour | 59 | Obstruction in every step |
| 52 | Gain of good friends | 61 | Bad luck and unhappy |
| 54 | Unexpected gain and profit | 62 | Unhappy, angry moments |
| 56 | Peacefull happy life | 63 | illluck, quarrel tendency |
| 57 | Very Good life | 64 | Disturbed mind and bad luck |
| 60 | Good favour from all | 65 | Failure and mental tension |
| 67 | Unexpected luck | 68 | Difficulties and obstruction |
| 71 | Royal-Raja life | 69 | All difficulties clubbed |
| 72 | Good royal life | 70 | Scarcity of food and luck |
| 73 -75 | Good Raja life | 76 | Miserable life, tension |
| 77, 79 | Very good life | 81 | Poverty and miserable life |
| 84 | Sri Lakshmi's grace | 82 | Bad life, deplorable stage |
| 88-90 | Life happy and peaceful | 83 | Very unhappy life |
| 92-93 | Happy and peaceful life | 91 | Bad effects and obstruction |
| 94 | Foreign travel | | |
| 95-96 | Happy home life | | |
| 97 | Become Minister | | |
| 98-99 | Raja position lucky travel | | |
| 100 | Raja Position | | |

• **Chimney:** It is usual to keep the smoke-emitting chimneys to the Northeast side of the house where no such construction is allowed. In other sides, it is of course, permitted because the head of the Vaastu purusha is positioned in that Northeast corner. Chimney's erection with emission coverage should be at Northwest region of vaayu kon. Agni corner also can be used as the best location suited for the purpose.

• **Cow Shed And Kennel:** During the consultation, a number of questions about shelters arise for keeping cows, goats, dogs or birds, bison etc. Buffalo are safe to be kept at gandharva or brunga paada. Cow shed is made in the area visible to house members. Kennels should be near the gate.

Cow shed is not allowed in Agni paadas and it can be in the eastern or northern paadas convenient to the cowmen. And the goat shed aalayam (house) is best at the Northwest side which is also good for storing fire wood. In other words, the sides of South, West, Northwest, or East are suited to keep cow, dog and sheep.

For birds, any direction side will be allowed since the cage does not touch the earth other than pillars or poles. Birds fly free and eat when given food grains.

However, the kanni moola corner Southwest should not be used as dog, cow, goat sheds as the area is under the seizure of Raahu (Sarpa).

• **Oxen/Bison Sheds:** Animals like Oxen and Bison have a separate area for happy living in the South side cells of No. 13 Yama, 14 Gandharva, 15 Brunga, a space in between South and Southwest corner. Some communities prefer to keep these animals at the eastern side.

• **Toilet Bowl (Commode):** No toilet bowl or commode should face East or South. The person using the same should not sit facing East side Sun, the provider of all happiness and prosperity. Nor should the person sit facing South side inviting Yama Raja's angers. These are applicable only when the latrines or toilets are constructed inside the main house as attached or otherwise. However, separate latrines or toilets made outside have no such problem.

• **Car Shed:** Car shed or garage for parking cars or other vehicles will be allowed in all sides and directions according to the convenience of the gate and main door. If the master bedroom is located at Southwest portion of the house, it is better to avoid such a side to be free from unwanted disturbances and sounds. Follow the rules of Vaastu main entrance gate and main door for the purpose.

## Outside Premises

Beautification of outside premises demands intelligence, care and nursing. Variety of plants, trees, shrubs, grass etc. should be grown in the surrounding areas to make the whole place beautiful and heart warming.

• **Landscaping:** Landscaping and greenery styled green grass are required to make the house vicinity beautiful and peaceful. Sometimes it become necessary to spread coloured stones or tiles with green grass in between them. Proper watering and caringare important to mainsuch grass field.

• **Gardening:** The house premises should be artistically designed with flowery and leafy plants and lush lawns. Pots of different sizes and colours with plants of attractive flowers, if arranged in order and at different levels, will be a pleasing sight.

• **Fountains:** Fountains with colourful light arrangement will add to the beauty of the garden. The water fountain can be used for watering the lawn and the plants. While arranging the landscaping process, necessary pipes are provided to keep fountains or streamlet at different locations. Provide perforated water pipes laid in the house premises for enabling timely watering. The fountains should provide a spectacular sight.

• **Plants & Shrubs:** Rose or jasmine and other variety of plants or shrubs of high yielding flowers, trees of small kinds, etc. can be artistically arranged inside the garden to attract more attention from visitors or friends.

**5. Colour Flowers:** Flower of different colours and fruits get attention of the visitors. For the beautification, such types of plants are to be grown in whatever space available in the premises. Attractive varieties of colour flower combination are always good.

• **Bridge over Channel:** A small bridge over the streamlet looks beautiful and attracts children to play over it. The people of all groups and tastes will appreciate it.

• **Railway tracks:** Along the garden borders in a round shape a track for the toy train can be laid to inculcate enthusiasm and vigourness in viewers' mind. It may promote greater ideas in children and youth.

• **Colour Pots:** Plants with flowers of various colours and sizes should be grown in pots painted in choice colours. Well arranged pots with colourful flowers will win the appreciation and attention.

• **Variety Plants:** The variety of plants with leaves and flowers of different shapes and colours will add the charm and beauty of the building.

• **Elevated Hill Mounts:** Hillocks and slopes artistically designed will beautify the garden and will provide a feeling of being in the nature.

• **Umbrella Tent:** Grass or Straw-thatched tent of round umbrella as a small sit-out will give a soothing feeling of living among the world of plants. The umbrella is a coloured straw-thatched shed where inmates can rest and relax in the proximity of their house.

• **Birds Collections:** A good cage sufficiently big and airy for the birds to live comfortably will be a source of enjoyment for the bird lovers. Love birds are a preferred lot. Watching and feeding the birds will provide great happiness and peaceful moments.

• **Dog Preference:** Kennels are not advisable if they are narrow and kept in a congested place. Dogs should have some space to run around when let out. Very big and ferocious dogs are not welcome if there is space limitation.

The tastes, needs and imagination will vary from one resident to another. Blind imitation of others will not help much. The design of the garden and choice of plants and birds should suit to the aesthetic sense and the financial capability of the inmates. The arrangement and beautification of the premises will reveal the personality and prosperity of the residents.

## Interior Decorations

Good interior decorations can make the life of the inmates at ease and peace. The happiness of being in one's own house should not be destroyed with costly but gaudy and sophisticated decorations. Rooms are to be designed according to the norms of Vaastu the style one likes and can afford.

1. Frontage, design carvings at entrance side wood paneling and at the top structural and sculptures designs of ancient or modern combined
2. Setting of sit out room
3. Designing of living room
4. Arrangement of dining room
5. Designing of drawing room
6. Bed room arrangement
7. Hall space setting arrangement ,designs
8. Kitchen, Platform, shelves, wash and zink
9. Bath rooms, latrine, toilets, wash basin

Personal choice and the designs play an important role while choosing materials for the following:-

Curtains
Lightings
Switches
Decorative
Tables
Chairs
Wardrobes
Shelves
Alamirahs

The actual users mind should not be in the following work:-

Painting work
Paneling
False ceilings
Carvings
Wood designs
Architectural designs

Various types of house utensils now in use function on solar power or electric energy.

Planning and execution are also important in modern living style.

卐

# Bhaagam 9

## The Scientific Concept of Vaastu Shastra

The Vaastu Science has proved beyond doubt its existence and credence on scientific footings. The acceptance of the Scientific Vaastu gained momentum when the rules are applied in all selected cases. The results of the application of Vaastu Principles are amazing. Certain yardsticks are applied specifically to prove the scientific origin of the Vaastu with the following approved concepts and various rules:-

- **Square and Rectangular shape:** The use of only square or rectangular shape of the land is accepted in Vaastu Parameter. No other size or shape of the land is approved. Even Diagonal shape of the land is considered to be very dangerous which needs rectification before use. To make the form of land like square or rectangular, it is imperative to have a rectification, leaving the non directional land as separate for gardening or plantation.

- **Law of Gravitation:** Sir Isaac Newton formulated Theories of Action and Reaction. That is the pull and push behavior of the nature. The Law of Earth's Gravitational force was brought to human light scientifically. Today, 'The Law of Motion' is approved and accepted by the modern community. The Vaastu Shastra deals with the unforeseen power of nature when the primary elements-Water, Air, Fire, Earth and Space clubbed together in combination. The combination of Law of actions and reactions is the basis of Vaastu Science.

The Earth factor has the gravitational power to pull down to earth any substance in solid form whether it is an apple or a mango from the trees. Why can't the other factors of Panchbhuta Elements have power to act like a magic work, especially when clubbed together?

The factor 'earth' is empowered to show its capability of 'the gravitational pull power' scientifically, which is proved and accepted by the world. The power of wind, the energy of Space, the gravity of Fire and efficiency of Water are not tested for its efficacy in combination.

- **Temple and Circular Design:** Every object in nature radiates energy in some form or other which is said to be amenable to Kirlian photography. The name of the Temple and Circular worship places, the abode of gods and goddesses, was known as Devalayam, Ambalam, Kshetram, Deva Bhavanam, Kovil, Mandhir, Pooja gruh, Prasadam etc. The Manasaara gave complete details of models of temple plan, construction of Vairaja (Square plan), Pushpaka (Rectangular Plan), Kailas (Circular plan), Manika (Elluptian Plan) and Trivishtaya (Octongular plan).

The land in rectangular or square is suitable to human beings or Manushyaalams. The Circular forms are not suitable to Manushyaalams or residential homes. Why are then circular forms unsuitable to human residences? This point is scientific.

• **The Theory of Magnetism & Vaastu Science:** 'Keep Head towards South' is the slogan of Vaastu Shastra while in rest or sleep. The approach of Vaastu and Magnetism principles and applications co-ordinate or co-operate very much with each other. The relation between Theory of Magnetism and Vaastu Science is established as magnetic Vaastu field.

A certain type of stones called magnetite ($Fe_3O_4$) has the property of attracting pieces of iron content. Such iron content bodies are called magnets. These are concentrated near the end point of South or North poles. These particles of magnets, collected together in a particular line at pole end have the power of great attraction. It has been noticed the opposite poles attract and the same poles repel. Magnetic field is the area round a magnet where a magnetic force is exerted.

The Molecular Theory of Magnetism formulated in principle by Mr. Weber, is effective when a person sleeps in North-South direction. The human body can be magnetized only when one lies in North-South position. It makes a lot of changes in the body by magnetic effect.

The application of magnetic theory has direct link with Vaastu shastra. The state of an unmagnetized and a magnetized view of a single iron rod are given below:-

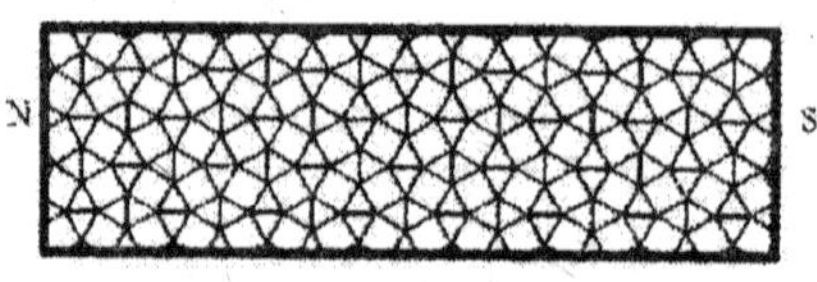

unmagnetized state

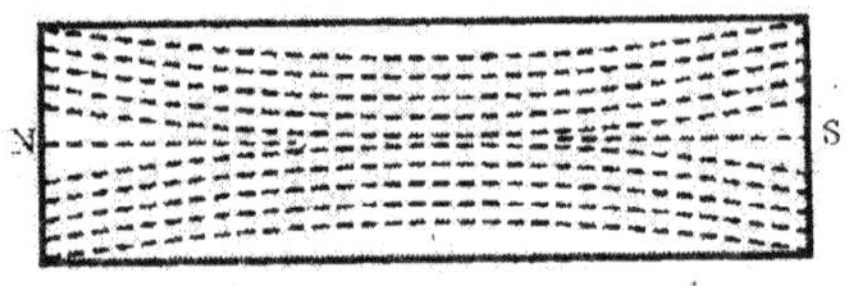

magnetized state

According to sages' belief, one can attain nirvana or sickness or death by sleeping in North-South direction with head at North. And at the same time one can acquire strength, enjoy perfect health and longevity of life by sleeping with head southwards. So the magnetic forces work at South Head direction favourably by maintaining the body calm, quiet with normal blood circulation and natural polarity. The tension and fatigue is automatically diminished. It tends to gain a momentum of vitality and strength in the body.

That may be the reason why almost all hospital beds are arranged in such a way that the patient can rest in bed keeping the head towards South. Sometimes alternatively, the patient's head is kept towards East direction. The Eastward head keeping has also the advantage of the excellent functioning of the brain and body.

The working of Vaastu Shastra and the application of Theory of Magnetism largely depend on the geographical meridians at a place where the earth's pole axis is in rotation. The magnetic elements of the earth are (1) Dip or Inclination (2) Declination (3) Horizontal intensity varying from place to place on the surface of the earth.

***Dip or Inclination:*** The intensity of earth's magnetic field is a Vector; at a place it is usually inclined to the horizontal. The angle between the total intensity of the earth magnetic field and the horizontal at a place is called the angle of Dip or Inclination at that place.

***Declination:*** The angle between the geographic and magnetic meridians at a place is called the Declination at the place.

***Earth's Magnetic Field:*** The Earth's total magnetic field 'I' in the horizontal direction at a place is called the horizontal component of the earth's induction field = B H

And vertical component is B v

$$\text{i.e.} \qquad I=\sqrt{(BH^2+BV^2)}$$

In other words, the earth behaves like a large magnet. The entire field is known as the earth's magnetic field. The power of such big magnetic earth is beyond the thinking of the human being. This is represented by :

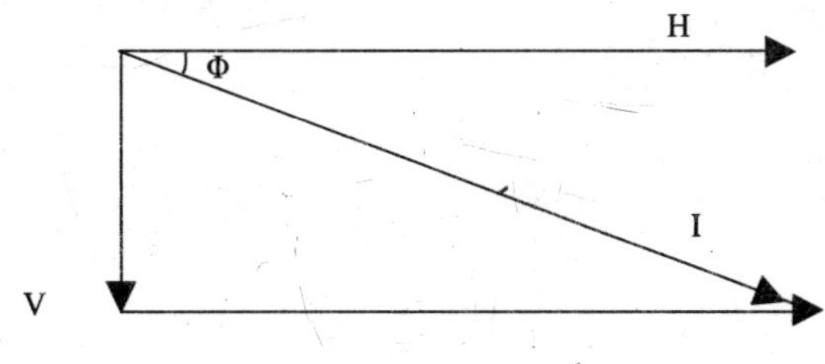

I = Magnetic field

$\Phi$ = Meridians

V = Vertical Component

H = I Cos meridian

V = I Sin meridian

$$I = \sqrt{(H^2+V^2)}$$

According to the position of the earth and its magnetic action, the combination or fusion line of process with solar rays, air power etc. is not uniform or similar. Likewise, the normal rotation of earth and its magnetic attraction or repulsion also deviate the power factor. But it differs in anti-clockwise direction and in cross sections everything will change with regard to rate and flux density. The magnetic attraction of earth's field is one of the real sources of Vaastu Shastra application.

• **Pyramids and Vaastu Shastra:** The Principle of Pyramids and Vaastu Science has a natural relationship in their hidden rules. The miraculous efficiency and capability is well established by the Egyptians in keeping human bodies under preservation for years together. The magnetic therapy of treatment for curing several diseases is famous. The Pyramidal structures are very useful for preservation of food items and for sharpening razor blades.

It has been the practice of constructing houses on semi-pyramidal style in India in general and South India in particular. It is visible even today in rural areas with houses thatched with palm leaves or straw, sand tiles etc. This kind of houses will provide a natural calm and comfortable living in rural areas. It becomes a fashion to make temples or prayer centres in semi pyramidal form. No one might have noticed such common phenomena as it continues from generations. Vaastu and Pyramidal principles prefer such houses and strongly recommend them for a good living.

The Egyptians probably considered it for the king's burial chamber. They blocked and concealed the entrance to the inner most part of the pyramid. The well known Egyptian Pyramid at Saggarsh has six series of giant steps and it preserves the mummy of King Zozer about 2650 BC. The dead bodies of Kings Khuful, Khafre and Kenkaure were preserved at Ciza in three large well preserved pyramids during 2600 to 2500 BC. It is proved beyond doubt that dead bodies in pyramids in Egypt were preserved around 5000 years ago.

***The Principle of Pyramids:*** The regular pyramid is like a polygon with four equal sides and angles. The vertex of a regular pyramid meets the base and its centre. The volume formula is as follows:-

V=1/3 BH (B-area, H-height of the pyramid)

L=1/2 PS (P-Perimeter slant height)

The Science of Vaastu is to be tested in human mind and laboratories to find out whether the Divine power emitting from the elements of nature is real or imaginary.

- **Practical Application Of Vaastu**: The Theoretical Rules of Vaastu Science are well known to most of the people. But its practical approach and actual practice are sometimes difficult to mention. There is nothing impossible in Vaastu Science to make it user friendly and helpful to lead a comfortable and happy life. The main Vaastu norms have their full value if they are transformed in the practical way. The divine product has to be utilized in a proper and useful manner to derive the best optimum benefit. Addition of this practical application of Vaastu Science is very useful for all purposes and occasions.

Some important aspects are given below based on the practical knowledge gained all these years of Vaastu consultancy:-

***Compass:*** An orientation specified Compass is good to check out the directions of the land in one's purview:

**a) <u>Diagonal:</u>** The land should not be in the shape of diagonal. If the land is in diagonal no construction is undertaken on it. The land owner has to face great misery if a land and a house are placed under diagonal dimension. This diagonal measurement selected for house direction will automatically affect the head of family and all others in matters of fear, troubles in service, education, promotion, and relation with colleague and delay of marriage or engagement.

For Example:

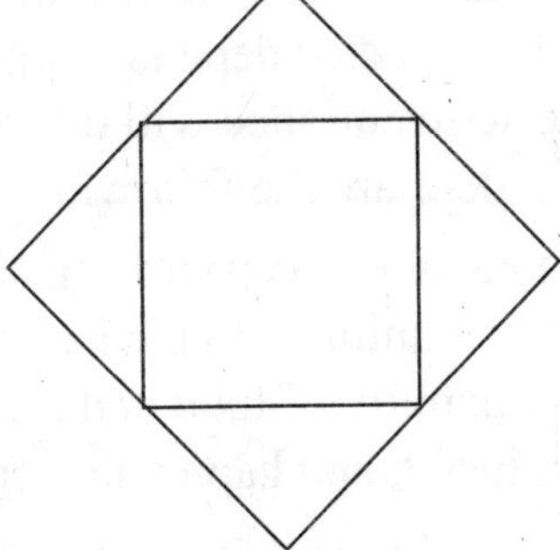

**Centre square is drawn from diagonal land for use after rectification.**

**b) Angles:** All the Corners of the land should maintain an angle of 90 degree and the angle of Northeast corner must be always below 90 degree.

**c) Rectification:** Rectification of the size of land is essential before a construction venture commences. The shape of the land should be converted to Square or rectangular form by maximum possible utilization of the area. The rectification has to be done under available land coverage by making an inner base line partitioned or with cemented foundation. The Inner land size should be like a

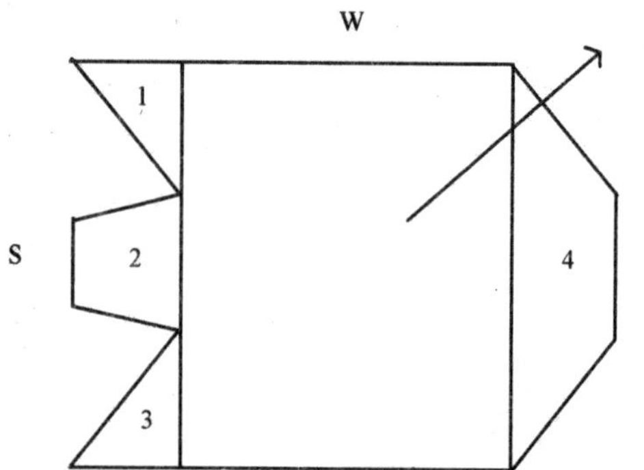


Rectified rectangular plot for use
Other positions separate with earth partitioned divider

**d) Road Face:** In any side-facing road, Northeast projection is good. A cut in any corner land is not at all good. It may cause accident or even death especially in Southwest or Northeast. It is better to avoid land if rectification is not possible to make to a square or rectangle. An addition of a purchase of land to the existing land definitely deviates from the present marma set up. Its results will be on the basis of present land extended criteria.

**e) Roads:**

**Having Road on one side:** If the land has the road only on one side the following results may be expected depending upon the side of North, South, West or East. The side-wise entrance will derive the merits to the road, the main gate and the main door are the following:-

North: Virtue in actions, respect from all.
East: Royal life admirable to the native.
South: Easy availability of food and fruits.
West: Wealth, health and happy atmosphere.

**Having Road on two sides:** If the land has road on two sides the best benefit diminishes from first double road combination and to the part in order.

East and North road
North and South road
South and East road
West and North road

**Having Road on three sides:** Roads on three sides are good. But construction of a house with East side open only is permissible like Sukshetram. Consultation and khanda determination is very important in the case of three sides road.

**Having Road on all four sides:** If there are roads on all the four sides, house construction is to be very sensitive and it involves much calculation since the land is surrounded by full open roads.

**Compound Wall:** It is better to have a compound wall around the total land area. The construction work should start from Southwest kanni moola or nairuti and extend to West or South. No common compound wall is permitted for two houses. However a single compound is permitted as joint colony boundary for more than three residences.

But Gupta Vaastu mentions that when constructing schools and teaching institutions, the walls in the East and North must be constructed first. The Southwest walls construction is made only after the completion of East and North walls. And no common wall for two buildings is permitted.

• **Colony Layout:** In the specimen of Colony Layout, it is advisable to keep the size of the each plot of land either in Square or Rectangular form.

The plots numbers 33, 22, 21, 10 and 4 are very good due to Northeast projections. Projections on Northwest are not good. Though plot number 28, 16 and 15 are in this category, they can be used after rectification. Plot number 27 is projected on Southwest side; it is not advisable to use it. If one purchased this plot due to reasons beyond control, the plot has to be rectified before its use. The Southeast plots 8, 7, 3, 2 and 1 are also to be rectified before construction. No rectification is done in Southeast or Southwest plots; it proved fatal and prone to accidents. Triangle plot number 9 is not at all recommended for a house. However, such lands are very useful for making Libraries, Temples, Churches or mosques.

Nowadays, Housing Colony is coming up in a large scale usually at the outskirts of all developing cities and towns. The Colony as a group will provide mutual help and finance for development of plot by leveling, plotting, keeping border stones, laying roads of inner passage, provision of electricity, water, bore-well, overhead tank, and other amenities or infrastructure that are required for the members.

Thereareanumberofsmall,medium and large scale land developers sprung up for construction of villas, houses, flats, commercial complexes, multistoried flats. The Construction Companies are as such engaged in a lucrative business and the Government of India has already declared construction as an infrastructure industry like hotel.

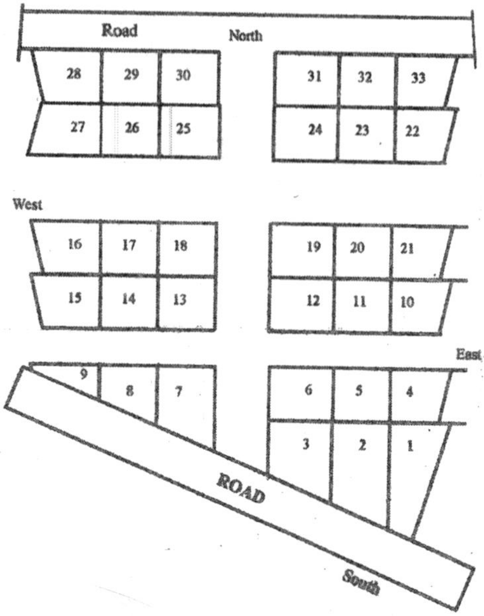


A Specimen Colony Layout is given below:-

## Conclusion

Vaastu Shastra rule will never change. Change has to come to one's stubborn attitude. The observance will bring a change to the level of stability, prosperity and permanent happiness.

The following are the main commands of Vaastu to be observed with care for enjoying the effectiveness and the fruits of Vaastu norms.

Ten commandments of Vaastu Shastra for excellent life are:

1. Select a land plot of rectangular or square shape, divide the plot into nine small part cells each, road direction-wise make a gateway at compound wall straight to enter to the main door. The main gate position will be fixed at any point of sides, the sixth cells from South corner Indra paada no.4, from Northeast Bhallada paada no. 28, from Northwest Pushpadinanda paada 20 and from Southwest Gruhaskshata paada no.12.

2. A good house plan drawn with much thought put into it, is needed to decide the perimeter of the house in running meters. The sum total of 2 lengths and 2 widths will make the measurement of basement perimeter as per Table 4. This decision is very prudent in selecting the excellent Uthama position of the house with Perimeter measurement with nakshatra, yoni, ayam, vyayam, and age. U is uthama, M is medium, and A is adhama.

3. The gap provision between four sides of the house and compound wall should keep measure one ninth (1/9) of the minimum space. More space is good especially at eastern or northern sides. This will enhance contact with people, reciprocal appreciations and mutual help.
4. During construction stage, care should be taken in providing more free space in the ground basement, in all rooms, in living and halls. The main doors, windows or ventilators are provided as per Vaastu marma.
5. Well, bore well or storage points should be made at the Northeast corner without intercepting the karna sutram lines. If one requires only storage of water, it is better to store the water only at Apan and Apatvalsa paadas.
6. Trees rule has to be followed while planting the trees in the residence compound. No lemon plant is grown inside the premises as it involves ladies naasham (or destruction) when the fruit is grown.
7. Kitchen is to be located at Southeast Agni corner where ladies are safe and healthy with East side platform for operator's East-face working. The side of the Kitchen should not be bigger than that of the master bedroom of the house. Work area provision is made separately.
8. No garage or car shed is constructed at the Northeast side by touching both sides of North or East walls. It will affect very adversely, by stoppage of incoming revenues. Serious accidents and diseases, heavy expenditure or danger to kith and kins will be the aftermath.
9. Special care has to be taken while fixing front main door and constructions pillars, walls, or other hindrances like veethi shoolas or any obstructions that jet into the main gateways and the main door.
10. Rooms should be spacious enough and well ventilated not only for fresh air but also for an atmosphere of liveliness.

Vaastu Miracle will definitely occur if one follows it.

# Table I

**Births & Deaths Perimeters**

**Births**

Good Perimeter Measurement as Birth

| Hasta/Angulam | In meters |
|---|---|
| 3-9 | 2.43 |
| 20-6 | 14.58 |
| 37-3 | 26.73 |
| 54-0 | 38.88 |
| 70-21 | 51.03 |
| 87-18 | 63.18 |
| 1o4-15 | 75.33 |
| 121-12 | 87.48 |

**Deaths**

Very Bad Perimeter Measurement as Death

| | |
|---|---|
| 16-21 | 12.15 |
| 33-18 | 24.30 |
| 50-15 | 36.45 |
| 67-12 | 48.60 |
| 84-19 | 61.05 |
| 101.6 | 72.90 |
| 118-3 | 85.05 |
| 135-0 | 97.20 |

# Table II

## Trees To Birth Star Combinations

| | | | | |
|---|---|---|---|---|
| 1. | Aswani | Kanjiram | Karaskaram | Strychnos nux-vomica |
| 2. | Bharani | Nelli/Amalaki | Goose berry | Phyllanthus emblica |
| 3. | Kirthika | Athi/Udumbara | Indian Fig | Ficus racemosa |
| 4. | Rohini | Jawal | perimodi | Synzygium cumini |
| 5. | Mrigasira | Karinjali | Khadira | Accia Catechu |
| 6. | Aridra | Karimaram | Black Tree | Diopyrosebenum |
| 7. | Purnarvasu Mula | Venu Bamboo | Bambus Valgaris | |
| 8. | Pushyami | Arayal | Aswattha | Ficus religiosa |
| 9. | Aslesha | Naaga maram | Naaga | Mesua ferrea |
| 10. | Maka | peral | Banyan | Ficus bengalensis |
| 11. | Pubba | Plasu | palasa | Butea frondosa |
| 12. | Uthara | Ethi | Plaska | Ficus microcarpa |
| 13. | Hasta | Ambazham | Ambara tree | Spondias pinnata |
| 14. | Citra | Koovalam | Bilwa | Aegle marmelos |
| 15. | Swathi | Nirmaruthu | Nirmarut tree | terminalia arjuna |
| 16. | Vishakha | Vaiyan kadavu | Kantakidruma | flacourtia jangomes |
| 17. | Anuradha | Elangi | Bhakula | Mimusops elengi |
| 18. | Jyeshta | Vetti | Kadumba | Aporusa lyndiana |
| 19. | Moola | Kundirikam | Vayanam | Canarium strictum |
| 20. | Purvashada | Vanji | Shanei | Salix tetrasperma |
| 21. | Utharashada | panasa | Jack fruit | Arto carpus integrilia |
| 22. | Sravana | Eruku | Kinsuka | Calotropis gigantia |
| 23. | Dhanishta | Muringa | Vagni/siguru | Moringa oleifera |
| 24. | Satabhisha | Kadambu | Abhayamavi | Anthecephalus chinesis |
| 25. | Purvabhadra | Mavu | Mango/Chuta | Magnifera Indica |
| 26. | Utharabhadra | Karinpana | Black palm | Borassus flabellifer |
| 27. | Revati | Erippa | Attilippa | Madduka inerifolia |

## Table III

### Glossary

Read pada as Paada and Vaastu as Vaastu

| | |
|---|---|
| Aarudam | Pivotal control starting point |
| Adhishtana | Basement under the ground & above |
| Adhiti | Pada Vaastu cell no.31 |
| Aditya | Sun, Pada Vaastu cell 5 |
| Advaitham | One God as per Adhi Shankaracharya siddhanth |
| Agama | Mode of worship, Idolor Shikhi, Shivaites or Vaishnavaits |
| Agni | God of Fire, cell no.9 |
| Akash | Sky entire atmosphere, open space |
| Alindah | Varandah, Corridor or passage |
| Amsam | fraction, division or part there of |
| Angulam | Ancient measurement one hasta/kolu equals to 24 angulam |
| Anganam | In front of house courtyard |
| Andarakshan | Pada Vaastu deity No. 8 |
| Anizham | Anuradha star of Zodiac belt star 17th |
| Apan | Inner pada deity cell no.33 |
| Apatvalsan | Inner pada deity cell no.34 |
| Ashta Dhik | Eight cardinal directions including 4 sides & 4 corners |
| Aswathi | Aswani, the 1st star of zodiac belt |
| Aridra | Thiruvathira the sixth star of zodiac belt |
| Aryaka | Inner pada deity cell no.35 |
| Arudotharam | Extra support for rafter between wall plate & ridge |
| Ayilyam | Aslesha star of zodiac belt no.9th |
| Ardha | Meaningfull or valuable |
| Ashram | Hermitage for a diciplined life of spiritual style |
| Asura | Pada Vaastu deity cell no.22 |
| Atman | The soul of each individual |
| Avanta | The ground leveling instrument for gnomon shanku |
| Avathara | Incarnation or manifestation of God |
| Ayam | Something accrued, income, benefit |
| Ayama | The building front elongation |
| Bhakhti | Devotion, the marga, path |
| Bhakhta | Devotee or spiritual person or pius |
| Bhalladan | Pada Vaastu deity cell no.28 |

| Bharani | Star of zodiac belt no. 2 |
|---|---|
| Bhoga | Sexual enjoyment or pleasure |
| Bhinna | Separately, partitioned or allocated |
| Bhoomi | One among the pacha bhootas of nature- Earth |
| Bhrusa | Pada Vaastu deity cell no.7 |
| Bindu | Nabhi or point of mandala grid |
| Brahma | The trinity creator, the God of Para Brahma |
| Brahmin | In varna division a super being Brahmin |
| Brahmashtan | Middle of the pada Vaastu control deity cell no.45 |
| Brahma nabhi | Middle of the mandala vinyasa pada |
| Brahmasutram | The line East- West axis in marma mandala Vaastu |
| Budha | The planet Mercury, God of wisdom & Knowledge |
| Charaki | External outer pada Vaastu deity cell no.50 |
| Chathuram | Equal four sided square |
| Chatu sala | Four direction house as single entity |
| Charana | Pillars or thunu |
| Chithira | Star of zodiac belt of 14th |
| Dandam | Linear measurement |
| Dhanam | Wealth, property, cash or money |
| Dhanalayam | A house of wealth or a bank |
| Daiva Khandam | One fourth part of land portion Southwest quarter |
| Devalayam | Place of worship or temple for offering prayers |
| Dharma | Righteousness in religion, ethics, Justice or Law |
| Dhanishta | A star of zodiac belt 23 |
| Dhanu | Sagittarius rasi or month |
| Dhanyam | Foodgrains of rice, wheat, corn, barley, bajra |
| Dwajam | Dwaja yoni No.1 yoni for construction |
| Dhik | 4 cardinal directions of sides NEWS |
| Dhinam | Dailly, everyday |
| Dwi | Two or double |
| Dhwitam | Twin houses or two wings of a house |
| Ekasala | One house or single roofed house |
| Eshana | Northeast zone, Manushya khandam |
| Gala | Neck or recess in basement |
| Gamanam | Offset or shift in uttaram |
| Ganitham | Mathematics for calculations |
| Gaja | Elephant or Gaja yoni |

| | |
|---|---|
| Gandharva | Vaastu pada deity cell no. 14 |
| Garba | Womb or temple sanctum santorium |
| Garba Gruha | Temple sanctum santorium |
| Gnomon | Direction to find by shadow of the sun motions by Sanku shtapana |
| Gramam | Village as envisaged in Vaastu |
| Gruham | House or sala or residence |
| Gruhashtan | Pada Vaastu deity no.12 |
| Gunamsam | Fraction of a semi perimeter of a rectangle is divided by Integrers from 9 to 32 widths is 4 parts remaining with length |
| Gunam | Virtue, quality, Character, merit from master, teacher or preceptor |
| Guru | Jupiter planet |
| Harmya | Build big type houses for different activities |
| Hasta | Linear measurement kolu of 24 angulam |
| Hasta | Also known by kolu, muzhakolu, kisku, kista |
| Eshta Dhirga | Selected or desired length or yoni |
| Eshta Devta | Deity of own choice |
| Indra padam | Pada Vaastu deity cell no.4 or Mahendra padam |
| Intriangal | The sensual organs eye, ear nose, skin and tongue |
| Janma | By birth |
| Jayantan | Pada Vaastu deity cell no.3 |
| Jyeshta | 18th star of Triketa in zodiac belt constellation |
| Jyothisha | Astrology or light from reasoning |
| Kalan | Yama Raja, God of death or time |
| Kala | Art ingenuity or skill or talent |
| Kalaham | Quarrel or strife |
| Khara | A mule or khara yoni |
| Karkidak | the month of Cancer or Rasi |
| Karna sutram | A diagonal axis line across SW to NE |
| Khandam | A divided sector or Quarter part or fragmented segment |
| Karma | Deeds, action, work, duty, fate or outlook |
| Kshetram | Segments for plots or portions. |
| Kolam | Art work for deity pooja at house frontage |
| Karthika | 3rd satr of the zodiac belt |
| Kubera | Pada Vaastu veedhi vidhana mandala division |
| Kumbham | Temple top or Aquarius month or raasi |

| | |
|---|---|
| Lingam | A symbolic Idol of Lord Shiva |
| Mana | Illam, house, residence or saala |
| Makara | Month of Capricorn or makara rasi |
| Mandala | Wheel or ring, path of heavenly body |
| Mandapam | Pavillion or open hall |
| Mantra | Sacred prayer, incantation |
| Mangalapalaka | Ornamental plank between wall plate door top |
| Marma vedha | Intersection with vulnerable points |
| Matrangulam | A measurement in angulam |
| Manusyalaya | Residence for human beings |
| Marma | Nerves intersection of lines in grid nodes, key points |
| Medam | A month or rasi of Aries |
| Meenam | A month or rasi of Pisces |
| Mitraka | Inner pada Vaastu deity cell no.41 |
| Moolam | Star of zodiac belt constellation no.19th |
| Mrigasira | A star of zodiac belt constellation no.5th |
| Mriga | Pada mandala Vaastu cell no 16 |
| Mukhya | pada mandala Vaastu cell no. 27 |
| Muzham | basic measurement of hasta, kista or kolu |
| Musthi | Firt or parva a measurement in angulam |
| Mukhti | Soul liberation from birth |
| Naadi | Sira or veins of orthogonal lines in Vaastu mandala |
| Nabhi | Cebtral of naval section |
| Nagara | Town, Rajadhani, pattana, with facilities |
| Nakshatra | Total 27 stars in zodiac belt from Aswani to Revati |
| Naga | Pada Vaastu cell no.26 |
| Narada | A celestial messenger, Divine Sage, son of Brahma Deva |
| Natya | Dance, Nirtha, |
| Nairuthy | Southwest corner pada Vaastu cell no.17 |
| Padam | A module or part grid, cusp |
| Padadevata | Deities of module cells |
| Padadhika | Ratio of length to width with integers adding |
| Padamana | The height between the bottomof wall plate with the top of foundation |
| Padayoni | A rule of proportioning rectangle |
| Padonam | A ratio of length to width integer substracting |
| Paduka | Underground the bottom course of basement |

| Paksha | 15 days Sukla or Krishna paksha waning or waxing of Moon |
|---|---|
| Panchabhuta | 5 Elements of Nature Fire, Water, Earth, Wind or Akash |
| Panchagam | 5 Angams of Astrology, Thithi, Varam, stars, Yogam, & karanams |
| Panchavarnam | 5 Colours green, Red, Blue, Yellow & White |
| Panayola | Palm leaves prepared for scripts writing or treatise |
| Patramana | Horizontal distance outside the wall plate basement offset of plinth |
| Puttanika | Pada mandala of outercell no. 52 |
| Pithruhara | Pada Vaastu deity cell no.17 |
| Peedam | A celebrated seat or grid |
| Pothika | A decorated bracket of pillar |
| Prishta | Back of land |
| Prasada | Temple Palace Buildings |
| Pooja | Worship or offerings |
| Prathima | Image, Statue |
| Punartham | Punarvasu the star of zodiac belt no.7th |
| Purusha | Male or gent |
| Pururutati | Purvabhadra the 25th star of zodiac belt |
| Puradam | Purvashada the 20th star of zodiac belt |
| Pooyam | pushyami the 11th star of zodiac belt |
| Pushpapada | Pada Vaastu deity cell no.20 |
| Ragam | Melody, music sound, tune |
| Rasam | Flavour, taste |
| Radham | Chariot, Royal carriage |
| Rasi | 12 Raasis steller months start from Aries to Pisces |
| Revati | 27th & last star of the zodiac belt |
| Rigvedha | Ancient Hindu Text of prominence |
| Roga | Pada Vaastu deity cell no.24 |
| Rohini | The 4th star of zodiac belt |
| Rudra | Inner Vaastu deity Shiva cell no.42 |
| Rajju | Diagonal mandala cross or rope |
| Sala | Residential rectangular hall with roof |
| Samatatayikam | A rectangular length equal to integral multiple of its width |
| Samhita | A generic compilation of Vaishnava Agamas |
| Sampathi | Benefit of abundance, Success & Prosperity |
| Samvrudhi | Growth and Prosperity |

| Sanadhana | Dharma Hindu Theory of Eternal Value, Value to all |
|---|---|
| Sangeetam | Music & Songs |
| Samskruti | Culture and refinement |
| Shanku | Gnomon, Shanku sthapana or conch sea shell |
| Sandhipalaka | A plank or reaper to conceal the gap of door panels |
| Shilpin | Artists or craftsman |
| Shishta | Combine or conjoined |
| Sthapaka | One who establishes or builds, founder |
| Sathyaka | Pada Vaastu deity cell no.6 |
| Shakhti | Strength or energy |
| Shani | Saturn the God of bad effects or Saturn planet |
| Shilpa | Crafts, Sculpture, creations |
| Shilpa shastra | Texts of Sculture & Archetectural science |
| Shrardham | Offerings of Bali darpan to deceased or expired parents or others |
| Shosha | Pada Vaastu deity cell no.23 |
| Shukran | The Venus planet the Guru of Asuras |
| Siddhi | Attainment or fulfillment |
| Soma | Pada Vaastu deity cell no 29 |
| Sneha | Tenderness or affection |
| Shravana | Tiruvaonam star of 22nd in zodiac belt |
| Shrishti | Creation or act of making, reprocreation |
| Sthoola | Material value grossily |
| Sthoopam | A monument of pillars or kodimaram |
| Shubham | Enjoyment or happiness, happy ending |
| Sugriva | Pada Vaastu deity cell no.19 |
| Swati | Chithi star of 15th in zodiac belt |
| Swastic | Symbol of Prosperity to Hindus |
| Sutram | Thread line or Formula or Theory, technique |
| Sutragrahi | Supervisor or shilpin of measurement and works |
| Thala | The Modular unit of dimension and palm hand |
| Thamo | Guna quality for ignorance |
| Thantra | Mysical rites of religious text of Hinduism |
| Thiru | A term of respect to great, honourable for Thiru |
| Thaliyola | Palm leaves grandhams books |
| Triguna | Three qualities |
| Trimurti | Three Deities: Brahma, Vishnu, Maheswara |

| Thula | Libra month & rasi of equality |
|---|---|
| Tejas | Sparkling energy, Splendour, aura of happiness |
| Trisala | Three Houses combination |
| Upanishad | Jnana Theological texts of Veda |
| Upagruha | Sub Houses like Cow shed, store etc |
| Uthama | The best or excellent |
| Uthara | North direction wall plate |
| Uthrutathi | 26th star of zodiac belt also known by Utharabhadra |
| Vaaram | Weeks Sunday to Saturday |
| Vaastu Devata | Vaastu Deities |
| Veedhanam | Vinyasa classifications |
| Vaastu Purusha | The Presiding Deity of Vaastu Shastra |
| Vaideha | Hasta measurement of 29 angulam 87 cms |
| Vanchanam | Fillet or projection from vertical plane basement, wall roof |
| Vamsam | Lineage, Hereditary to generations |
| Vardhaki | Shilpin engaged in the work of construction of buildings |
| Varnam | Class or groups of Brahmins, Kshertiyas, Vaishyas or Shutras |
| Varnam | Specificied in colours of White, red, yellow or Black |
| Veedhi | Road, ways, path |
| Varunan | Water and Sea God Pada Vaastu deity cell no21 |
| Vayu | Pada Vaastu Deity cell no.25 |
| Vedanta | Ensyclopedia of Veda ie Upanishads |
| Vedas | Text of Hinduism Rig, Yayur, Sama or Adharva Vedas |
| Vithari | Vaastu pada deity cell no. 51 |
| Viman | Aeroplane, Tower Structure erected above sanctum santorium |
| Vishakha | Star 16th of zodiac belt |
| Vishudha | Clear, clean or pure |
| Vithara | Pada Vaastu deity cell no.11 |
| Vidhik | Corner Houses NE, SW, SE, NW or kons |
| Vruksha | Trees |
| Vyama | Measure of tips middle fingers. Hands stretched both ways 8 padas |
| Vruchika | Month of Scorpio & Rasi |
| Vrushabha | Month, Rasi or yoni Edava month or rasi |
| Veeryam | Heroism, prowess, courage, boldness, gallantry |
| Yajamana | Owner who makes the construction |
| Yaana | Vehicle used for travel |

| Yavam | Measurement, grain of barley 1/8 angulam |
|---|---|
| Yama | Dharma Raja, God of execution and pada Vaastu deity cell no.13 |
| Yamaloka | The land of Yama Raja or dead |
| Yantra | Instrument, machine, mystical diagram |
| Yochana | 1000 Rajju or 8000 dhanda measurement |
| Yoga | Meditation, art of keeping in good health |
| Yoni | Womb or orientation of buildings |
| Yugma | Even Number, Double |

# Table IV

## Easy Reckoner

### Perimeter & Yoni Measurement Plans & Designs For Buildings

Perimeter = length x width x 2 = 4 sides total. Hasta (Kolu) = 72 cms, Angulam = 3 cms. Yoni No.1 = Dwaja Yoni, No.3 = Simha yoni, No.5 = Virshabha yoni, No.7 = Gaja yoni. H = Hasta, A = Angulam, C = Childhood, A = Adolescent, Y = Youth, O = Old Age, D = Death. Remarks: U = Uthama (Good), M = Medium, A = Bad (Adhama).

### How to make use of Perimeter Chart

At any construction or alteration point of residential or other building, the foundation based perimeter has to be ascertained as per Perimeter Chart given below. The calculation of perimeter will involve by adding the sum total of two lengths and two widths measurement in running meters. This will cover fully the paduka or foundation measurement in total around house foundation.

Take an excellent position of uthama with age youth per perimeter chart. For example perimeter is decided with 68.88 meters with length 18 meters one side and width 16.44 meters totaling around foundation will be 68.88 meters. This example will hold good for Uthama with age youth, ayam, vyayam, sapta yoni and in hasta measurement of 95-16 Kolu. This perimeter measurement lands you in happiness, peace and prosperity.

| Perimeter H-A | Yoni No. | Aya H-A | Vyaya No. | Age in metres | Perimeter G:M:B: | Star name | Remarks |
|---|---|---|---|---|---|---|---|
| 3-0 | 1 | 12-0 | 9 | - | 2-16 | Satabisa | M |
| 3-16 | 3 | 5-8 | 11 | C | 2-64 | Krithika | A |
| 4-08 | 5 | 10-16 | 5 | C | 3-12 | Pushyami | M |
| 5-00 | 7 | 4-0 | 1 | C | 3-60 | Hasta | U |
| 5-16 | 1 | 9-8 | 3 | C | 4-08 | Moola | U |
| 6-08 | 3 | 2-16 | 5 | C | 4-56 | Satabisa | A |
| 7-00 | 5 | 8-0 | 7 | A | 5-04 | Bharani | M |
| 7-16 | 7 | 1-8 | 9 | A | 5-52 | Pushyami | A |
| 8-08 | 1 | 6-16 | 11 | A | 6-00 | Hasta | U |
| 9-00 | 3 | 12-0 | 13 | A | 6-48 | Jyeshta | M |
| 9-16 | 5 | 5-8 | 1 | A | 6-96 | Satabisa | U |
| 10-8 | 7 | 10-16 | 3 | Y | 7-44 | Bharani | M |
| 11.0 | 1 | 4-0 | 5 | Y | 7-92 | Punarvasu | M |
| 11-16 | 3 | 9-8 | 7 | Y | 8-40 | Hasta | M |

|  |  |  |  |  |  |  |  |
|---|---|---|---|---|---|---|---|
| 12-8 | 5 | 2-16 | 9 | Y | 8-88 | Jyeshta | A |
| 13-0 | 7 | 8-0 | 11 | Y | 9-36 | Dhanishta | M |
| 13-16 | 1 | 1-8 | 13 | O | 9-84 | Bharani | A |
| 14-8 | 3 | 6-16 | 1 | O | 10-32 | Punarvasu | M |
| 15-0 | 5 | 12-0 | 3 | O | 10-80 | Uttara | U |
| 15-16 | 7 | 5-8 | 5 | O | 11-28 | Jyeshta | M |
| 16-8 | 1 | 10-16 | 7 | O | 11-76 | Dhanishta | U |
| 17-0 | 3 | 4-0 | 9 | D | 12-24 | Aswani | A |
| 17-16 | 5 | 9-8 | 11 | D | 12-72 | Punarvasu | A |
| 18-8 | 7 | 2-16 | 13 | D | 13-20 | Uttara | A |
| 19-0 | 1 | 8-0 | 1 | D | 13-68 | Anuradha | A |
| 19-16 | 3 | 1-8 | 3 | D | 14-16 | Dhanishta | A |
| 20-8 | 5 | 6-16 | 5 | C | 14-64 | Aswani | U |
| 21-0 | 7 | 12-0 | 7 | C | 15-12 | Aridra | M |
| 21-16 | 1 | 5-8 | 9 | C | 15-60 | Uttara | M |
| 22-8 | 3 | 10-16 | 11 | C | 16-08 | Anuradha | M |
| 23-0 | 5 | 4-0 | 13 | C | 16-56 | Sravana | A |
| 23-16 | 7 | 9-8 | 1 | A | 17-04 | Aswani | U |
| 24-8 | 1 | 2-16 | 3 | A | 17-52 | Aridra | M |
| 25-0 | 3 | 8-0 | 5 | A | 18-0 | Pubba | U |
| 25-16 | 5 | 1-8 | 7 | A | 18-48 | Anuradha | M |
| 26-8 | 7 | 6-16 | 9 | A | 18-96 | Sravana | A |
| 27-0 | 1 | 12-0 | 11 | Y | 19-44 | Revati | U |
| 27-16 | 3 | 5-8 | 13 | Y | 19-92 | Aridra | A |
| 28-8 | 5 | 10-16 | 1 | Y | 20-40 | Pubba | M |
| 29-0 | 7 | 4-0 | 3 | Y | 20-88 | Visakha | U |
| 29-16 | 1 | 9-8 | 5 | Y | 21-36 | Sravana | U |
| 30-8 | 3 | 2-16 | 7 | Y | 21-84 | Revati | A |
| 31-0 | 5 | 8-0 | 9 | O | 22-32 | Mrigasira | A |
| 31-16 | 7 | 1-8 | 11 | O | 22-80 | Pubba | A |
| 32-8 | 1 | 6-16 | 13 | O | 23-28 | Visakha | A |
| 33-0 | 3 | 12-0 | 1 | O | 23-76 | Uttarashada | U |
| 33-16 | 5 | 5-8 | 3 | O | 24-24 | Revati | U |
| 34-8 | 7 | 10-16 | 5 | D | 24-72 | Mrigasira | A |
| 35-0 | 1 | 4-0 | 7 | D | 25-20 | Maka | A |
| 35-16 | 3 | 9-8 | 9 | D | 25-68 | Visakha | A |
| 36-8 | 5 | 2-16 | 11 | D | 26-16 | Uttarashada | A |

| 37-0 | 7 | 8-0 | 13 | D | 26-64 | Uttarabhadra | A |
|---|---|---|---|---|---|---|---|
| 37-16 | 1 | 1-8 | 1 | C | 27-12 | Mrigasira | U |
| 38-8 | 3 | 6-16 | 3 | C | 27-60 | Maka | U |
| 39-0 | 5 | 12-0 | 5 | C | 28-08 | Swati | U |
| 39-16 | 7 | 5-8 | 7 | C | 28-56 | Uttarashada | A |
| 40-8 | 1 | 10-16 | 9 | C | 29-04 | Uttarabhadra | U |
| 41-0 | 3 | 4-0 | 11 | A | 29-52 | Rohini | A |
| 41-16 | 5 | 9-8 | 13 | A | 30-00 | Maka | A |
| 42-8 | 7 | 2-16 | 1 | A | 30-48 | Swati | M |
| 43-0 | 1 | 8-0 | 3 | A | 30-96 | Purvashada | M |
| 43-16 | 3 | 1-8 | 5 | A | 31-44 | Uttarashada | A |
| 44-8 | 5 | 6-16 | 7 | Y | 31-92 | Rohini | A |
| 45-0 | 7 | 12-0 | 9 | Y | 32-40 | Aslesha | A |
| 45-16 | 1 | 5-8 | 11 | Y | 32-88 | Swati | U |
| 46-8 | 3 | 10-16 | 13 | Y | 33-36 | Purvashada | A |
| 47-0 | 5 | 4-0 | 1 | Y | 33-84 | Purvashada | U |
| 47-16 | 7 | 9-8 | 3 | O | 34-32 | Rohini | U |
| 48-8 | 1 | 2-16 | 5 | O | 34-80 | Aslesha | A |
| 49-0 | 3 | 8-0 | 7 | O | 35-28 | Chitra | U |
| 49-16 | 5 | 1-8 | 9 | O | 35-76 | Purvashada | A |
| 50-8 | 7 | 6-16 | 11 | O | 36-24 | Purvabhdra | M |
| 51-0 | 1 | 12-0 | 13 | D | 36-72 | Krithika | A |
| 51-16 | 3 | 5-8 | 1 | D | 37-20 | Aslesha | A |
| 52-8 | 5 | 10-16 | 3 | D | 37-68 | Chitra | A |
| 53-0 | 7 | 4-0 | 5 | D | 38-16 | Moola | A |
| 53-16 | 1 | 9-8 | 7 | D | 38-64 | Purvabhadra | A |
| 54-8 | 3 | 2-16 | 9 | C | 39-12 | Kritika | A |
| 55-0 | 5 | 8-0 | 11 | C | 39-60 | Pubba | U |
| 55-16 | 7 | 1-8 | 13 | C | 40-08 | Chitra | U |
| 56-8 | 1 | 6-16 | 1 | C | 40-56 | Moola | U |
| 57-0 | 3 | 12-0 | 3 | C | 41-04 | Satabisa | U |
| 57-16 | 5 | 5-8 | 5 | A | 41-52 | Kritika | U |
| 58-08 | 7 | 10-16 | 7 | A | 42-00 | Pubba | U |
| 59-0 | 1 | 4-0 | 9 | A | 42-48 | Hasta | M |
| 59-16 | 3 | 9-8 | 11 | A | 42-96 | Moola | M |
| 60-8 | 5 | 2-16 | 13 | A | 43-44 | Satabisa | A |
| 61-0 | 7 | 8-0 | 1 | Y | 43-96 | Bharani | M |

| | | | | | | | |
|---|---|---|---|---|---|---|---|
| 61-16 | 1 | 1-8 | 3 | Y | 44-44 | Pubba | A |
| 62-8 | 3 | 6-16 | 5 | Y | 44-92 | Hasta | U |
| 63-0 | 5 | 12-0 | 7 | Y | 45-36 | Jyeshta | M |
| 63-16 | 7 | 5-8 | 9 | Y | 45-84 | Satabisa | M |
| 64-8 | 1 | 10-16 | 11 | O | 46-32 | Bharani | M |
| 65-0 | 3 | 4-0 | 13 | O | 46-80 | Punarvasu | A |
| 65-16 | 5 | 9-8 | 1 | O | 47-28 | Hasta | U |
| 66-8 | 7 | 2-16 | 3 | O | 47-76 | Jyeshta | A |
| 67-0 | 1 | 8-0 | 5 | O | 48-24 | Dhanishta | U |
| 67-16 | 3 | 1-8 | 7 | D | 48-72 | Bharani | A |
| 68-8 | 5 | 6-16 | 9 | D | 49-20 | Punarvasu | A |
| 69-0 | 7 | 12-0 | 11 | D | 49-68 | Uttara | A |
| 69-16 | 1 | 5-8 | 13 | D | 50-16 | Jyeshta | A |
| 70-8 | 3 | 10-16 | 1 | D | 50-64 | Dhanishta | A |
| 71-0 | 5 | 4-0 | 3 | C | 51-12 | Aswani | U |
| 71-16 | 7 | 9-8 | 5 | C | 51-60 | Punarvasu | A |
| 72-8 | 1 | 2-16 | 7 | C | 52-08 | Uttara | M |
| 73-0 | 3 | 8-0 | 9 | C | 52-56 | Anuradha | M |
| 73-16 | 5 | 1-8 | 11 | C | 53-04 | Dhanishta | A |
| 74-8 | 7 | 6-16 | 13 | A | 53-52 | Aswani | A |
| 75-0 | 1 | 12-0 | 1 | A | 54-00 | Aridra | M |
| 75-16 | 3 | 5-8 | 3 | A | 54-48 | Uttara | U |
| 76-8 | 5 | 10-16 | 5 | A | 54-96 | Anuradha | U |
| 77-0 | 7 | 1-8 | 7 | A | 55-44 | Sravana | U |
| 77-16 | 1 | 9-8 | 9 | Y | 55-92 | Aswani | U |
| 78-8 | 3 | 2-16 | 11 | Y | 56-40 | Aridra | A |
| 79-0 | 5 | 8-0 | 13 | Y | 56-88 | Pubba | M |
| 79-16 | 7 | 1-8 | 1 | Y | 57-36 | Anuradha | M |
| 80-8 | 1 | 6-16 | 3 | Y | 57-84 | Sravana | U |
| 81-0 | 3 | 12-0 | 5 | O | 58-32 | Revati | M |
| 81-16 | 5 | 5-8 | 7 | O | 58-80 | Aridra | A |
| 82-8 | 7 | 10-16 | 9 | O | 59-28 | Pubba | M |
| 83-0 | 1 | 4-0 | 11 | O | 59-76 | Visakha | A |
| 83-16 | 3 | 9-8 | 13 | O | 60-24 | Sravana | U |
| 84-8 | 5 | 2-16 | 1 | O | 60-72 | Revati | U |
| 85-0 | 7 | 8-0 | 3 | D | 61-20 | Mrigasira | A |
| 85-16 | 1 | 1-8 | 5 | D | 61-68 | Pubba | A |

| 86-8 | 3 | 6-16 | 7 | D | 62-16 | Visakha | A |
|---|---|---|---|---|---|---|---|
| 87-0 | 5 | 12-0 | 9 | D | 62-64 | Purvashada | A |
| 87-16 | 7 | 5-8 | 11 | D | 63-12 | Revati | A |
| 88-8 | 1 | 10-16 | 13 | C | 63-60 | Mrigasira | M |
| 89-0 | 3 | 4-0 | 1 | C | 64-08 | Maka | U |
| 89-16 | 5 | 9-8 | 3 | C | 64-56 | Visakha | U |
| 90-8 | 7 | 2-16 | 5 | C | 65-04 | Uttarashada | A |
| 91-0 | 1 | 8-0 | 7 | C | 65-52 | Uttarabhadra | U |
| 91-16 | 3 | 1-8 | 9 | A | 66-00 | Mrigasira | A |
| 92-8 | 5 | 6-16 | 11 | A | 66-48 | Maka | A |
| 93-0 | 7 | 12-0 | 13 | A | 66-96 | Swati | M |
| 93-16 | 1 | 5-8 | 1 | A | 67-44 | Uttarashada | M |
| 94-8 | 3 | 10-16 | 3 | A | 67-92 | Uttarabhadra | U |
| 95-0 | 5 | 4-0 | 5 | Y | 68-40 | Rohini | A |
| 95-16 | 7 | 9-8 | 7 | Y | 68-88 | Maka | U |
| 96-8 | 1 | 2-16 | 9 | Y | 69-36 | Swati | A |
| 97-0 | 3 | 8-0 | 11 | Y | 69-84 | Purvabhadra | M |
| 97-16 | 5 | 1-8 | 13 | Y | 70-32 | Uttarabhadra | A |
| 98-8 | 7 | 6-16 | 1 | O | 70-80 | Rohini | U |
| 99-0 | 1 | 12-0 | 3 | O | 71-28 | Aslesha | M |
| 99-16 | 3 | 5-8 | 5 | O | 71-76 | Swati | M |
| 100-8 | 5 | 10-16 | 7 | O | 72-24 | Purvashada | M |
| 101-0 | 7 | 4-0 | 9 | O | 72-72 | Purvabhadra | A |
| 101-16 | 1 | 9-8 | 11 | D | 73-20 | Rohini | A |
| 102-8 | 3 | 2-16 | 13 | D | 73-68 | Aslesha | A |
| 103-0 | 5 | 8-0 | 1 | D | 74-16 | Chitra | M |
| 103-16 | 7 | 1-8 | 3 | D | 74-64 | Purvashada | A |
| 104-8 | 1 | 6-16 | 5 | D | 75-12 | Purvabhadra | A |
| 105-0 | 3 | 12-0 | 7 | C | 75-60 | Kritika | A |
| 105-16 | 5 | 5-8 | 9 | C | 76-08 | Aslesha | M |
| 106-8 | 7 | 10-16 | 11 | C | 76-56 | Chitra | M |
| 107-0 | 1 | 4-0 | 13 | C | 77-04 | Moola | U |
| 107-16 | 3 | 9-8 | 1 | C | 77-52 | Purvabhadra | M |
| 108-8 | 5 | 2-16 | 3 | A | 78-00 | Kritika | A |
| 109-0 | 7 | 8-0 | 5 | A | 78-48 | Pushyami | U |
| 109-16 | 1 | 1-8 | 7 | A | 78-96 | Chitra | A |
| 110-8 | 3 | 6-16 | 9 | A | 79-44 | Moola | M |

| | | | | | | | |
|---|---|---|---|---|---|---|---|
| 111-0 | 5 | 12-0 | 11 | A | 79-92 | Satabisha | U |
| 111-16 | 7 | 5-8 | 13 | Y | 80-40 | Kritika | A |
| 112-8 | 1 | 10-16 | 1 | Y | 80-88 | Pushyami | M |
| 113-0 | 3 | 4-0 | 3 | Y | 81-36 | Hasta | U |
| 113-16 | 5 | 9-8 | 5 | Y | 81-84 | Moola | U |
| 114-8 | 7 | 2-16 | 7 | Y | 82-32 | Satabisha | A |
| 115-0 | 1 | 8-0 | 9 | O | 82-80 | Bharani | A |
| 115-16 | 3 | 1-8 | 11 | O | 83-28 | Pushyami | U |
| 116-8 | 5 | 6-16 | 13 | O | 83-76 | Hasta | A |
| 117-0 | 7 | 12-0 | 1 | O | 84-24 | Jyeshta | M |
| 117-16 | 1 | 5-8 | 3 | O | 84-72 | Satabisha | U |
| 118-8 | 3 | 10-16 | 5 | D | 85-20 | Bharani | A |
| 119-0 | 5 | 4-0 | 7 | D | 85-68 | Punarvasu | A |
| 119-16 | 7 | 9-8 | 9 | D | 86-16 | Hasta | A |
| 120-8 | 1 | 2-16 | 11 | D | 86-64 | Jyeshta | A |
| 121-0 | 3 | 8-0 | 13 | D | 87-12 | Dhanishta | A |
| 121-16 | 5 | 1-8 | 1 | C | 87-60 | Bharani | A |
| 122-8 | 7 | 6-16 | 3 | C | 88-08 | Punarvasu | U |
| 123-0 | 1 | 12-0 | 5 | C | 88-56 | Uttara | U |
| 123-16 | 3 | 5-8 | 7 | C | 89-04 | Jyeshta | A |
| 124-8 | 5 | 10-16 | 9 | C | 89-52 | Dhanishta | U |
| 125-0 | 7 | 4-0 | 11 | A | 90-00 | Aswani | A |
| 125-16 | 1 | 9-8 | 13 | A | 90-48 | Punarvasu | U |
| 126-8 | 3 | 2-16 | 1 | A | 90-96 | Uttara | U |
| 127-0 | 5 | 8-0 | 3 | A | 91-44 | Jyeshta | A |
| 127-16 | 7 | 1-8 | 5 | A | 91-92 | Dhanishta | A |
| 128-8 | 1 | 6-16 | 7 | Y | 92-40 | Aswani | U |
| 129-0 | 3 | 12-0 | 9 | Y | 92-88 | Aridra | M |
| 129-16 | 5 | 5-8 | 11 | Y | 93-36 | Uttara | A |
| 130-8 | 7 | 10-16 | 13 | Y | 93-84 | Anuradha | M |
| 131-0 | 1 | 4-0 | 1 | Y | 94-32 | Sravana | U |
| 131-16 | 3 | 9-8 | 3 | O | 94-80 | Aswani | M |
| 132-8 | 5 | 2-16 | 5 | O | 95-28 | Aridra | A |
| 133-0 | 7 | 8-0 | 7 | O | 95-76 | Pubba | A |
| 133-16 | 1 | 1-8 | 9 | O | 96-24 | Anuradha | A |
| 134-8 | 3 | 6-16 | 11 | O | 96-72 | Sravana | A |
| 135-0 | 5 | 12-0 | 13 | D | 97-20 | Revati | A |

| | | | | | | | |
|---|---|---|---|---|---|---|---|
| 135-16 | 7 | 5-8 | 1 | D | 97-68 | Aridra | A |
| 136-8 | 1 | 10-16 | 3 | D | 98-16 | Pubba | A |
| 137-0 | 3 | 4-0 | 5 | D | 98-64 | Visakha | A |
| 137-16 | 5 | 9-8 | 7 | D | 99-08 | Mrigasira | U |
| 138-8 | 7 | 2-16 | 9 | D | 99-60 | Revati | A |
| 139-0 | 1 | 8-0 | 11 | C | 100-08 | Mrigasira | U |
| 139-16 | 3 | 1-8 | 13 | C | 100-56 | Pubba | A |
| 140-8 | 5 | 6-16 | 1 | C | 101-04 | Visakha | U |
| 141-0 | 7 | 12-0 | 3 | C | 101-52 | Uttarashada | U |
| 141-16 | 1 | 5-8 | 5 | C | 102-00 | Uttarabhadra | M |
| 142-8 | 3 | 10-16 | 7 | A | 102-48 | Mrigasira | M |
| 143-0 | 5 | 4-0 | 9 | A | 102-96 | Maka | A |
| 143-16 | 7 | 9-8 | 11 | A | 103-44 | Visakha | M |
| 144-8 | 1 | 2-16 | 13 | A | 103-92 | Uttarashada | A |
| 145-0 | 3 | 8-0 | 1 | A | 104-40 | Uttarabhadra | U |
| 145-16 | 5 | 1-8 | 3 | Y | 104-88 | Mrigasira | U |
| 146-8 | 7 | 6-16 | 5 | Y | 105-36 | Maka | U |
| 147-0 | 1 | 12-0 | 7 | Y | 105-84 | Swati | U |
| 147-16 | 3 | 5-8 | 9 | Y | 106-32 | Uttarashada | A |
| 148-8 | 5 | 10-16 | 11 | Y | 106-80 | Uttarabhadra | U |
| 149-0 | 7 | 4-0 | 13 | O | 107-28 | Rohini | U |
| 149-16 | 1 | 9-8 | 1 | O | 107-76 | Maka | U |
| 150-8 | 3 | 2-16 | 3 | O | 108-24 | Swati | A |
| 151-0 | 5 | 8-0 | 5 | O | 108-72 | Purvashada | M |
| 151-16 | 7 | 1-8 | 7 | O | 109-20 | Uttarashada | A |
| 152-8 | 1 | 6-16 | 9 | D | 109-68 | Rohini | A |
| 153-0 | 3 | 12-0 | 11 | D | 110-16 | Aslesha | A |
| 153-16 | 5 | 5-8 | 13 | D | 110-64 | Swati | A |
| 154-8 | 7 | 10-16 | 1 | D | 111-12 | Purvashada | A |
| 155-0 | 1 | 4-0 | 3 | D | 111-60 | Purvabhadra | A |
| 155-16 | 3 | 9-8 | 5 | C | 112-08 | Rohini | U |
| 156-8 | 5 | 2-16 | 7 | C | 112-56 | Aslesha | A |
| 157-0 | 7 | 8-0 | 9 | C | 113-04 | Chitra | M |
| 157-16 | 1 | 1-8 | 11 | C | 113-52 | Purvashada | A |
| 158-8 | 3 | 6-16 | 13 | C | 114-00 | Purvabhadra | M |
| 159-0 | 5 | 12-0 | 1 | A | 114-48 | Kritika | U |
| 159-16 | 7 | 5-8 | 3 | A | 114-96 | Aslesha | U |

| | | | | | | | |
|---|---|---|---|---|---|---|---|
| 160-8 | 1 | 10-16 | 5 | A | 115-44 | Chitra | U |
| 161-0 | 3 | 4-0 | 7 | A | 115-92 | Moola | A |
| 161-16 | 5 | 9-8 | 9 | A | 116-40 | Purvabhadra | M |
| 162-8 | 7 | 2-16 | 11 | Y | 116-88 | Kritika | U |
| 163-0 | 1 | 8-0 | 13 | Y | 117-36 | Pushyami | M |
| 163-16 | 3 | 1-8 | 1 | Y | 117-84 | Chitra | U |
| 164-8 | 5 | 6-16 | 3 | Y | 118-32 | Moola | U |
| 165-0 | 7 | 12-0 | 5 | Y | 118-80 | Satabisha | M |
| 165-16 | 1 | 5-8 | 7 | O | 119-28 | Kritika | A |
| 166-8 | 3 | 10-16 | 9 | O | 119-76 | Pushyami | U |
| 167-0 | 5 | 4-0 | 11 | O | 120-24 | Hasta | U |
| 167-16 | 7 | 9-8 | 13 | O | 120-72 | Moola | A |
| 168-8 | 1 | 2-16 | 1 | O | 121-20 | Satabisha | U |
| 169-0 | 3 | 8-0 | 3 | D | 121-68 | Bharani | A |
| 169-16 | 5 | 1-8 | 5 | D | 122-16 | Pushyami | A |
| 170-8 | 7 | 6-16 | 7 | D | 122-64 | Hasta | A |
| 171-0 | 1 | 12-0 | 9 | D | 123-12 | Jyeshta | A |
| 171-16 | 3 | 5-8 | 11 | D | 123-60 | Satabisha | A |
| 172-8 | 5 | 10-16 | 13 | C | 124-08 | Bharani | A |
| 173-0 | 7 | 4-0 | 1 | C | 124-56 | Punarvasu | M |
| 173-16 | 1 | 9-8 | 3 | C | 125-04 | Hasta | U |
| 174-8 | 3 | 2-16 | 5 | C | 125-52 | Jyeshta | A |
| 175-0 | 5 | 8-0 | 7 | C | 126-0 | Dhanishta | U |
| 175-16 | 7 | 1-8 | 9 | A | 126-48 | Bharani | M |
| 176-8 | 1 | 6-16 | 11 | A | 126-96 | Punarvasu | M |
| 177-0 | 3 | 12-0 | 13 | A | 127-44 | Uttara | A |
| 177-16 | 5 | 5-8 | 1 | A | 127-92 | Jyeshta | U |
| 178-8 | 7 | 10-16 | 3 | A | 128-40 | Dhanishta | U |
| 179-0 | 1 | 4-0 | 5 | Y | 128-88 | Ashwani | U |
| 179-16 | 3 | 9-8 | 7 | Y | 129-36 | Punarvasu | U |
| 180-8 | 5 | 2-16 | 9 | Y | 129-84 | Uttara | A |
| 181-0 | 7 | 8-0 | 11 | Y | 130-32 | Anuradha | A |
| 181-16 | 1 | 1-8 | 13 | Y | 130-80 | Dhanishta | A |
| 182-8 | 3 | 6-16 | 1 | O | 131-28 | Ashwani | M |
| 183-0 | 5 | 12-0 | 3 | O | 131-76 | Aridra | M |
| 183-16 | 7 | 5-8 | 5 | O | 132-24 | Uttara | M |
| 184-8 | 1 | 10-16 | 7 | O | 132-72 | Anuradha | U |

| | | | | | | | |
|---|---|---|---|---|---|---|---|
| 185-0 | 3 | 4-0 | 9 | O | 133-20 | Sravana | A |
| 185-16 | 5 | 9-8 | 11 | D | 133-68 | Ashwani | A |
| 186-8 | 7 | 2-16 | 13 | D | 134-16 | Aridra | A |
| 187-0 | 1 | 8-0 | 1 | D | 134-64 | Pubba | A |
| 187-16 | 3 | 1-8 | 3 | D | 135-12 | Anuradha | A |
| 188-8 | 5 | 6-16 | 5 | D | 135-60 | Sravana | A |
| 189-0 | 7 | 12-0 | 7 | C | 136-08 | Revati | M |
| 189-16 | 1 | 5-8 | 9 | C | 136-56 | Aridra | A |
| 190-8 | 3 | 10-16 | 11 | C | 137-04 | Pubba | M |
| 191-0 | 5 | 4-0 | 13 | C | 137-52 | Visakha | A |
| 191-16 | 7 | 9-8 | 1 | C | 138-00 | Sravana | U |
| 192-8 | 1 | 2-16 | 3 | C | 138-48 | Revati | A |
| 193-0 | 3 | 8-0 | 5 | A | 138-96 | Mrigasira | U |
| 193-16 | 5 | 1-8 | 7 | A | 139-44 | Pubba | A |
| 194-8 | 7 | 6-16 | 9 | A | 139-92 | Visakha | M |
| 195-0 | 1 | 12-0 | 11 | A | 140-40 | Uttarashada | M |
| 195-16 | 3 | 5-8 | 13 | A | 140-88 | Revati | U |
| 196-8 | 5 | 10-16 | 1 | Y | 141-36 | Mrigasira | M |
| 197-0 | 7 | 4-0 | 3 | Y | 141-84 | Maka | U |
| 197-16 | 1 | 9-8 | 5 | Y | 142-32 | Visakha | M |
| 198-8 | 3 | 2-16 | 7 | Y | 142-80 | Uttarashada | A |
| 199-0 | 5 | 8-0 | 9 | Y | 143-28 | Uttarabhadra | M |
| 199-16 | 7 | 1-8 | 11 | O | 143-76 | Mrigasira | M |
| 200-8 | 1 | 6-16 | 13 | O | 144-24 | Maka | M |
| 201-0 | 3 | 12-0 | 1 | O | 144-72 | Swati | M |
| 201-16 | 5 | 5-8 | 3 | O | 145-20 | Uttarashada | U |
| 202-8 | 7 | 10-16 | 5 | O | 145-68 | Uttarabhadra | U |
| 203-0 | 1 | 4-0 | 7 | D | 146-16 | Rohini | A |
| 203-16 | 3 | 9-8 | 9 | D | 146-64 | Maka | A |
| 204-8 | 5 | 2-16 | 11 | D | 147-12 | Swati | A |
| 205-0 | 7 | 8-0 | 13 | D | 147-60 | Purvabhadra | A |
| 205-16 | 1 | 1-8 | 1 | D | 148-08 | Uttarabhadra | A |
| 206-8 | 3 | 6-16 | 3 | C | 148-56 | Rohini | A |
| 207-0 | 5 | 12-0 | 5 | C | 149-04 | Aslesha | U |
| 207-16 | 7 | 5-8 | 7 | C | 149-52 | Swati | M |
| 208-8 | 1 | 10-16 | 9 | C | 150-00 | purvashada | A |
| 209-0 | 3 | 4-0 | 11 | C | 150-48 | Purvabhadra | U |

| 209-16 | 5 | 9-8 | 13 | A | 150-96 | Rohini | M |
|---|---|---|---|---|---|---|---|
| 210-8 | 7 | 2-16 | 1 | A | 151-44 | Aslesha | U |
| 211-0 | 1 | 8-0 | 3 | A | 151-92 | Chitra | U |
| 211-16 | 3 | 1-8 | 5 | A | 152-40 | Purvashada | A |
| 212-8 | 5 | 6-16 | 7 | A | 152-88 | Purvabhadra | A |
| 213-0 | 7 | 12-0 | 9 | Y | 153-36 | Kritika | M |
| 213-16 | 1 | 5-8 | 11 | Y | 153-84 | Aslesha | A |
| 214-8 | 3 | 10-16 | 13 | Y | 154-32 | Chitra | M |
| 215-0 | 5 | 4-0 | 1 | Y | 154-80 | Moola | U |
| 215-16 | 7 | 9-8 | 3 | Y | 155-28 | Purvabhadra | U |
| 216-8 | 1 | 2-16 | 5 | O | 155-76 | Kritika | A |
| 217-0 | 3 | 8-0 | 7 | O | 156-24 | Pushyami | U |
| 217-16 | 5 | 1-8 | 9 | O | 156-72 | Chitra | M |
| 218-8 | 7 | 6-16 | 11 | O | 157-20 | Moola | A |
| 219-0 | 1 | 12-0 | 13 | O | 157-68 | Satabisha | U |
| 219-16 | 3 | 5-8 | 1 | D | 158-16 | Kritika | A |
| 220-8 | 5 | 10-16 | 3 | D | 158-64 | Pushyami | A |
| 221-0 | 7 | 4-0 | 5 | D | 159-12 | Hasta | A |
| 221-16 | 1 | 9-8 | 7 | D | 159-60 | Moola | A |
| 222-8 | 3 | 2-16 | 9 | D | 160-08 | Satabisha | A |
| 223-0 | 5 | 8-0 | 11 | C | 160-56 | Bharani | A |
| 223-16 | 7 | 1-8 | 13 | C | 161-04 | Pushyami | A |
| 224-8 | 1 | 6-16 | 1 | C | 161-52 | Hasta | M |
| 225-0 | 3 | 12-0 | 3 | C | 162-00 | Jyeshta | M |
| 225-16 | 5 | 5-8 | 5 | C | 162-48 | Satabisha | U |
| 226-8 | 7 | 10-16 | 7 | A | 162-96 | Bharani | M |
| 227-0 | 1 | 4-0 | 9 | A | 163-44 | Punarvasu | M |
| 227-16 | 3 | 9-8 | 11 | A | 163-92 | Hasta | A |
| 228-8 | 5 | 2-16 | 13 | A | 164-40 | Jyeshta | A |
| 229-0 | 7 | 8-0 | 1 | A | 164-88 | Dhanishta | U |
| 229-16 | 1 | 1-8 | 3 | Y | 165-36 | Bharani | A |
| 230-8 | 3 | 6-16 | 5 | y | 165-84 | Punarvasu | U |
| 231-0 | 5 | 12-0 | 7 | Y | 166-32 | Uttara | U |
| 231-16 | 7 | 5-8 | 9 | Y | 166-80 | Jyeshta | A |
| 232-8 | 1 | 10-16 | 11 | Y | 167-28 | Dhanishta | M |
| 233-0 | 3 | 4-0 | 13 | O | 167-76 | Ashwani | A |
| 233-16 | 5 | 9-8 | 1 | O | 168-24 | Punarvasu | U |

| | | | | | | | |
|---|---|---|---|---|---|---|---|
| 234-8 | 7 | 2-16 | 3 | O | 168-72 | Uttara | A |
| 235-0 | 1 | 8-0 | 5 | O | 169-20 | Anuradha | U |
| 235-16 | 3 | 1-8 | 7 | O | 169-68 | Dhanishta | M |
| 236-8 | 5 | 6-16 | 9 | D | 170-16 | Ashwani | A |
| 237-0 | 7 | 12-0 | 11 | D | 170-64 | Aridra | A |
| 237-16 | 1 | 5-8 | 13 | D | 171-12 | Uttara | A |
| 238-8 | 3 | 10-16 | 1 | D | 171-60 | anuradha | A |
| 239-0 | 5 | 4-0 | 3 | D | 172-08 | Sravana | A |
| 239-16 | 7 | 9-8 | 5 | C | 172-56 | Ashwani | U |
| 240-8 | 1 | 2-16 | 7 | C | 173-04 | Aridra | A |
| 241-0 | 3 | 8-0 | 9 | C | 173-52 | Pubba | A |
| 241-16 | 5 | 1-8 | 11 | C | 174-00 | Anuradha | A |
| 242-8 | 7 | 6-16 | 13 | C | 174-48 | Sravana | M |
| 243-0 | 1 | 12-0 | 1 | A | 174-96 | Revati | M |
| 243-16 | 3 | 5-8 | 3 | A | 175-44 | Aridra | M |
| 244-8 | 5 | 10-16 | 5 | A | 175-92 | Pubba | U |
| 245-0 | 7 | 4-0 | 7 | A | 176-40 | Visakha | A |
| 245-16 | 1 | 9-8 | 9 | A | 176-88 | Sravana | U |
| 246-8 | 3 | 2-16 | 11 | A | 177-36 | Revati | A |
| 247-0 | 5 | 8-0 | 13 | Y | 177-84 | Mrigasira | M |
| 247-16 | 7 | 1-8 | 1 | Y | 178-32 | Pubba | M |
| 248-8 | 1 | 6-16 | 3 | Y | 178-80 | Visakha | U |
| 249-0 | 3 | 12-0 | 5 | Y | 179-28 | Uttarashada | U |
| 249-16 | 5 | 5-8 | 7 | Y | 179-76 | Revati | A |
| 250-8 | 7 | 10-16 | 9 | O | 180-24 | Mrigasira | A |
| 251-0 | 1 | 4-0 | 11 | O | 180-72 | Maka | Ap |
| 251-16 | 3 | 9-8 | 13 | O | 181-20 | Swati | A |
| 252-8 | 5 | 2-16 | 1 | O | 181-68 | Uttarashada | U |
| 253-0 | 7 | 8-0 | 3 | O | 182-16 | Uttarabhadra | A |
| 253-16 | 1 | 1-8 | 5 | D | 182-64 | Mrigasira | A |
| 254-8 | 3 | 6-16 | 7 | D | 183-12 | Maka | A |
| 255-0 | 5 | 12-0 | 9 | D | 183-60 | Swati | A |
| 255-16 | 7 | 5-8 | 11 | D | 184-08 | Uttarashad | A |
| 256-8 | 1 | 10-16 | 13 | D | 184-56 | Uttarabhadra | A |
| 257-0 | 3 | 4-0 | 1 | C | 185-04 | Rohini | U |
| 257-16 | 5 | 9-8 | 3 | C | 185-52 | Maka | U |
| 258-8 | 7 | 2-16 | 5 | C | 186-00 | Swati | A |

| 259-0 | 1 | 8-0 | 7 | C | 186-48 | Purvashada | U |
|---|---|---|---|---|---|---|---|
| 259-16 | 3 | 1-8 | 9 | C | 186-96 | Uttarashada | A |
| 260-8 | 5 | 6-16 | 11 | A | 187-44 | Rohini | M |
| 261-0 | 7 | 12-0 | 13 | A | 187-92 | Aslesha | M |
| 261-16 | 1 | 5-8 | 1 | A | 188-40 | Swati | U |
| 262-8 | 3 | 10-16 | 3 | A | 188-88 | Purvashada | M |
| 263-0 | 5 | 4-0 | 5 | A | 189-36 | Purvabhadra | A |
| 263-16 | 7 | 9-8 | 7 | Y | 189-84 | Rohini | U |
| 264-8 | 1 | 2-16 | 9 | Y | 190-32 | Aslesha | A |
| 265-0 | 3 | 8-0 | 11 | Y | 190-80 | Chitra | M |
| 265-16 | 5 | 1-8 | 13 | Y | 191-28 | Purvashada | M |
| 266-8 | 7 | 6-16 | 1 | Y | 191-76 | Purvabhadra | U |
| 267-0 | 1 | 12-0 | 3 | O | 192-24 | Kritika | U |
| 267-16 | 3 | 5-8 | 5 | O | 192-72 | Aslesha | M |
| 268-8 | 5 | 10-16 | 7 | O | 193-20 | Chitra | M |
| 269-0 | 7 | 4-0 | 9 | O | 193-68 | Moola | M |
| 269-16 | 1 | 9-8 | 11 | O | 194-16 | Purvabhadra | M |
| 270-8 | 3 | 2-16 | 13 | D | 194-64 | Kritika | A |
| 271-0 | 5 | 8-0 | 1 | D | 195-12 | Pushyami | M |
| 271-16 | 7 | 1-8 | 3 | D | 195-60 | Chitra | A |
| 272-8 | 1 | 6-16 | 5 | D | 196-08 | Moola | A |
| 273-0 | 3 | 12-0 | 7 | D | 196-56 | Satabisha | A |
| 273-16 | 5 | 5-8 | 9 | C | 197-04 | Purvabhadra | A |
| 274-8 | 7 | 10-16 | 11 | C | 197-52 | Pushyami | M |
| 275-0 | 1 | 4-0 | 13 | C | 198-00 | Hasta | A |
| 275-16 | 3 | 9-8 | 1 | C | 198-48 | Moola | U |
| 276-8 | 5 | 2-16 | 3 | C | 198-96 | Satabisha | A |
| 277-0 | 7 | 8-0 | 5 | A | 199-44 | Bharani | U |
| 277-16 | 1 | 1-8 | 7 | A | 199-92 | Pushyami | A |
| 278-8 | 3 | 6-16 | 9 | A | 200-40 | Hasta | U |
| 279-0 | 5 | 12-0 | 11 | A | 200-88 | Jyeshta | U |
| 279-16 | 7 | 5-8 | 13 | A | 201-36 | Satabisha | A |
| 280-8 | 1 | 10-16 | 1 | Y | 201-84 | Bharani | U |
| 281-0 | 3 | 4-0 | 3 | Y | 202-32 | Punarvasu | M |
| 281-16 | 5 | 9-8 | 5 | Y | 202-80 | Hasta | U |
| 282-8 | 7 | 2-16 | 7 | Y | 203-28 | Jyeshta | M |
| 283-0 | 1 | 8-0 | 9 | Y | 203-76 | Dhanishta | M |

| | | | | | | | |
|---|---|---|---|---|---|---|---|
| 283-16 | 3 | 1-8 | 11 | O | 204-24 | Bharani | A |
| 284-8 | 5 | 6-16 | 13 | O | 204-72 | Punarvasu | A |
| 285-0 | 7 | 12-0 | 1 | O | 205-20 | Uttara | U |
| 285-16 | 1 | 5-8 | 3 | O | 205-68 | Jyeshta | U |
| 286-8 | 3 | 10-16 | 5 | O | 206-16 | Dhanishta | U |
| 287-0 | 5 | 4-0 | 7 | D | 206-64 | Ashwani | A |
| 287-16 | 7 | 9-8 | 9 | D | 207-12 | Punarvasu | A |
| 288-8 | 1 | 2-16 | 11 | D | 207-60 | Uttara | A |
| 289-0 | 3 | 8-0 | 13 | D | 208-08 | Anuradha | A |
| 289-16 | 5 | 1-8 | 1 | D | 208-56 | Dhanishta | A |
| 290-8 | 7 | 6-16 | 3 | C | 209-04 | Ashwani | U |
| 291-0 | 1 | 12-0 | 5 | C | 209-52 | Aridra | M |
| 291-16 | 3 | 5-8 | 7 | C | 210-00 | Uttara | M |
| 292-8 | 5 | 10-16 | 9 | C | 210-48 | Anuradha | M |
| 293-0 | 7 | 4-0 | 11 | C | 210-96 | Sravana | A |
| 293-16 | 1 | 9-8 | 13 | A | 211-44 | Ashwani | M |
| 294-8 | 3 | 2-16 | 1 | A | 211-92 | Aridra | M |
| 295-0 | 5 | 8-0 | 3 | A | 212-40 | Pubba | U |
| 295-16 | 7 | 1-8 | 5 | A | 212-88 | Anuradha | M |
| 296-8 | 1 | 6-16 | 7 | A | 213-36 | Sravana | A |
| 297-0 | 3 | 12-0 | 9 | Y | 213-84 | Revati | U |
| 297-16 | 5 | 5-8 | 11 | Y | 214-32 | Aridra | A |
| 298-8 | 7 | 10-16 | 13 | Y | 214-80 | Pubba | M |
| 299-0 | 1 | 4-0 | 1 | Y | 215-28 | Visakha | U |
| 299-16 | 3 | 9-8 | 3 | Y | 215-76 | Sravana | M |
| 300-8 | 5 | 2-16 | 5 | O | 216-20 | Revati | A |
| 301-0 | 7 | 8-0 | 7 | O | 216-72 | Mrigasira | M |
| 301-16 | 1 | 1-8 | 9 | O | 217-20 | Pubba | A |
| 302-8 | 3 | 6-16 | 11 | O | 217-68 | Visakha | M |
| 303-0 | 5 | 12-0 | 13 | O | 218-16 | Uttarashada | M |
| 303-16 | 7 | 5-8 | 1 | O | 218-64 | Revati | M |
| 304-8 | 1 | 10-16 | 3 | D | 219-12 | Mrigasira | A |
| 305-0 | 3 | 4-0 | 5 | D | 219-60 | Maka | A |
| 305-16 | 5 | 9-8 | 7 | D | 220-08 | Visakha | A |
| 306-8 | 7 | 2-16 | 9 | D | 220-56 | Uttarashada | A |
| 307-0 | 1 | 8-0 | 11 | D | 221-04 | Uttarabhadra | A |
| 307-16 | 3 | 1-8 | 13 | C | 221-52 | Mrigasira | A |

| 308-8 | 5 | 6-16 | 1 | C | 222-00 | Maka | U |
|---|---|---|---|---|---|---|---|
| 309-0 | 7 | 12-0 | 3 | C | 222-48 | Swati | U |
| 309-16 | 1 | 5-8 | 5 | C | 222-96 | Uttarashada | U |
| 310-8 | 3 | 10-16 | 7 | C | 223-44 | Uttarabhadra | U |
| 311-0 | 5 | 4-0 | 9 | A | 223-92 | Rohini | U |
| 311-16 | 7 | 9-8 | 11 | A | 224-40 | Maka | M |
| 312-8 | 1 | 2-16 | 13 | A | 224-88 | Swati | U |
| 313-0 | 3 | 8-0 | 1 | A | 225-36 | Purvashada | U |
| 313-16 | 5 | 1-8 | 3 | A | 225-84 | Uttarabhadra | U |
| 314-8 | 7 | 6-16 | 5 | Y | 226-32 | Rohini | U |
| 315-0 | 1 | 12-0 | 7 | Y | 226-80 | Aslesha | A |
| 315-16 | 3 | 5-8 | 9 | Y | 227-28 | Swati | U |
| 316-0 | 5 | 10-16 | 11 | Y | 227-76 | Purvashada | M |
| 317-0 | 7 | 4-0 | 13 | Y | 228-24 | Purvabhadra | M |
| 317-16 | 1 | 9-8 | 1 | O | 228-72 | Rohini | U |
| 318-8 | 3 | 2-16 | 3 | O | 229-20 | Aslesha | A |
| 319-0 | 5 | 8-0 | 5 | O | 229-68 | Chitra | U |
| 319-16 | 7 | 1-8 | 7 | O | 230-16 | Purvashada | A |
| 320-8 | 1 | 6-16 | 9 | O | 230-64 | Purvabhadra | M |

# Table V

**Test Chakra to find Vaastu Good or Bad**

In the given below chart, there are twelve different results. By praying to the God of your choice, ask a small kid below 8 years to touch one column cell of the Good/Bad Test Chakram. You have to connect to the 13th word on either side or club together to arrive the exact position of the good or bad result of the present house or land.

| Decided | Your | Your | Your | You | House | Show | Though |
|---|---|---|---|---|---|---|---|
| You | Trees | Your | Residence | Land | Own | Difficulties | House |
| will | Is | Your | No | Will | Planted | Present | Land |
| Is | Decision | Are | Has | Have | Afflicted | House | Defects |
| become | Around | Occupied | Diagonal | Good | Is | The | Defects |
| Financial | With | Plot | In | Financially | Land | Land | Shape |
| For | Correct | Cause | In | Prosperity | Arudam | To | Your |
| Strong | Are | Is | Is | Making | It | Of | Perimeter |
| If | Causing | Expert | House | And | Against | Subjected | Against |
| House | Will | House | Calculation | House | Progeny | Sthapati | Exists |
| Lead | Vaastu | To | Vaastu | With | Enable | Placements | Of |
| is | Or | And | It | A | Which | Sarpa | Hence |
| Happy | Good | Hamper | Age | Constructed | Animals | Get | Can |
| Happy | Will | And | Troubles | And | Beneficial | Growth | Yoni |
| Per | Will | It's | Not | And | Cause | Blood | Will |
| prosperous | Family | And | And | Decided | Not | Mistakes | Overrule |
| prosperous | Difficulties | Yakshas | Occur | Life | Life | Progress | Paadas |
| plan | Prosper | Corrected | Dangers | Life | Demotion | Troubles | Frequently |

You can engage a Vaastu expert accordingly if remedial measures have to be undertaken wherever necessary. By adding you will get the following twelve answers:

1. Decided land is good for making house with happy and prosperous life.
2. Your own decision is correct. It will enable good beneficial family life.
3. Your difficulties are the cause of house placement hamper growth and progress.
4. Your house has defects in perimeter, calculation of age, yoni and paadas.
5. You will have financial prosperity if house is constructed per decided plan.
6. House is afflicted with arudam causing progeny or animals will not prosper.
7. Show your house plot to expert shtapathi and get its mistakes corrected.
8. Though no defect in your house exists, it can not overrule dangers.
9. You will become financially strong and lead a happy and prosperous life.
10. Trees planted around land are against Vaastu which will cause difficulties, demotion.
11. Your present occupied land is subjected to Sarpa and Blood-yakshas troubles.
12. Residence land diagonal shape is against Vaastu hence troubles will occur frequently.